KENNY MACASKILL has been a Loth[...]em-
ber of the Shadow Cabinet sinc[...]has
held portfolios covering enterpri[...]uni-
cations and justice. He is deputy leader of the [...]rood
Parliamentary Group and has been National Treasurer and Vice
Convener of Policy. Kenny was also the SNP's Poll Tax spokesperson,
leading the party's popular 'Can Pay, Won't Pay' campaign. Kenny
was educated at Linlithgow Academy and Edinburgh University and
was a senior partner in a law firm until becoming an MSP. He is married with two sons.

RT HON HENRY MCLEISH began his political career as an elected member in local government in 1974, and was leader of Fife Regional
Council for five years. In 1987 he was elected as a member of the UK
Parliament and acted as Minister for Devolution and Home Affairs
in the Labour government from 1997 to 1999. In the first Scottish
Parliament he was Minister for Enterprise and Lifelong Learning
from 1999, and in 2000 he became First Minister of Scotland until
2001. Resigning from politics in 2003, he is now an adviser and consultant and lectures in the USA and elsewhere on a variety of topics.

All royalties generated from sales of this book will be paid to
The Scotland Funds, a non-government charitable organisation
dedicated to connecting people of Scots descent back to Scotland
via philanthropic giving.
Luath Press is an independently owned and managed book
publishing company based in Scotland, and is not aligned to any
political party or grouping.
The authors acknowledge the generous assistance from BAA
Scotland, Standard Life and Scottish & Newcastle towards the
publication of this book.
All photographs inside and on the front cover are reproduced by
kind permission of the interviewees.
Photograph of Dario Franchitti: Voorhees Studios.
Photograph of Harry Benson: John Kirkby.

Global Scots

Voices From Afar

Kenny MacAskill
and
Henry McLeish

Luath Press Limited
EDINBURGH
www.luath.co.uk

First published 2005

The paper used in this book is recyclable. It is made from low chlorine pulps produced in a low energy, low emission manner from renewable forests.

Printed and bound by Digisource (GB) Ltd., Livingston

Typeset in Sabon 10.5 by Catriona Vernal

To Scots the world over

Acknowledgements

THERE ARE COUNTLESS PEOPLE to whom we are indebted for their support and assistance in writing this book. The sponsorship was pivotal in allowing it to happen. Without the support from BAA Scotland, Standard Life and Scottish & Newcastle this book could not have been written. We are grateful for their trust and faith given the adverse publicity that political figures can carry. Moreover, the willingness and indeed the continued support throughout from all at Luath Press were essential, especially from Gavin MacDougall and Catriona Vernal.

This book was much more of a team effort than simply the collaboration between two authors. We appear on the cover but so many more were instrumental. None more so than Karen Newton. Euan Lloyd, Craig Milroy and David Hutchison equally and ably assisted. Tom Brown's skill and experience helped enormously. A great deal of effort was expended on their part for no real reward; not for them the jaunts abroad but the slog of seeking to improve the final outcome. We are eternally grateful for their contribution. We also owe a deep debt of gratitude to our respective families for their support.

Many others provided names or contacts. John McCann at Global Scots showed incredible patience in seeking out contacts he had made and was unsparing in sharing them with us. Friends of Scotland were also happy and willing to use their website and network to make connections for us. Bob Creighton, who appears in the book, took time not simply to be interviewed but to suggest names and help make contacts with other Scots. We hope the final product lives up to the trust they have placed in us.

Finally, we must thank each and every one of the Scots interviewed. They were happy to co-operate when most neither knew us nor anything about us. They took us on trust because they believed in the project that we had embarked upon. They remain proud of their roots whether or not they will ever seek to return for good. This will forever be their native land. We hope that they will be proud of their contribution. Scotland should certainly be proud of them.

Kenny MacAskill and Henry McLeish

Contents

CONTENTS

Introduction

For we're no awa tae bide awa
For we're no awa tae le'e ye
For we're no awa tae bide awa
We'll aye come back an' see ye

THIS IS A SONG WHICH SCOTS HAVE SUNG for many a year – at home and abroad, at Hogmanay and at farewell gatherings, in sadness and with pride – and still it rings out. Emigration and 'expat' Scots are part of who we are and what has created modern Scotland. They are not lost to us but remain part of us. With a Parliament now restored to Scotland there is an opportunity to reach out and link up with our fellow Scots worldwide. Why they left and whether they will permanently return is to some extent irrelevant. What matters is that we recognise them as our kinfolk. We are all Scots – some of us live in this beautiful land of ours, while others reside abroad. These people are not our past but part of our future.

As authors, we belong to separate tribes in Scottish politics. The Labour and Nationalist communities have fought over common turf for decades. We have different views on the constitutional relationship between Scotland and England, but we share a common belief that Scotland can achieve so much more. Fundamentally, what needs to be done involves a change of attitudes by the Scots themselves. Reaction to our co-operation was of some shock and surprise – perhaps indicative of the distance that still has to be travelled in Scottish politics towards a recognition of a broader national interest, rather than narrow party benefit.

However, Scotland has changed and continues to do so, following the restoration of its Parliament. The initial delight that turned to despondency is now being replaced by a desire simply to see progress made and tangible improvements occur in all facets of Scottish life and society. There are clear signs of growing optimism in Scotland and a resurgence in national self-confidence. Both are essential if Scotland is to prosper and live up to the First Minister's sobriquet of 'the best small nation in the world'. Work remains to be done and some of our travails must be in addressing attitudes of the Scots.

Having previously worked together on a book in which resident Scots provided a vision of where Scotland could be in 2020, it seemed a logical progression to have Scots who live abroad reflect on their native land. Migration has defined Scotland throughout the centuries and moulded our nation. In a fast-changing world and an increasingly global economy, where does Scotland stand, and how should it position itself?

Other nations, not least the Irish, have cherished their émigrés or depended on their diaspora for support; and as a result these exiles have been able to make a significant contribution. Scotland, it seemed to us, has had an ambivalent attitude – at best, pride in the success of many high-flying Scots but, equally, disparagement if they dared to comment on their native land. Why should that be? Scotland should welcome the success of its diaspora, and listen and learn from their experiences. If we fail to do that, we not only lose their indigenous talent but we also squander their experience and deprive ourselves of freely-given valuable advice and guidance.

No Scot, resident or otherwise, can be unaware of the 'kent yer faither' syndrome that exists in our homeland. In moderation, it can be a good thing, maintaining the egalitarianism on which we pride ourselves. Beyond that, it becomes caustic and corrosive, dragging down individuals and denigrating success. It seemed to us that there were clear signs of that negative attitude being applied to the Scottish diaspora. At best, it is an unworthy resentment of obvious success; at worst, a refusal to recognise 'oor ain folk' as Scots. We should be a nation comfortable with success and hungry for more, not a nation uneasy with success and bedevilled by 'begrudgery'. Self-defeating pessimism needs to be overcome. We need to believe in ourselves, having confidence, ambition, and optimism.

A period of absence abroad can be an advantage in reflecting on our nation's situation; it can be difficult to have perspective when too close-up. A measure of dispassionate consideration from someone sympathetic, but not immersed, can be beneficial. Too much in Scottish society is mildly accepted because 'it has always been this way'. Why? If there are kinfolk who can see what needs to be changed, or have found a different and better way, then why not learn from them?

For these reasons, we wanted to seek out these members of the wider Scottish family and write this book. The views of many high-flying Scots are well known, but what of others who have been successful in less prominent fields or simply have not been visible to the Scottish eye? What do they think and what could we learn from them? What did Scotland give them and fail to provide for them? What should be adopted or adapted and retained or rejected? Though Scots are scattered to the winds and have settled on every continent on this planet, on this occasion we have been restricted to seeking the views of those in North America and Europe. However, a broad mixture has been obtained. They are in the New World and the Old; men and women; in the private sector and public service; the young and not-so-young; from our major cities, small towns, the central belt and the rural hinterland. Attitudes and values vary depending on the era as well as the area they come from and we have sought to reflect that. Yet we found, as the reader will, that certain values and feelings are universal and transcend age, class, gender or locality.

Beyond that there was no agenda, and no constraints were set on what could be said or commented on. Some indicated a desire to be unflinchingly frank and, indeed, wondered if their views would be welcomed. We assured them they would. If they felt there were aspects of our society that are unpleasant or attitudes that need changing, then so be it. Scotland cannot live a lie; deluding ourselves with false pride is fundamentally damaging. As it transpired, even those with some bitter memories remain committed to the land they left and their overall impression was highly favourable. Notwithstanding some blighted memories, all are eager to see

Scotland improve and remain willing to play their part. These Scots abroad cherished the opportunity to contribute and comment in a way that may allow them to repay what they received. They seek to help in improving the land they love.

Any fixed perceptions came from us. We, as authors, shared the same blinkered perceptions many do in Scotland about the diaspora. It has been eye-opening and illuminating for us, not only to discover so many hidden Scottish talents but to learn so much from them. The attributes and achievements of these people made us wonder why we had never, as a society, sought their views before. Typically modest and self-deprecating, they played down their obvious talents and abilities. They have much to offer us back home and we could certainly do with their assistance.

Through them, aspects of our history are highlighted or brought to light that were unknown to us. Attitudes are challenged and social customs and behaviour commented on. Advice is freely and fondly dispensed as to how our common homeland can best adapt and make progress in the modern world. At the same time, what is quintessentially Scottish, whether part of our soul or simply the sensible attitudes of a down-to-earth and pragmatic people, must be cherished. We were also afforded an insight into the lot of an emigrant, which is not always a happy one, and the things that money and quality of life cannot replace. Some of our interviewees are on a temporary posting or sojourn abroad and will return. For others, the move is permanent as they have made a new life with their families and taken on the nationality of their new land. However, even for those to whom a permanent return is not an option, there remains a commitment to the homeland they left – and a clear and strong heritage which they have passed on to future generations, whatever their passports may say.

For Scotland to progress, it needs to come to terms with itself. To become less inward-looking and recognise that many problems are not the fault of London rule (let alone Margaret Thatcher) but are ingrained in our own attitudes and opinions. To define Scotland as a nation in the modern world, without harbouring prejudice against our southern neighbours. To recognise that being self-critical need not mean being self-destructive and that, equally, there is much to be proud of and to cherish and retain at all costs. Self-delusion is unhelpful; self-confidence remains essential.

The interviews were a fascinating journey for us, hence the contributions are chronological as matters were raised or points made allowing the book to unfold. It will be for our readers to take from each of the interviewees what they will. For us, there were clear threads that ran through the diverse expatriate community. There was a pride in their identity and a gratitude for what they had received. Education and egalitarianism were acknowledged uniformly. Most acknowledged a work ethic and strong community values.

In many instances, what they found lacking from Scotland was opportunity – although it could be said this is inevitable in a small country with a limited population. However, it became clear to us that many of the constraints upon Scotland were not due to its size but to our people's 'state of mind' – limitations and ambitions were self-imposed not imposed upon us. Many testified to a lack of confidence or at least a failure to promote and instil it through our otherwise exemplary education system. Sectarianism, it became obvious, is a problem that ran deeper than we had first thought. As resident Scots, we can become inured to its pernicious effects, simply accepting it as part of our society. Our kinfolk abroad, quite correctly, see it differently, as a poison which must be purged.

They wish to see us progress as a society but, in doing so, not to reject or lose what has made us and them distinctively Scottish. That is a valid point which we overlook at our peril. It is not simply a question of what we must acquire but equally what we must retain. If we lose what makes us uniquely and distinctly Scottish, then who are we? There is a general view, though, that Scots need to 'lighten up' – being less down on each other and more confident in ourselves. A larger neighbour and political union have created concerns about assimilation and absorption throughout the centuries. This has manifested itself in negativity and anti-English attitudes. Some of our interviewees referred to the Irish, who similarly have made a move from a negative perception of Britain to a confident realisation of a

European Ireland. They are confident in themselves, but not condemnatory of their larger neighbour.

Scots abroad are our greatest overseas asset. More than others, they appreciate the new importance of internationalism, the interconnectedness and the interdependence of the new modern world. They sense more keenly the importance of building on our historic reputation as an outward-looking nation, while acknowledging the testing challenges of an increasingly competitive and changing world.

The lesson we have learned from those we interviewed is this: where you live is much less important than who you are and what you can do for your country. Scots abroad want to do more for their native country. They want to be asked not ignored, valued not dismissed, and they are keen to be part of a Scottish goodwill force.

In past times, Scots abroad could keep in touch with friends and family back home only at great cost and with considerable difficulty. Links with other Scottish communities were difficult and fragmented. Moreover, there was no single point of reference for Scots or national body to foster or sustain links and identity. Caledonian Clubs and St Andrew's Societies could seek to forge links but with no central focus or driving force, momentum stalled.

Now, thanks to modern communications, the Internet, the information revolution and travel, we live in a shrinking world where distance, boundaries and borders no longer matter. More importantly, the new Scottish Parliament provides a source of funding and encourages the forging of stronger links between Scotland and its diaspora. Scotland is on the world stage once more and all her communities must be given a chance to play their part. The Parliament is not just an opportunity to transform Scotland itself, but it can also create closer links with Scottish communities across the world. The time has come for Scots to 'come home', if not physically then at least in spirit.

This embrace of Scots abroad is about kinship; embracing our common humanity; the romance, nostalgia and sentiment associated with being Scottish; the pride we feel for our country. The idea of 'Scottishness' is not just about place but must also be global, an idea reaching out and making an impact on the world. Identity and association is more important than where we live. No matter where Scots live in the world, they are all part of the same history and the same family.

Five million of us may reside in Scotland, but many, many more now reside elsewhere – and there needs to be an understanding that we are all Scottish, with a shared identity, history and commitment to our homeland. Some will have the right to vote and the responsibility to pay taxes as a result of residency. Others will miss out on those dubious privileges, never mind certain other benefits of being home-based.

Devolution has created a new mood and a new momentum, but our restored Parliament is more than devolved powers, buildings and politicians. It was also formed to change Scotland's state of mind and open up our thinking to new possibilities; created in a spirit of optimism and hope that we can find new solutions to old problems and provide a new focus for our changing relationships with the UK, Europe and the rest of the world.

It must be the Parliament's duty to ensure that Scots never again feel forced to leave and that there is an economy which is robust enough to prevent the perpetual haemorrhaging of the young and talented. Some Scots will still choose to leave – whether for love, lifestyle or job opportunity, it will inevitably happen. Such is the way in a modern world where travel is cheap and the economy is global. Rather than seeing this as a disadvantage, it should be an opportunity for us. We must make a virtue out of what is necessity in the twenty-first century. Our international kith and kin allow us access and influence that other nations can only envy.

For the first time in 300 years, Scottish communities around the globe have a fixed point of reference in our newly-restored Parliament. It is time to bring all our communities together and allow the diaspora to be seen as fellow and equal Scots. They are, after all, 'no awa tae bide awa'.

Kenny MacAskill and Henry McLeish
November 2005

Andy Mooney

CHAIRMAN OF DISNEY CONSUMER
PRODUCTS, LOS ANGELES

From Whitburn to Walt Disney

FROM WHITBURN TO WALT DISNEY is a considerable distance to have travelled, and from a council house in West Lothian to chairman of a global company even more so. Yet this is precisely the journey made by Andy Mooney. As Chairman of Disney Consumer Products he oversees the worldwide promotion of the Disney brand in a range of merchandise, from toys to interactive games, through outlets including Disney Toys, Buena Vista Games and the Disney Store. It's been a meteoric – but meritocratic – rise for a Whitburn lad.

I meet with him at the EuroDisney offices in France, having been told that whilst happy to be interviewed there are some points he wishes to make which may be hard-hitting. Intrigued, I explain to his staff that as well as learning about him, it's important that we learn from him. I want to hear what he thinks of his native land and what it provided for him, as well as what it failed to do.

The offices are located in a new – albeit rather non-descript – development, adjacent to the EuroDisney Parc on the outskirts of Paris. Being chairman of a global brand company, his time is at a premium, but correspondence and communications with offices in Los Angeles and London eventually find a gap in his tight schedule. He has flown in from LA for a regular series of meetings with corporate staff that appear to be both whirlwind and intense, but we manage to fit in a brief opportunity for a chat. He is smart but casually dressed, and looks fit and well for his 49 years. A Scottish twang is still audible in an otherwise neutral accent. Confident and relaxed, he appears a man who is driven and who does not suffer fools gladly – a manner befitting a lad born in Bangour and brought up in Whitburn, who has risen to the very top in corporate America.

Los Angeles is now home for Andy Mooney, with his wife Vizhier, an immigrant from the Philippines. He enjoys America and its way of life, considering himself American. He and Vizhier have both taken out American citizenship and feel they have found a home they enjoy and feel comfortable in. He recalls that he has only ever worked for North American companies, no matter what side of the Atlantic he has been situated on. He felt at ease in the American corporate climate and when he was given the opportunity to travel to the US it became clear that was where he wanted to be. That said, he will continue to return to Scotland and would be happy to spend regular time back in his native land should the opportunity arise.

His background reads like a social and economic history of his home county of West Lothian – industries that have come and gone and attitudes that afflicted the area figure highly in his story. The sectarian divide that plagues Scotland has clearly left some scars. He considers his perspective on Scotland as from a central belt and working class background. He jokes that he has 'lots of American friends who travel to Scotland for various reasons. They come back and tell me what fun they have had in the Highlands or the Borders, and I laugh because I never went to these places. I spent most of my time in the central belt between Edinburgh and Glasgow.' It's clear, though, that he still retains a genuine affection for the country of his birth and the county of his childhood.

His parents, Paul and Esther, were a religious mixed marriage and accordingly moved from their respective villages of Fauldhouse and Blackburn to a new home in Whitburn. His father worked in the mines, initially in shale when it predominated, and then in coal. He subsequently left the pits and worked in the British Leyland plant that had opened in Bathgate. His mother worked with Levi Jeans at their factory in Whitburn for over 20 years. Today, the pits have gone and the factories have closed. His father has passed away but his mother still resides in the town, and his younger sister, Janette, still lives and works in the area. He keeps in touch with home and family with annual visits, and also arranges for them to visit him.

Schooling was at St Joseph's Primary School, Armadale and then at St Mary's High School in Bathgate. Being bussed to school and with both parents working, he describes himself as a 'latch key kid'. With only a few Catholic kids in the area he spent a lot of time at home on his own but had a wide circle of friends at school. It was clearly a happy childhood with fond memories, even if some of Scotland's social ills still rankle.

'A good education which has served me well over the years' was the most important thing that Scotland gave him. Intellect is important to him and is a critical factor for him when recruiting. He still believes that the educational system in Scotland is 'one of the better education systems', producing very smart people, even if, unfortunately, many end up leaving.

Leaving school as he neared 16, he started as a trainee - accountant with Uniroyal at Newbridge following summer work elsewhere. After a year he moved on to Cameron Iron Works in Livingston for five years. In the mid 1970s he moved south to Leeds with the same company. These companies provided him with time and training to do his ICMA examinations, something which he is clearly grateful for, as he became close to qualified by the age of 22. That move to Leeds was what took him furth of Scotland, and it has been onwards and upwards since then.

Following a stint at Perkins Diesel Engines, he joined Nike Incorporated as UK Division Chief Financial Officer and spent 20 years there; moving into marketing in 1982 and holding numerous senior posts. In 1994 the benefits of working for a global company afforded him the opportunity of becoming Chief Marketing Officer for Nike in the USA. As head of their £3 billion Global Apparel organisation, with responsibility for Nike and Jordan brands, he was credited with introducing new advertising strategies.

He joined the Walt Disney Company at the start of 2000, becoming President of Disney Consumer Products and acceding to Chairman in May 2003. His chairmanship is acclaimed as having strengthened the brand and developed stronger relationships with many of the world's largest retailers.

His upbringing has been pivotal in motivating him to succeed, leaving marks as well as driving him on to the top. His contempt of the Scottish focus on religion is mirrored by his disdain for the English emphasis on class. 'In Scotland, when I grew up anyway, your religious background could potentially make a difference in the type of work that you were doing. You didn't have to state your religion on the job application form but you still had to put down what school you attended, so it was known. South of the border, the question is, which university did you go to? Every step of the way in the UK I was in some minority group, either a Catholic up north, or uneducated down south, in terms of not going through a college education.' He recalls a pecking order down south as he remembers a religious divide up north and hence his affinity with the USA – 'because the premises were in Peterborough, it was Oxbridge and then there were even colleges in Oxbridge that had a higher status than others, then there were other universities, and then me. I was the only person that they had as professional staff that hadn't actually gone to university. It seemed to me, therefore, that the States, and the west coast in particular, seemed to be the best place in the world in terms of finding somewhere people could rise to their natural level, independent of their ethnic or social background or their education.'

Though settled in America with only the possibility of limited holidays back in Scotland, he still has a desire to help and advise those back home. Scotland did influence him, and he is happy to try to assist his native land. It's not only in words, but also in deeds, as he is part of Scottish Enterprise's Global Scot network.

Scotland gave Andy much more than an education. Through his parents' influence, but what he also sees as a Scottish characteristic, he had instilled a capacity and belief in hard work. He acknowledges that this is not unique to Scotland, but feels it is typical of the Scots, transcending social classes and being a national trait. The values that were instilled in him were not so much of wealth accumulation, but of self-improvement: 'It was really just doing better that was the driving goal.' His parents, particularly his father, were competitive, and that was passed on to him. He sees that as being peculiar to, if not unique of, the Scots who he describes as 'pretty fearless.' He adds, 'You find that a lot of people who cross the border to go somewhere else are usually quite outspoken compared to their peers of whatever country they are going to. That can be a good thing or a bad thing. I actually think the notion of being fearless and competitive, not combative and warrior like, if packaged properly, can be positive.' That is covered, though, with a caveat that there appears to be an air of acceptance, if not resignation, by many resident Scots, which he thinks could be dramatically improved if leaders emerged to try and give a direction.

Another aspect he recalls, which still impresses him even if it somewhat perplexes him, is the hospitality of the people. He describes Scotland as a 'very welcoming nation. People are friendly, and strangely they are more hospitable to people who come from outside than they are often to each other inside.' It's a virtue that he sees as being an asset for his kinfolk and one to build on in the global world that now exists.

However, there are aspects of Scottish life that he did not enjoy, and if they did not restrict him, certainly rankled with him. He accepts assurances from family and friends that the religious divide and sectarian attitudes, whilst if not crossed and resolved, have improved. Although the totality of his recollections and reminiscences are positive, sectarianism is an aspect of Scotland which has left an unfavourable scar.

His distaste for bigotry is matched by his disdain for prejudice. Whether in church or class limitations, Scotland and the UK fair badly in comparison to his new home. He remembers television soap operas when growing up. He found American ones, such as *Dallas*, to be aspirational, as opposed to the home-grown products such as *Eastenders* which seemed to have 'working class folks, more often than not, putting each other down rather than pushing each other up.' It's a trait he believes is damaging. 'As soon as you aspire and you self-improve, you are pulled down by your peers or friends, like a reverse snobbery. There is definitely a degree of a "kent yer faither" which is unique not just to Scotland, but UK wide.'

He has seen change evolve and hopes ebb and flow over the years for his homeland. That is epitomised for him in his home county which has changed as industries have arrived and departed. 'My experience of it since leaving has been somewhat of a rollercoaster because I was very conscious of how well the economy was doing in the area at the time. You could sense a palpable vibe of whether things were good or not so good. At the time I left, things were very good. Livingston New Town had just been created. The government grants were bringing a lot of industry there. I come back every year and see changes, and places coming and going. The backdrop created a different atmosphere. People had less money, they were less optimistic. Seven or eight years ago companies like Motorola and new technology companies were opening up, and people were buying big houses. The last couple of years it seems to have subsided again. Motorola has now gone.'

He recognises the double-edged sword of Scotland being a place where it's easy for business to get into and simplest to get out of. For him, that means offering something 'other than the financial incentive that would make the country a more sustainable employer's choice.' His solution is to have 'a sustainable competitive management, either in the form of intellect, products, costs, or whatever it might be.'

When asked what Scotland could do to learn from his experiences and his new home, his position as major corporate player in a global enterprise who has risen from the office floor to the very top shines through. He believes Scotland needs to get focused and then properly market itself. 'I think the country has to decide, then communicate, what it wants to be known as a centre of excellence for – is it medicine? Is it biotechnology? Politically, that has to be done. I have worked in other industries where if you aren't on a pedestal then the best thing to do in the marketplace is to say "Hey, I've got a range of products, but these are the ones I am going to focus on and make myself stand out in this competitive landscape."'

He cites an example from his own recent experience with Walt Disney, which is actively expanding in the video gaming industry. 'Canada – both coasts – have been quick to create not just the financial environment to encourage that, but they have been vocal about saying "Come to Canada", because they are going to be one of the future centres of video gaming, so already there have been fairly robust communities that have gone there. My understanding is that Scotland has done some of the same but you really have to dig deep to find out if that is true.'

He is scathing of the stereotypical 'Brigadoon' image of sheep, tartan, bagpipes and golf. Scotland 'should be presenting itself as a contemporary nation of highly educated people. If I were to brand a country like Scotland today to succeed in the contemporary world I would focus on being one of the leading countries in terms of not only creating a highly educated, highly motivated workforce, but also welcoming with open arms anybody of a kindred spirit from anywhere else in the world.' There he sees the friendliness of the folk as a positive advantage.

He senses that things are changing in Scotland. He's proud of its past as well as trying to assist in its future. 'We have got a history of great architecture and great design, just look at Mackintosh. Look at the history of medicine.' That takes him back to focus and branding. He believes 'Glasgow is developing a buzz and striking out a little more in the contemporary scene' even if 'Edinburgh is still on the historical and cultural side of things'. He 'would like to see Scotland become increasingly known as a wellspring of innovation – a place of being hip and contemporary, and capable of producing people and extraordinary products.'

Andy Mooney is evidently genuinely fond of his native land, without the need for misty-eyed romanticism. It has been important in making him who he is, even if that could only be achieved outwith it. That said, it often frustrates him, and he concludes that 'Scotland is a small country in the big world. In the highly competitive world you have got to focus on the things you want to stand out for.'

Interviewed by Kenny MacAskill
March 2005

Professor Neil Walker

PROFESSOR OF EUROPEAN LAW AT
THE EUROPEAN UNIVERSITY
INSTITUTE, FLORENCE

The Lad o' Pairts and the Democratic Intellect

NEIL WALKER AND I SHARED A FLAT in Glasgow 25 years ago. He was a young student from Coatbridge studying law at Strathclyde University, while I was a legal apprentice. For him, a PhD and a lectureship at that university followed. The last time we met was a decade or so ago, when he was a lecturer in the law faculty at the University of Edinburgh, tutoring and publishing in areas from the police to the poll tax. A Chair at the University of Aberdeen came thereafter, and constitutional matters came to the fore in both Scottish devolution and European law.

Today, he is Professor of European Law and Dean of Studies at the European University Institute in Florence. He remains Professor of Legal and Constitutional Theory at Aberdeen, and is considered one of the foremost experts on European law and constitutional matters, not just in Scotland, but throughout the world, writing and lecturing extensively on that and other related issues. Indeed, after we had met and I sought to clarify a few matters with him, I found he had relocated for a month to New York. He records his CV rather modestly but those in the know have already told me that he is flying high in his career and is well respected. Given the ongoing debate on the constitution and overall direction of Europe, Professor Walker is clearly going to be playing an important role in the years to come.

But he hasn't changed much. He remains a tall, easygoing man, bordering on the gregarious. Although he has been in Italy since 2000, his accent sounds as if he has never been away from Scotland. Initially meeting in the new Parliament building (which he has not previously visited, despite his expertise and knowledge in devolution matters), we later adjourn to a nearby hotel to meet Henry and have a coffee. Neil chats freely about his work and life in Italy and is neither a stuffy academic nor stuck in an ivory tower. Instead, he's knowledgeable and down to earth. A learned academic, he has given great thought to our questions, and his answers range wide and deep.

Born in Bellshill Maternity Hospital in 1960, he was brought up in the Townhead area of Coatbridge. There was no history of academia or law in his family: his mother was a housewife, and his father was a manager in the freight sector. Neither attended university. They lived in what he describes as a 'bought' house in the town. His parents now live in Falkirk, and he has a brother who is a tax inspector in Glasgow. He returns reasonably often to meet up with them and maintains regular contact with family and friends back in Scotland. The beautiful city of Florence in Tuscany is now his home, with his wife Gillian and their son. Since our meeting in March she has given birth to another child. He also has a son from a previous relationship back in Scotland.

He attended Coatbridge High School and it's obvious that the Scottish education he received here has played a significant part in making him the character he is and allowing him to achieve the heights he has reached. He is very much the archetypal Scottish lad o'pairts; something his response reflects when asked what Scotland gave to him. Although there was no university background, education was important to his family and there was never anything other than a belief in a meritocracy. Coatbridge was not an affluent town and the high school was not the most illustrious of alma maters – but that was not considered an impediment. If you were bright and studied hard, you would succeed. His views reflect a warmth and gratitude to where he came from and the community that created him.

'That made a huge difference. I took it for granted that I was going to Coatbridge High School, a good school, and I didn't think it was lower down the hierarchy than other schools. The democratic education system in Scotland is good in the sense that as someone who went to a normal comprehensive school, I never felt that I was occupying the second tier of an educational structure. It is particularly important when you are young to realise that.'

But to Neil it was more than simply the opportunity offered by a comprehensive education, but the very nature of the educational system provided. Although now a Professor in European Law, his studies have ranged far and wide, leaving their imprint. He is very much a committed believer in the democratic intellect. 'The other aspect is the idea of it being a broad-ranging education for its own sake, and not an instrumental education where you specialise early in order to achieve a particular purpose. That is very important. Most Scots I know have inquiring minds. One of the reasons they have intellectual curiosity is, deep down, the nature of their education. You were told that languages are as important as maths, which is as important as English and so on. I think that is absolutely vital and that goes all the way through the system.'

Neil also remembers the community which Coatbridge formed, and the importance of this. Travelling extensively, he recognises that all areas universally provide something for their citizens and create a sense of community. It occurs in Italy but is distinct from that which forged him in Coatbridge. What was provided for him was important in creating not just the opportunity for him to prosper but the values and views that he holds. It's something he sees reflected in Scottish beliefs and sense of humour. The distinctive community has created a unique perspective.

'No one coming from anywhere would say they didn't get their sense of community, but you have to take it a bit further than that. The Scottish sense of community is not particularly close. Having lived in Italy for five years, I see a much closer and more smothering sense of local community which has its advantages and disadvantages. There is a sense of abstract community in Scotland. An egalitarian sense – the needs of strangers and being part of a civilised community is very important.'

That sense of community has remained with him and manifests itself in recognition of the role that the community plays in individuals' success. Scots remember where they came from and who created them and that runs deep from a belief in egalitarianism to the sense of humour. 'One thing that is important is a sense of not taking yourself too seriously, nor of taking your successes or failures too seriously. I think it is related to the community thing. Most Scottish people I know have a sense of the contingency of their own life. Any success or failure you have is actually very much dependent on a wider part of your circumstances. They may be the beneficiary or they may be the fall guy.'

Listening to him brings to mind the oft used Scottish phrase, that we are 'all Jock Tamson's bairns'. He says: 'What I mean is that there is a strong sense of being part of a broader society or a broader community. When I hear Scots talking about themselves, I don't often get the sense of "I made it myself without any help". All of these things are important and it is certainly what Scotland gave to me.'

Neil did not leave because Scotland failed him, but because opportunities arose elsewhere. There are natural limitations in Scotland to the number and variety of posts available, not just in his sector but many others. 'My reason for leaving Scotland was not dissatisfaction – it was a personal desire to do something else.'

Scotland is a small country and some posts and opportunities are therefore restricted or impossible to attain. He points out that being part of the Anglophone community opens up possibilities for self-improvement and advancement that may be denied to others, something which is sometimes ignored by Scots. 'The horizons of a small country are naturally limited. In many ways Scotland is better placed than other countries, for example, Finland, which I know well.' He jokes, 'Guys there know 15 years in advance whether they have got the next job, as there are only seven jobs going.' But, he adds, 'There is a lot of cross border mobility, and a lot of mobility in the English-speaking world in general. I would never say I outgrew my roots, not at all. I may well go back. We have to accept that the larger the place the more diverse the opportunities that are available.'

Although Scotland cannot provide all potential employment wants, he believes it can address the question of self-confidence. That is something which he feels is still lacking, impacting on the ability for Scots to take up opportunities and achieve their true potential. He sees it in his son and recalls it from his own youth. If not a Scottish cringe there is most certainly a Scottish constraint on self-promotion and as a result a constriction on success. Being self-effacing is one thing; lacking self-confidence quite another. He's been absent from the country since the publication of Carol Craig's book *The Scots Crisis of Confidence*, and indeed the creation of the Centre for Confidence and Well Being in Glasgow. His remarks show why they have been apposite and appropriate.

'When I went to university my friends from England called it the "wee Mary" syndrome. Wee Mary from Cowdenbeath or wherever was more intelligent than the English yas, but didn't say anything. Interestingly, it is something that you don't realise – you are actually in the situation, you don't grow up thinking "we lack confidence" – you just suddenly meet the situation. I mention this because you meet it in university but you also meet it throughout life. People with what I would call cosmopolitan ease that you don't have, and that is about a lot of things. Again it goes back to the education system.'

He's clearly somebody confident of his own abilities but recognises an inner trait that he has overcome but others still possess. It's a complicated situation, to which he sees no simple solution – but believes education and self-confidence are fundamental.

A change has been noted in his own son who has moved with him from Aberdeen to Tuscany. The learning of a new language and the opening up of another culture has been beneficial for him and in marked contrast to his situation in Aberdeen. 'He is far more confident now than he was as a five or six year old in Aberdeen because he was a quiet guy there. Having to learn another language and another culture – he just couldn't be passive and he had to find a way.'

He sees this reflected in other Scots, resulting in a trait not just of being self-effacing but missing out on possible success. 'Often the things that Scots succeed in are reasonably quiet low level tasks, like building an empire through bureaucracy and all the rest of it. These activities are not necessarily public activities. Even myself, in the university profession, which may not be high profile but is something which is hard work and you could do quietly and effectively (or ineffectively for that matter). I think Scots are good at that, saying "look, I don't worry much about the lack of self-publicity, but I will show that I can do these things." Scots are not lacking in substance.'

Although grateful for his Scottish education, it's obvious that he thinks it failed in that regard, and this needs to be addressed. I have never known him to brag in his life, notwithstanding much justification for it given his intellect and talent. That for him, though, is not the Scottish way, nor does he seek to create that. He simply seeks an ability to be more vocal and public rather than reticent and retiring when we have sensible things to say and useful things to contribute. Being modest as he is should not mean being silent as he has shown.

'It's more a sense of being. A lack of self-confidence in some situations. Scottish people don't apologise for their Scottishness but they do tend to be a bit defensive about it. I meet every nationality and I don't find them saying "despite the fact I come from Portugal" or wherever. Whereas Scots don't actually say that but it's implicit in their attitude.'

Being absent from Scotland has also given him a sense of his homeland's beauty. Coatbridge does not figure highly in Visit Scotland's list of visitor attractions, but he talks fondly of his hometown and longingly of Scotland, comparing his native land favourably with the much quoted Tuscany he now resides in. 'I lived for 40 years in one of the most beautiful countries in the world. It's one of the things I take pride in and never stop telling people about, and they all agree.' Even the weather is not something that detracts from the grandeur of the landscape. Indeed, he lightly adds, 'My wife once described me as liking drizzle – as if to say how absurd it was that someone would like it. But I like the greyness of Scotland. I love bright sunny days too, but I think a lot of our architecture, whether in Edinburgh or Aberdeen, sees the colour and beauty heightened by it.'

So what can his native land learn from this itinerant academic? As befits an intellectual who has given a great deal of thought to the question, he stands it on its head and says that, first and foremost, it's what it must not change or lose. That doubtless reflects the lad o' pairts who has blossomed with the democratic intellect.

'There may be a few things that Scotland can change but there are also things that it has to work hard to preserve. There is a sense in which many of the things I like most about Scotland – democratic education, the upstanding communities, the inter connectiveness and not taking itself too seriously. I think we have to work hard to retain these things.'

He sees that as a challenge in today's global world. However, in terms of change, he sees an outward looking and less insular Scotland as essential. Education and culture are at the root of that. He is now well qualified to comment on both the virtues and failings of a Scottish education, having been given an opportunity to succeed by it, to seeing the limitations of it from on high both at home and abroad. Meritocracy must be maintained, but self-confidence must be nurtured. Current insularity is displayed not simply in poor linguistic skills but ultimately in bigotry. That has to be addressed. 'Scotland has to build its sense of a cosmopolitan community very strongly, both internally and externally. We want to give people the confidence to live with cosmopolitan ease. That doesn't necessarily mean going abroad like I did. It means living with cosmopolitan ease here as well.'

Neil Walker is grateful for what his Scottish education and community enabled him to achieve but is aware of the limitations which certain aspects of Scotland continue to impose. Self-improvement is required, but self-confidence equally so. Who are we to disagree?

Interviewed by Kenny MacAskill and Henry McLeish
March 2005

Reverend Bill Reid

RETIRED MINISTER OF THE SCOTS
KIRK IN PARIS

In the Footsteps of the Tartan Pimpernel

REVEREND BILL REID TENDED TO THE congregation at the Scots Kirk in Paris from 1993 until his retirement in February 2005 when he turned 65. I experienced some difficulty in tracking him down; those to whom I spoke at the Church of Scotland offices in Edinburgh were not aware of his recent retirement and it was only late in the day that members of the congregation kindly passed on his contact details. However hard he may be to trace, he is both courteous and accommodating.

I arrange to meet him, at short notice, the following morning outside a metro station in central Paris and we adjourn to a small, pleasant café in Montmartre, near to where he lives with his wife Esther. He is a fundamentally decent and kindly man with a clear Scottish accent underpinned by the city of Glasgow, in which he was born and brought up. He had described himself as elderly and balding on the phone, but appears active and exuberant in person. Clearly a man eager to enjoy his recent retirement and make the most of the opportunity, he and his wife have decided to spend a few more years in a city they evidently adore. He keeps a very busy schedule – this is no idle retirement.

He is unassuming and queries why I should wish to interview him for a book on the diaspora. Instead he refers me to his three grown-up children who are also Scots scattered to the wind. Alasdair is an economist in Brussels, Ewan works with computers in Amsterdam, and Kirsty is an academic in Bristol. I explain that the diaspora are not all high-flying businessmen or learned academics and I am keen to have a broader point of view. Spiritual service abroad offers another perspective and one appropriate to listen to and learn from. The history of the Kirk is an important part of our country's heritage and in Paris it has been made famous by the Tartan Pimpernel, Donald Caskie. He was a predecessor of Bill Reid's who, following the German invasion of France in World War II, chose to remain in Paris, and was involved in assisting the wartime escape of Allied servicemen from France – a true story of courage that has been covered extensively in film and literature.

That leads him on to giving an outline not just of his service to the Church in Paris but of the Kirk's presbytery abroad. 'The Presbytery of Europe has roughly 12 congregations. That presbytery geographically stretches from Lisbon in the west to Budapest in the east and it goes as far south as Malta. There is a Church of Scotland congregation in almost every mainland European capital in Western Europe, with the exception of Germany. Most of these came about because of Scots travelling and working over many years. Amsterdam's goes back at least to the 1500s. There was a strong link between Scotland and the Netherlands which led traders to have a base in the Netherlands. We have one in Amsterdam, Rotterdam, Brussels, Malta, Rome and Paris, and two in Switzerland.'

He's visibly proud of his roots and the history of his Church. The Church in Paris itself was founded in the 1850s and has occupied several buildings for worship. It started out using a French Reform church, before acquiring what was then the American cathedral and finally moving to a new building in the late 1990s. 'Scots have moved away from their homeland either through employment or through trade. For a long time in the twentieth century the Scottish congregation have made their presence felt in Paris.'

The Scots Kirk in Paris, as indeed elsewhere, was never simply a Scottish enclave but an international one. The reasons are manifold. 'We do our worshipping in English. Having said that, a very real part of my ministering was to the growing number of French members.

We have always had French members, but I saw an increase in the number of French that we had. Outside the French, people come here for a variety of reasons, some of them because of marriage to a Scottish member of the congregation, some of them to improve their English, some of them perhaps don't have any reason. The congregation consists of about 100 to 120 people. Currently we have between eight and 12 different national origins. These stretch from Australians through Africans – we have Malawian families – to Americans; almost any English-speaking country. It is very much a multinational congregation and that is something which is reflected in other congregations in Europe.'

Resident in Paris for over a decade, and with his children furth of his native land, Bill Reid, though a Europhile, still considers himself Scottish. A house is retained in Forres where he previously ministered for many years. He and Esther return there for several weeks a year to relax and catch up with friends. Though born and brought up in Glasgow, Morayshire is now home. 'It's great to have that base. Whilst we love being in France we are conscious of our roots. We discussed years ago the fact that we couldn't sell our house in Scotland as we wanted to keep our base. I think one day we will go back. Perhaps in the post-retirement period – beyond that we are not looking any further. Forres is where our family grew up and I think we would head back there.'

He spent his childhood in the Carntyne area of Glasgow, which he recalls as an upper working class area. Though no parental background in the ministry, he was brought up in the church, with his father an elder and his mother a regular churchgoer, and attending Scripture Union himself. His father was a slater and his mother a housewife. Both parents have since died but he has a sister who lives in the south west of Scotland. He attended Carntyne Primary School and then Whitehill Secondary. He describes himself as having had a conversion experience which he remembers as a significant moment. Studying at Glasgow University and obtaining an MA and BD, he then served as an assistant in his home church in Carntyne. In 1966 he moved to his own parish in Hurlford, Ayrshire, where he stayed until

1973, moving on to Forres where he administered for 20 years, before the opportunity arose to go to Paris.

When asked what Scotland gave him, his faith and the commitment it brought with it is foremost. 'The first thing I derived from Scotland was my religious belief. I was conscious of the rich feeling of religion in Scotland despite some of the problems that go with it.' He viewed Scotland as having a distinct take on faith and its application. Doubtlessly, this is partly explained by growing up in postwar Glasgow, but it is something that he sees as general throughout the land. 'Being born in Scotland, there is a tremendously strong social awareness. I was conscious early on that we Scots had a philosophy or attitude to the social concerns that you don't always find in other countries. I think it is a very positive factor which I think, as a Scot living abroad for 12 years or more, Scotland is still retaining.'

He views both France and Scotland as welcoming countries. He is mindful of past intolerance of religion in Scotland and has read of recent problems with immigration. However, he remains optimistic. 'It's still a country in principle with a very open attitude to people in need, although obviously there are social pressures and other worrying trends. Outbreaks of what we could call racism. I think it reflects on the pressure on people, when societies change and we have a lot of incomers. When we look back, we had a problem with Irish immigration.' He remains positive and upbeat, seeing Scots as diverse; perhaps reflecting his residency in various parts of the country, whether in the city of Glasgow, the coalfields of East Ayrshire, or rural Morayshire.

Growing up in Carntyne, poverty was not an issue he was conscious of (located as it is in the east end of Glasgow). However, on moving to Ayrshire he became involved with many social organisations and saw clear evidence of it. He's proud of his church's involvement in social issues. Faith was a motivating factor but its application equally so. 'The Church has done a great deal to contribute to the social welfare of Scotland. Chalmers, way back in the nineteenth century, had a social welfare programme which some social work departments still don't have. I think it was always wider than religion – and rightly so.' He adds, 'One of my fundamental convictions, which I am sure goes back to my Scottish upbringing, has always been that the gospel has an application to daily life and to those issues. If I didn't have that then it is not worth the candle. From time to time you run into difficulties with that. Church people who want to segregate things and have their wee cosy meeting on a Sunday and not relate that to Monday mornings. Earthed Christianity is part of our rich Scottish heritage; even in the church it has been a feature right back to John Knox's time. The emphasis is on applied religion.'

Though he has commented sadly on past religious intolerance and recent racial disharmony, he didn't depart Scotland because it was lacking in anything, and it is his intention to return at some stage. 'I simply felt it was time to move on and I wanted something very different. The prospect came up and I was attracted to it. I didn't accept because I felt Scotland had let me down or failed to provide anything.'

But he does see things that could be changed and improved in Scotland, learning from his experience in France, mostly on aspects of our society and the actions of people and institutions as opposed to economics. Affairs of state are also mentioned, which is perfectly understandable given his belief in a gospel with an application to daily life. 'There is a greater conviviality built into French thinking and into French society. For instance, cafés where we are sitting now, or restaurants – you can come in at any point during the opening hours of the day. Some of them here in this area will open from seven in the morning until seven at night, or later. You can get anything from a glass of mineral water through to strong spirits. You still occasionally see people here under the weather but it is very rare. Over the past 12 years I can't remember often seeing people rolling about drunk. I wouldn't exaggerate that in Scotland, but I know it exists. Whilst in some ways better than the English, there is a lot to learn with Scots' attitudes to alcohol, pubs etc.' The warmth towards French attitudes extends beyond alcohol to meals. 'One of the things that my wife and I like here, and most visitors from Scotland enjoy, is that a meal is primarily a social event. The French love their food. If you are invited into someone's home for lunch, it is a family convivial atmosphere, which I think we still have in Scotland, but not to the same extent as we used to.'

There are other aspects of French life that contrast favourably with Scottish society. He keeps in touch with events in his native land by reading local and national newspapers online. 'The French also benefit from having no papers which come close to what I would call the gutter press back home. I feel very strongly about this because I detest papers like *The Sun*. France is well served by its press, in the best possible sense. In general, it's a responsible press. To my mind, Scotland used to be well served by the press – *The Herald* is still a good paper, but generally I am disappointed.' But it's not just the press that print the stories, but the people that read them. 'The French are not as pathologically interested in the private lives of public people.' It's said more in sorrow than anger at a society that glees in sin, and individuals who gloat at salaciousness.

He feels he has benefited from his stay abroad. That's evident from his healthy demeanour and a zest for enjoyment following a lifetime of service. He is at pains not to disparage his native land but simply to make observations that he has picked up and he feels would be enhancements not detractions from. He feels qualified to comment but not uniquely so. 'Looking in from the outside, I needed to live outwith Scotland to see some things in a slightly different light. I wouldn't exaggerate it – there are a lot of people with open learning attitudes who have contributed to Scotland. I think Scotland contributes to the international community and the European community elsewhere.' Saying that, he does think it could be improved if it were governed better. 'Living in France has given me a greater perspective on Europe. I think even in Scotland we tend to talk about Europe as if it were "over there" – we forget that we are part of Europe. Thankfully, in some political circles people hammer the idea that Europe and Scotland are one and the same. Scotland has lots to learn from other parts of Europe; to be more open in its potential participation in European affairs. As Scots in Scotland we need to be conscious of trying to improve on that. It is quite frustrating that in the UK setup we are run by UK government policies which tend, in my opinion, to be very blinkered and tunnel-visioned.'

As someone who chose to go abroad out of preference rather than necessity, he has a particular viewpoint but does not feel it to be unique to himself. Moreover, as someone who, whilst absent, keeps in touch and is intent on returning, he is both well informed about contemporary Scotland and harbours a clear affection for it and its people. Moral values are important to him. They found and formed his faith and helped define his Scottish identity. In that respect, he is positive about the nation. 'I don't think Scotland has much to learn in that sense. We have an inbuilt sense. Fundamentally within Scottish society, there is a good understanding of moral issues and a good basis on which we make moral judgements.'

The opportunity to live abroad has been enjoyed by him and it's clearly something that his children have inherited. They were all educated in Scotland and appear to have prospered in it, even if they, like their parents, have moved abroad, whether temporarily or permanently. Confident of his identity, he is anxious not to detract from what he sees as a positive side to being Scottish, though there is room for enhancement and self-improvement in a variety of ways. Values and behaviour are pivotal to that, with the opportunity for the country to improve spiritually as well as physically.

How the Scots see themselves is important to Bill, as befits a man whose vocation has had him examine not just people's exteriors but their very soul. He's a man of faith not just in his God but in his kinfolk. 'It is important that while we learn a lot from other countries we don't downplay what we have to offer. Perhaps we are a bit slow to put ourselves forward. Particularly to learn other languages, but we also have things to contribute. The worst thing that could happen would be if Scots began to think that we are country cousins and that only people who go to other places have a wider perspective. That is rubbish. That's wrong.'

Interviewed by Kenny MacAskill
April 2005

Donald MacLaren

UK AMBASSADOR TO GEORGIA
AND CHIEF OF THE CLAN
MACLAREN

Our Man in Tbilisi

DONALD MACLAREN IS THE UK AMBASSADOR to Georgia and Chief of the Clan MacLaren. An interview has been arranged and I set off for Tbilisi, the Georgian capital. A formal invitation is needed to enter the former Soviet Republic and I am in possession of a letter to the Georgian Embassy in London. The document is stamped by the British Embassy in Tbilisi and signed 'The MacLaren of MacLaren, HM Ambassador'. Passing through Amsterdam Airport on my way there, I bump into an old friend of my brother's, who I have only ever met once in almost thirty years. What a strange world we Scots inhabit: I have a chance encounter in a foreign airport with someone from my hometown, and, having spent almost my entire life in Scotland, I am travelling all the way to the Caucasus for my first ever meeting with a clan chief.

I arrange to meet Donald MacLaren the following day for lunch in a restaurant near the Embassy. Georgia is a country that does not have its troubles to seek. Ethnic and linguistic divisions are compounded by a continuing Russian presence and endemic poverty. The people are friendly but much of their city is dilapidated and fading. There are some pretty buildings, but also some Soviet concrete monstrosities.

The Ambassador's reputation precedes him. I have heard talk of him from locals at meetings earlier in the day, and from others before who have known of him or previously met him. He is highly thought of by all. The Georgians that I speak to are genuinely fond of him, viewing him as open and effective. His Scottishness is viewed as an endearing, if somewhat disarming, trait. Stories of him playing the bagpipes at the Prime Minister's funeral and wearing the kilt on a regular basis are legion, and seem to have passed into local folklore, with clear respect and warmth towards him as an individual. British interests in the world are not always the easiest to sell or to promote, and he is evidently doing an effective job in a challenging country.

He appears in the restaurant true to form: kilted but casually dressed. It is somewhat disconcerting, and on first glance he could easily be mistaken for a Scottish rugby fan on a trip abroad – a casual shirt and shoes offsetting the clan tartan. His bonhomie is evident. He's recognised, and is popular, speaking amicably to staff and other diners. Over lunch he tells me about himself, the Clan MacLaren, his Scottish identity and his hopes for the country. He's lively, intelligent and very passionate, not just about the Highlands, but all things Scottish. His accent, whilst public school, has a distinct Scottish influence, with clear pronunciation of the 'r's and 'ch's. His sense of belonging seems only to have increased with his sojourns abroad. Prior to being 'our man in Tbilisi' he has been in Berlin, Moscow, Cuba, Venezuela and Kiev, alongside stints back in London at the Foreign and Commonwealth Office.

Ironically, he was not born in Scotland, but in St Albans in Hertfordshire. However, that seems only to have made him more aware of his roots, and become more fiercely attached to his identity. 'Alba', he reminds me with a smile, is another name for Scotland. Both his parents were Scottish, with his mother coming from Edinburgh and his father from Turriff, where his paternal grandfather had been the Minister. His father was an officer in the Queen's Own Cameron Highlanders, and then worked in the City. His mother had initially studied medicine at Edinburgh University, before becoming a bookseller and writer. They had met in London and married. Donald was an only child of that union, but each of his parents had been married before and he has a half brother and half-sisters. Both parents are now deceased.

His parents ensured that their offspring would have a knowledge and affection not only for their country, but also their clan. Balquhidder in Perthshire is the ancestral home of the Clan MacLaren and has been since the twelfth century. The family house was tenanted, so his childhood holidays were spent in Dunblane. However, Balquhidder is home. It's not just his village but part of his soul. Summers in Dunblane were not simply for rest and recuperation, but an opportunity for his mother to research clan and highland social history. Family history was passed on down the generations. At a very early age, he imbibed Scottish legends and folklore. He was educated at Glenalmond in Perthshire, followed by Edinburgh University, where he met his wife, Maida, who is also Scottish.

He tells me about the Clan MacLaren. It is something that he is both proud of and takes seriously. Being chief is not just a title but a responsibility. His uncle was the previous chief, but his female cousin had neither interest nor issue to follow. Rather than allow the line to die out, inheritance passed to his father, as recognised by the Lord Lyon, so that the lineage could continue with Donald as heir. The Clan Society was formed in the 1960s, and his father published a history of the clan in 1961. Both parents were active in attending and hosting Clan Society events and highland gatherings. The annual games continue to this day in Lochearnhead, and there are societies around the globe – in Australia, New Zealand and North America – as befits a clan with its chief in Georgia. He acceded to the chiefship at the age of 11 when his father died. Initially he had the guidance of a chieftain of the clan, known as a 'tutor', then at 18 he was inaugurated in his own right at a formal ceremony. The occasion was sombre, following the loss of a loved parent, but significant with the consequent responsibility as chief.

It is principally the clan and family connection that maintains Donald's roots and links with Scotland. His employment with the Foreign Office has resulted in him not just working outwith Scotland, but often being based overseas. But the clan, and duties related to it, ensure regular visits and constant involvement. He makes an effort to be seen not as a chief-in-exile, but head of a strong and active clan society. Some years ago the family house in Balquhidder was restored as home. It has been more than simply a summer holiday residence, with his family living there and his children attending the village school when he was posted back to London. The home in Balquhidder acts as the fulcrum for the family, as the clan did for him. He and his wife Maida have three boys and two girls, their places of birth testifying to his service in the Foreign Office. Two boys were born in Berlin and the third near London; one daughter was born in London and the other in Cuba. Their lives, as well as their births, are international. One son is in the army and served in Iraq; another is working for the International Association for Business and Parliament; and the eldest daughter works with UNICEF. Balquhidder, he tells me, remains home to all of them, and they too are proud of their Scottish identity and clan ancestry.

When asked what Scotland gave to him it is clearly a sense of being and of identity, both with clan and with nation – one whose history and character have been forged not just in adversity but in the overcoming of adversity. 'Scotland gave me my identity. There is a distinctiveness about being Scottish. I feel this strongly as a highlander, as a member of a clan and as head of that extended family. This was given to me by my parents and my kinsmen from an early age, as something to be taken very seriously.'

He believes that being Scottish displays itself in a number of ways. 'There is a sense of inner strength. If things are difficult or if a situation becomes a problem, you tackle it and you get over it. We have always had a defiance, together with resilience and resourcefulness. But Scots are also known for their creativity and their imagination: whether in the arts or sciences, the Scots have a particular talent.' There is neither a sense of superiority towards other peoples nor hostility to other countries, simply a pride in his kinfolk and an awareness of where he belongs. He's proud of the number of Scots like himself who are in the Foreign and Commonwealth Office and who, proportionately, number far more than our percentage share of the UK population. Perhaps, as the saying goes, absence makes the heart grow fonder, but his time south of the border and his sojourns abroad have only heightened his feelings and attachment to Balquhidder, the Clan MacLaren and Scotland.

However, he is no romantic nationalist. His children may have enjoyed the movie *Braveheart*, but he himself did not, mainly because of its historical inaccuracies. 'You could tell a better story about Sir William Wallace by sticking to the real events.' Ambitious for his country, he wishes to participate in its future. As befits a man with a lifetime of public service he wishes to continue that, once his days in the FCO are over. He is genuinely interested in the way the Scottish Parliament will develop. 'This is an exciting moment in Scotland's history. The Parliament obviously has huge potential. There is a great opportunity for Scotland to take stock of where it stands, and what it should be, and can be doing next, to get us over what has been a long period of demoralisation and resignation. We need to break out of that, do things better and move on. Scotland is a great nation and it is time that Scotland proved that today, and I would love to be part of that.'

He is optimistic for Scotland's future but is under no illusions. 'I think that creating opportunity is the real challenge for Scotland today. Traditionally, Scots have thought of opportunity as being abroad, whether that be North America or the Far East – or just England. I think it would be good if more and more Scots saw their future as staying in Scotland itself, but then this goes back to economic opportunity.'

However, he is clear about the solution: 'Make Scotland an attractive place for talented Scots to stay and work in, and make it a place where people believe in themselves.' He sees the constitutional change having a cultural effect. 'Scots will take advantage of the Parliament to build up a greater sense of self-confidence, to rely on ourselves more, not constantly looking round for someone to blame, and certainly not just blaming others for whatever state Scotland finds itself in today.' He is keen for Scots to take responsibility for their own destiny. Interestingly, he argues in favour of fiscal autonomy, or Scotland having its own Exchequer as he puts it. 'That will enable us to take more responsibility, be more competitive, and create more opportunity for ourselves. We should be accountable for our actions.'

As with many who have worked abroad he sees how other small nations have succeeded. 'We certainly can, and should look at countries of a similar size to Scotland who have gone through their own transformation, for example Ireland or the Nordic countries. Scotland shouldn't simply be copying someone else. Every community, every nation is different. But there are lessons to be learned from others' mistakes and successes, and from the sharing of best practice.'

Donald MacLaren is a likeable man and a likeable Scot. I sense a certain self-consciousness about his public school accent. He tells a story of entering a bar in Tbilisi, where a group of Scottish oil workers are watching a Scotland international match. There is much banter and a reference to him being akin to the character 'Jamesie' in Rab C Nesbit. He adds, 'they knew I was from the Embassy and said "c'mon, when we are in trouble you will get us out of prison"'. That said, he was accepted as one of them, and several 'cranberry juices' were despatched. All Scots abroad, one big clan.

He and I grew up in different Scotlands. He was a public school boy in Perthshire and I was a state school lad in West Lothian. But who is to say who is more Scottish? We are equally so; clan chief or shipwright, there is no prerogative on being Scottish. I may have grown up reading Tom Johnston and *The Making of the Scottish Working Class* rather than a history of the clans. Robber barons and idle lairds rather than warrior chiefs. Much of Tom Johnston's history is true and not the romantic picture often portrayed. But Donald MacLaren is equally irked by inaccuracies in history and perception, as his views on *Braveheart* show.

However, this is the twenty-first century. That was then, and this is now. It's not just attitudes to religion but to class that Scotland has to get over and move on from. Prejudice about the school you went to or the accent you have needs jettisoned. Ambassador or oil worker, what matters is whether you identify with Scotland as your country and wish to make it your home. Donald is a talented man, with much to offer. He's keen to contribute, and a small nation which has haemorrhaged talent needs all it can get. As he says, 'I would like to do something myself more directly for Scotland.'

He asks me about opportunities and politics in Scotland. It occurs to me that the Scottish Executive is seeking representatives abroad, from Beijing to Brussels. He has served the UK well, and could equally do so for his native land. With his CV, the Executive need look no further. He asks about which party he might join on his return to Scotland. I offer to sign him up for the SNP there and then: Scottish parties should be forming an orderly British queue to sign up this talent for their team.

Interviewed by Kenny MacAskill
April 2005

Ifeoma Dieke

INTERNATIONAL FOOTBALLER,
MIAMI

Gregory's Girl

IFEOMA DIEKE IS A 24 YEAR OLD FOOTBALLER in Miami. Previously a professional player with Atlanta Beat, she now plays with Soccer Locker whilst coaching at Florida International University. She also plays at an international level for Scotland, and today she's back in Glasgow, having played against England in Liverpool the night before. I arrange to meet her at Hampden Park, home of Scottish football, for a chat before she departs back across the Atlantic. The bus is delayed and I kill time in the café in the Scottish National Football Museum. It's adorned with pictures and memorabilia from the past relating to our national game; a game which we claim to have invented in its modern form. The greats from the glory days – Baxter, Law, Dalglish – are all portrayed with pride.

The previous night I had caught the end of the match on television. Ifeoma was playing centre back. She is quite small and slight but wiry and quick with it: more Willie Miller than Jim Holton, I think. Prior to the game, Scotland's chances were not rated highly. But there's nothing like adversity to bring out the best in Scottish teams. They fought and harried throughout, even though they had a physical disadvantage of being smaller and slighter. Ifeoma played well, showing pace and a good touch on the ball. One Scottish player in particular, Julie Fleeting, strikes me as one of the best players – male or female – whom I have seen in a long time wearing a dark

53

blue jersey. As a disconsolate foot soldier in the Tartan Army, I ponder as to whether the solution to the difficulties in the men's game is not to find players with a distant Scottish grandmother but to bring in some of our own females.

After 90 minutes the game is tied 1-1. A deflection that deceived the Scottish goalie had put England ahead but a spectacular free kick from Julie Fleeting drew Scotland level. Three minutes of extra time were played. One and a half minutes beyond regulation and extra time, a last attack from England saw a ball cut into the Scottish penalty area. Going nowhere, it struck a Scottish defender who was unable to get out of its path. It deflected goalwards, where the Scottish goalie had gone the wrong way. She valiantly arched back and reached a forlorn hand to it but the ball still trundled over the line. The ball was centred and the whistle blew. Scotland had lost 2-1. The Scots girls were devastated and many in tears. It was a typical Scottish defeat. They had not deserved to lose and certainly not in that manner.

I commiserate with Ifeoma and congratulate her on her own game and the team's performance. I have seen it all before, I tell her, whether Argentina in 1978, Italy in 1990 or even when standing on the terraces in the Stade de France in Paris in 1998, when a similar type of goal was conceded resulting in a 2-1 defeat to Brazil. So near and yet so far; to try so hard and fail so cruelly. It's so typically Scottish to lose in such a heartbreaking fashion, I begin to wonder if we are cursed.

Ifeoma is smaller and slighter than she appears on the television. She's friendly and self-confident, even if she's clearly exhausted from the efforts of the night before and the journey home. We chat in the reception area in the main stand at Hampden Park as she awaits her brother coming to collect her. She speaks with a distinctive west of Scotland accent, unchanged by residence in the United States.

Born in America to Nigerian parents, Ifeoma was brought up in Cumbernauld. Scotland is her country and she considers herself Scottish, representing it internationally. She says: 'I view Scotland as my home. Obviously, I was born in America and had the opportunity to play for America, Nigeria or Scotland, but if people ask me where my home is and where I want to play, it's Scotland. I was supposed to trial with the American team but I couldn't go through with it because I think when you do play for a national football team your heart has got to be in it. My heart wasn't in it. I feel Scottish. I don't know much about my family's background in Nigeria. Scotland is my home.'

Her father is a consultant in tourism development, previously a senior lecturer in tourism at Strathclyde University. It's a job that takes him around the world – last year seeing him in Dubai, this year located in the USA – and it explains Ifeoma's global background. Her father's job brought the family to Scotland and, apart from a brief sojourn to Norwich, it has been her home until she moved to Miami. Her parents return regularly to Nigeria but it's not a country that she identifies with other than in her name. Her younger brother who is collecting her today is studying at university in Stirling, and her older sister works in Glasgow. She also has an older brother located in New York.

There was no football background in the family but it's something that she credits Scotland with providing for her. The national game has helped to forge her national identity. She's the embodiment of the movie *Gregory's Girl*, which revolved around a girl growing up in Cumbernauld New Town and wanting to play football. Attending St Mary's and St Joseph's primary schools and then Our Lady's High School in the New Town, football was at the centre of her life let alone her identity. 'The main thing about Scotland is that it gave me the first opportunity to play football. When I went to school in England, girls were not allowed to play football during PE. I always wanted to play football and they wouldn't let me down there. I was one of two girls who played football with the boys' team at St Mary's where I was spotted by the coach of Cumbernauld Cosmos who asked me to join them. That got me into women's football in Cumbernauld which I loved. So that is what Scotland gave to me. I don't know what would have happened if I had stayed in England.'

Her career went from strength to strength. Trophies abounded at her club, Cumbernauld Cosmos, with them winning all three domestic competitions both years she played with them. Her talent was recognised not just at home but abroad. 'After that, I felt I had won every honour there was in Scotland and I needed a new challenge. I was young and ambitious. I went to America, as everyone considers America to be the best, so I went there to challenge myself.' A scholarship in the United States followed. Not only did her football career progress but she also obtained a BA in Management. Following graduation, she played professionally with a team in Atlanta before moving two years ago to her current team in Miami. It's a life she evidently loves – playing the game she adores in a preferable climate. Though she will continue to return to Scotland on a regular basis to meet with family and friends and play for Scotland, she looks destined to be a permanent fixture in Florida. She may be a loss to Scotland but not to the national team.

However, it wasn't just football which Scotland gave to her. She compares education and the health service favourably to her new abode. 'When I was in Scotland we were taught about the world and I think the education system in Scotland is a lot better than the American education system. The health service is better, too. If you don't have insurance in America, that's you.'

Being Scottish has created an attitude and culture of being able to get on with people that she thinks is sometimes not replicated south of the border. She sees that particularly in international football. 'Being Scottish is different. People can distinguish our attitude and demeanour. People enjoy Scottish company more than English company. We are not as arrogant, particularly in football. In Scotland we don't have much expectation – we just go, take part, enjoy ourselves, and if we get far – good. We're not arrogant like the English, who say, straight up, "we're going to win the World Cup". That's a good thing – we are not over-confident, but we don't lack confidence. I see us like the Irish.'

Where Scotland compares less favourably with the USA is in sporting opportunities. 'Facilities are better in America than Scotland. Our big problem in Scotland is money. Sport is not high on the government's agenda. In America they give local, state and national funding. In Scotland, one level of funding is available.' She believes this impacts on the opportunities for individuals and also the performance of the team. Full size indoor and outdoor pitches are essential, and all-weather ones at that.

Although she's conscious both of the sectarian divide in Scotland and of a less racial mix than in the States, it's issues that have never affected her in terms of her footballing career, and which she believes is improving, even if there's still a long way to go. She is supportive of government initiatives to promote anti-racism, including getting footballers themselves involved. It's something which she has not seen done in the States and thinks is helpful here, with footballers acting as role models to impressionable youngsters.

Ifeoma is optimistic for her country even if it's unlikely to be her home again. She's aware of the recent difficulties in the Scottish game and uses that as a point of reference. 'The history of football is a classic example – we have been successful in the past and I think we can get back there. We can be as good as we want to be if we find the right chemistry. The last few years in particular, we saw a foreigner coming in to lead the national team, not understanding the culture and what Scots are based on. But now we have Walter Smith, who knows what Scotland is all about. It's a passionate game and I think if we build a strong squad we will go from strength to strength.'

I could almost be talking to Billy Bremner. Ifeoma is passionate about her country and is proud to represent it. I ask if she is aware of the tale often credited to the late Bill Shankly, the former Liverpool manager who said that when you pull on the dark blue jersey the rampant lion on the chest shouts 'get up, get out and get intae them!'. She replies: 'When I pull on the jersey I get spurred on. I am proud to wear the jersey. There are plenty of other people on the bench who are desperate to play. If you don't have pride and passion then you shouldn't be playing football for your country. We played England last night. You get spurred on because of their arrogance. They think we don't have a chance. That encourages us more. The Scottish mentality is just to fight and never give up. We have a never say die attitude.'

I leave Ifeoma at Hampden Park and daydream about a great day for Scotland and the national team. A full crowd at the national stadium, having seen revenge gained on the Auld Enemy, joyfully streaming out of the ground singing 'Who put the ba' in the English net, Ifeoma, Ifeoma!'

Interviewed by Kenny MacAskill
April 2005

Duncan MacLaren

SECRETARY GENERAL OF
CARITAS INTERNATIONALIS, ROME

Scotland International

DUNCAN MACLAREN IS SECRETARY GENERAL of Caritas Internationalis, a confederation of 162 Catholic relief, development and social service organisations, operating in over 200 countries worldwide, which seeks to build a world of justice and peace. It's the social action arm of the Catholic Church, rooted in the gospel and Catholic teaching but working for all those in need, regardless of race, creed, gender or ethnicity. The organisation has a special status with the Holy See, so Duncan is based in the Vatican City, living in a flat a few bus stops away in Rome. I meet with him today in a small pied-à-terre which he owns in Glasgow. Scotland is still home to him and provides a base for regular sojourns, allowing the prospect of a permanent return at some stage in the future. On this occasion he's back for a friend's wedding anniversary celebrations. He tells me it's a flying visit, and the frequent low cost flights between Scotland and Italy make it all possible, if a little tiring.

When I first considered writing this book, Duncan was an obvious choice for inclusion. He is a man I have known and respected for many years, who is eminently approachable and amenable. He's in as senior a position as they come, in what is arguably the biggest international aid agency in the world, so however obliging he may be, catching up with him is difficult. An initial plan to meet up when he is home for a break between Christmas and New Year is cancelled as he rushes back to Rome following the tsunami disaster in Asia. This is followed by a trip to North Korea, then the turmoil of the death of Pope John-Paul and the appointment of Pope Benedict. He tells me about his trip to North Korea, mentioning that Gothenburg and Tonga are next on his itinerary.

As friendly and considerate as ever, we chat over coffee and croissants in his flat in central Glasgow. He's looking slightly tired, as work has been hectic and his flight here meant an early start. Slightly built, he's bright and cheery. His accent is still clearly Scottish and has not changed at all since I first met him. To assist me in the interview he has kindly prepared a brief biography and obviously given a great deal of thought to my questions and his answers.

What's most surprising about Duncan, given his position and career, is the lack of any Catholic or even religious background. He was in fact notionally Protestant in affiliation at birth. However, his family were very involved in social justice through political and trade union matters. His biography narrates that he was born in Dumbarton in 1950 into what he says Scots erroneously call 'an ordinary working class family'. His father was a printer and an ardent trade unionist, who ended up as father of the chapel. His mother was a housewife and he was an only child. Both parents have now passed away. He was brought up in Clydebank, apart from a brief stay in London when his father was forced to find work there, which, he recalls, left a few bruises as he was picked on by pupils and teachers as a result of his Scottish accent. The family returned to Clydebank and stayed initially with grandparents before obtaining a council tenancy of their own elsewhere in the town.

He attended Elgin Street Primary School and then Clydebank High School. His grandfather, Willie Ireland, influenced him considerably. He remembers him as 'an old communist', but possessing decency and humanity. He recalls the funeral of Pope John XXIII on television and his grandfather commenting that he had been 'a good man' – the first nice thing he could recall him saying about a Catholic, never mind a Pope.

Leaving school, he studied languages at Glasgow University. A year in Switzerland followed, which improved his skiing if nothing else. His mother's ill health brought him home and he worked as a researcher in the Celtic department at Glasgow University, part of which saw him recording the last Gaelic speakers in Perthshire where his father's family originated from, one of whom was in fact his grandfather's cousin. As well as his degree in languages he later did a postgraduate in Theology and Development Studies at New College in Edinburgh.

Notwithstanding his grandfather's communism and his father's union activism, Duncan had been very active in the SNP and he applied for and obtained the post of researcher with the SNP Parliamentary Group in Westminster. He spent two years in London, then six years back with the Party in Edinburgh.

His introduction to Catholicism came through a girlfriend whilst at university in Glasgow. Through her he was introduced to Father Gerry Hughes at the Chaplaincy, who embodied the social justice that he had been brought up with, together with a burgeoning spirituality within himself. He started going to mass in Switzerland, even though he had still not officially become a Catholic. His route into the Church was laid when he was working in Edinburgh and was introduced to the late Father Anthony Ross. His faith is now evident but it is clearly rooted in his past through a commitment to social justice.

He considered becoming a Dominican Friar, but instead became a co-founder of a new lay group within the order, and remains a member to this day. He's very proud of his Catholicism, and of the Church in Scotland, as befits someone with nationalist sympathies. Scotland, he tells me, is the only country in the world where the Church is recognised even though the state is not. 'There is no other country or state in the world that has this situation. The Bavarian Bishops will meet together but they belong to the German Bishops Conference, the same with the Catalan Bishops and the Québécois Bishops in Canada. This is the only state in the world where the Catholic Church is recognised even if Scotland is not a state. The reason was that the Scottish Catholic Church has always been a church that has been oppressed but has remained alive and has remained loyal to the Pope and to Rome. So Scottish Catholics, far from being intruders into Scottish society, are, on the contrary, part of its history. The English bishops told Rome to ignore the Scots, but Rome rejected this and continued to recognise Scotland.'

He subsequently left his job with the SNP to become the first Director of Scottish Catholic International Aid Fund (SCIAF), the overseas aid organisation of the Catholic Church in Scotland, and the Scottish branch of Caritas Internationalis, of which he is now Secretary General. He was there for 12 years before being approached in 1995 to become Head of International Relations for Caritas. In 1999 he was elected Secretary General and was re-elected, unopposed, in 2003. His contract will end in 2007 and he thinks it will then be time for pastures new.

He is a highly influential and respected man, yet is modest and unassuming, both in his biography and in his chat with me. Even in his position, there is never a hint of arrogance or boastfulness. It's simply a matter of steely determination based on faith and commitment. It's evident that he thoroughly enjoys his job, not least because it allows him to practise the faith and the principles that he is committed to. He spends about 40 per cent of his time abroad, overseeing the international plan that the organisation approves every four years. The current plan includes advocacy for the poor; peacebuilding and reconciliation training; the co-ordination of dealing with major emergencies; liaison with the seven global regional structures; humanitarian standards; work on issues such as gender; and relations with the United Nations, Vatican and other organisations, both secular and of other faiths. He's also currently Chair of the Steering Committee for Humanitarian Response (SCHR) which brings together all the chief executive officers of the large international humanitarian networks, from the International Red Cross to Oxfam International.

Until recently, he has been penning an occasional column in a Sunday newspaper on his reflections from Rome, and that leads me into asking him what he feels Scotland gave to him. His answer befits someone who has followed a path of spirituality blended with justice and fairness – community, education and values. 'Scotland gave me a sense of community, of belonging to a community, which

I have taken into my work. It has given me a sense of openness too, and my colleagues in other parts of the world say I am extremely open to them. It gave me an excellent education. Clydebank High School was a good school with nearly all working class kids. My grandfather, from a humanist point of view, gave me a sense of humour, and one of my delights is to get off a plane here and just hear the wit on an ordinary Glasgow bus.'

Scotland has also provided the platform for his international work and outlook. 'I was interested in international work. I had lots of penpals all over the world so I am not surprised that I ended up doing international things, and I think Scottish society encouraged me, especially my education, particularly the languages – looking outwards and looking at foreign countries. I remember going on a school cruise to Morocco and I had learned two words of Arabic and I used them and people were absolutely delighted. The very fact you had taken the time to attempt to learn a tiny bit of their culture was something that stayed with me. I think it is part of the Scottish attitude to the outside world. Scotland could be even more outward looking if it had a political role in the international scene.'

As you would expect from someone who has worked in politics, he sees it expressed in that arena, adding that 'it is significant that UKIP have got 12 seats across England but none here. The BNP have never been able to take much of a hold here. I am proud of that and I think it is part of our democratic tradition when you go away back to the Declaration of Arbroath. All of those things I take into my work.'

His departure from Scotland was not due to any disgruntlement with the country, but simply that there was nowhere further for him to progress to. That's something he is disappointed in, not just for himself, but for the country. It's obvious he wishes that there were not just more job opportunities, but also international involvement here in Scotland. 'I think Scotland has given me a great deal. It has helped me in so many ways. I feel quintessentially Scottish but in my kind of field and one in which I may want to continue, there is no way I can return to Scotland in 2007. I was director of the only independent Scottish Aid organisation. If I had left that and gone to another organisation here it would have been a branch of a British Organisation which basically does two things: fundraising, and awareness and developmental education work in Scotland. They don't deal with projects, appraisals and humanitarian standards, and so on that SCIAF does. So after SCIAF there was nowhere for me to go, except either England or abroad. The limitations were the political limitations within Scotland.'

He also sees a dark side to Scotland, mostly due to sectarianism. He is pleased to see it being addressed with some vigour, even if there have been recent shameful incidents. He recalls that when he was Director of SCIAF, he and the then Secretary of Christian Aid in Scotland thought it might be a good idea to merge the two organisations into one Church agency, partly as a sign of ecumenical commitment and partly for efficiency's sake. A concept paper was written and he took it to the Scottish Bishops who pronounced it interesting and said they would consider it. His colleague took it to the board of Christian Aid in Scotland who rejected it. Duncan narrates that his colleague left disappointed shortly thereafter. He adds, 'It was at that point I thought that there is a narrowness of vision in this country. This was a radical idea, an innovative idea; but to nip it in the bud, not even think about it and just discard it completely, was bad. The relations between the churches are good but actually getting together is out of the question.'

I am assured, not only by Duncan but by others involved in the churches, that the relationships between them are as good as he professes. Moreover, that there are doctrinal issues together with practical implications that impact on co-operation. However, it does begin to appear that sectarianism and tribalism may run deeper in Scottish society than simply hooliganism at football matches and general ignorance.

Duncan is ambitious for Scotland. He, as you would expect from a former SNP member of staff, believes in independence. 'I joined the SNP at 15, although I was supposed to be 16. My feelings haven't changed. The concept of independence has changed, and I am a passionate believer in the European Union. I think that the Scottish

Parliament will only go so far and will be stopped unless it has the political powers to do so as an independent nation.'

Those views might be considered as typical of many, but it's what he believes Scotland could do in the field of international aid that is interesting. He is ambitious not just for his country to be recognised in the international community as in the Catholic Church, but to participate in world affairs. 'I think the more countries that are peace-brokers in the world such as Norway and Finland, the better. It is important to have partnerships between Scottish communities and African communities and so on. I think there is a sense of community in Scotland. There is a lot we can do in that area as an independent country. If you look at Norway, it was a major peace-broker in East Timor and is a major broker in Sri Lanka. They are trusted and are therefore called upon to aid conflicts. I feel that Scotland, with its history and community-based society, could play a similar kind of role.'

There are matters at home that need addressed. 'Every time I come back to Scotland I am appalled by the poverty I see on the street on the faces of the people of Glasgow. I don't live very far from Buchanan Street. You go down there and look into people's faces – appalling poverty needs to be tackled. I would like the churches to be even more involved in tackling poverty than they are already. Caritas Germany, for example, is an overseas programme, but is in fact the largest employer after the German state for poverty and health related organisations within Germany. We don't do that in Scotland. Churches are involved in these kinds of things but it's voluntary. To tackle endemic poverty that we have in Scotland we need much more political will.'

On a happier note, he's appreciative of immigrants and refugees, who he believes add vibrancy and culture to the city. 'These people become Scots. I used to live in Maryhill and the corner shop was owned by a Bangladeshi family but they were adopted Glaswegians. They appreciate being Scottish. We should appreciate them.'

His time in Rome has left him with the view that there's politically little to learn from Italy. He sees it as a country corrupt from top to bottom, though he whimsically recognises that socially it has things to offer. 'We have to make sure we have checks and balances in Scotland so that we don't go down the same way. Particularly when it is one particular political party that dominates politics. What Scotland hasn't given me in a personal sense? People tell me that I dress slightly better now. I certainly prefer drinking wine to lager. I don't feel guilty about any of it.'

Duncan MacLaren radiates as a man of deep faith and integrity. Practising what he preaches, he has put Scotland on the international stage but he is keen for it to do more. He is grateful for what it has given to him but recognises problems that still exist within its society, whether economic, social or political. But he remains eager that Scotland should have the opportunity to provide more for others as well as to address the flaws within. I can't help thinking there's something sadly lacking when Scotland is unable to provide a platform for a talented and committed individual to create a better land at home and a fairer world abroad.

Interviewed by Kenny MacAskill
April 2005

Bill Sim

SENIOR VICE PRESIDENT OF PEPCO
HOLDINGS INC., WASHINGTON DC

Gorgie Boy Lights Up Washington

BILL SIM HAD BEEN MENTIONED TO ME by several people when enquiring about expatriate Scots to interview in America. They told me that not only was he a highly successful businessman in his own right, but he was also very active in promoting Scottish interests across the Atlantic – one of a hardy band of people seeking to promote Scotland economically and not just participate in cultural Caledonian society events. A quick Internet search for William Sim at Pepco confirmed his status as a senior corporate executive in the United States. A page of news reviews and profiles, both informative and laudable, is instantly conjured up. He's the Senior Vice President of Pepco Holdings Inc., responsible for all utility operations in an energy company which provides gas and electricity to more than 1.8 million customers in America's capital and the eastern seaboard states of Maryland, Delaware and New Jersey. Power and light are provided from New Jersey down to Washington DC and from Atlantic City across to Philadelphia.

His CV narrates that he joined the Potomac Electric Power Company as a manager in 1977, and has worked his way successfully up the company ladder ever since. He was born in Edinburgh but graduated from Glasgow University, and has an MBA from Maryland. Aside from his business prowess, he's on the Board of Visitors for the Engineering School at the University of Maryland,

and a member of the Leadership Washington, Class of 2003. He has also been involved in numerous civic and charitable organisations, from the Board of Trustees of the Round House Theatre, through numerous boys' and girls' clubs, to being the past chairman and founder of the Soccer Association of Columbia, Maryland.

An e-mail to him brought an immediate and positive response. He departed for the United States in 1970 but has returned to Scotland annually ever since. When his children were younger his wife brought them back for much of the summer and he joined them for several weeks. Both his parents have since passed on but the annual pilgrimage continues. His mother's twin sister is still alive and well, fiercely independent and residing in Morningside, Edinburgh. As fortune has it, he's due back in the coming weeks to visit his aunt and reconnect with Scotland, so we arrange to meet up when he is on this side of the Atlantic.

As with many participants in this book, we meet in the new Parliament building. The thought occurs to me that Holyrood is providing not just a visitor attraction for tourists but a fulcrum around which the diaspora can focus. Rather than each Caledonian Club or Clan Society operating in isolation, there is a heart in the Scottish Parliament building to return to, and a hand in the Scottish Executive to steer them.

Bill Sim has been in the building previously and is clearly pushed for time as he finalises affairs in Edinburgh and prepares to return to the States. However, he never says a word about that and is patient and obliging throughout. At 60 years old he looks well and is courteous and considerate – an amalgam of Scottish decorum with American manners. He is modest and unassuming, completely devoid of airs or graces. His accent is no longer east of Scotland, nor is it east coast American – it belongs somewhere in the mid-Atlantic. He reminds me of my late father, though I don't tell him that. I can't help thinking that there is something about Scots of that generation that is universal and thoroughly decent. He tells me, with obvious pride, that he's a Gorgie Boy. His father was from Macduff in Banffshire, his mother from the capital, but he grew up in Wardlaw Place, adjacent to Tynecastle Park Stadium, home of Heart of

Midlothian Football Club. He's a lifelong Hearts fan, and he tells me that one of the first games his father took him to was that in which Hearts won the League Cup in 1958. He proudly tells me he can name the team to this very day, and does so! His passion for football continues to this day with his involvement in the Maryland Soccer Association.

His father was a painter, in an artisan rather than artistic sense, while his mother was a housewife, and he was an only child. As his relationship with his aunt testifies, it was a close family. He attended Craiglockhart Primary and then the Royal High School. In 1958 his father did some work abroad and saved a bit of money, allowing the family to buy a newly-built house in Penicuik, though he continued to attend the Royal High. His memories of Midlothian are as fond and happy as those of Gorgie. He wistfully recalls long summers, endless football games with his friends, and acting as a tourist guide during the Edinburgh Festival with the Scouts.

Education was important to his family and it is something that he is both proud of and grateful for. His background is not atypical, but he is well aware of the sacrifices his family made for him and the chances his society gave him – allowing him to achieve what he has. 'It started in high school and continued through university. The whole education system benefited me. I was the first in my family to go to university. My parents were keen for me to get a good education, although there was not much money going around. It was bad enough coming up with money for the school uniform each summer.'

Glasgow University offered a degree in engineering. But university was more than just an education, as he was actively engaged in the social scene, serving as Secretary of the Students' Union and President of the Scottish Engineering Students Association. During a summer job, whilst still studying, he was dispatched to Runcorn in England, where he met Anne. They married before his graduation and have been together ever since. The Scottish education system is something that he is deeply grateful for and supportive of, and believes it compares favourably with that across the Atlantic. He welcomes the breadth of its studies and the width of its activities. 'Scotland gave me an education that was broad. You see people in the US who are very insular. Once you get your education you see where you are going. The education we had in the late fifties and sixties gave you a chance to get out there.'

And get out there he did. After graduation, numerous job offers followed. He was keen to be involved not just in design but also in construction, and accepted a job in London. A few years on, as his experience grew, he was offered the opportunity to go to the United States where a major building project was underway. He and Anne left with the intention of enjoying a few years in another country and absorbing a different culture. The job that had taken him across the Atlantic ended but he and his wife were not for returning, and employment in other major construction projects followed, some in the USA and some elsewhere. A few years became many years. As his CV states, he joined the Potomac Electric Power Company in 1977 as Manager, and is now the Senior Vice President for the holding company. His son Christopher and his daughter Joanna were born in America, and in 1995 he became an American citizen.

Scotland, though, has never stopped being part of what made him and who he is. His education was pivotal in that; provided by parents eager for him to improve himself, in a country that valued education in itself. Like many Scots, he is reticent about his achievements, though they are many, but he is vocal about what he sees as the basis of them. He is long gone from his native land, having taken out citizenship in his new home, but he has not forgotten Scotland and never will. His family came back for six weeks every summer, even if he could only return for two or three himself. His children consider themselves Scottish Americans, even though their mother is English. His son works in retail in New York and his daughter is an artist in Florida, but Scotland is where they identify with in the American milieu. Bill Sim's love of football has been passed on through the generations to his son, who played at high school and college, and to his first grandchild who has already received a football and a Scotland top. A shopping trip for the football strip had been a vital part of the visit home.

As with numerous kinfolk before and doubtless more to come, Bill Sim did not consciously choose to leave Scotland – it just happened that way. The nature of the work he was involved in and the opportunities available to him meant that it was almost destined to happen. 'When I came out of college I knew I wanted to be in the construction business, and in the project manager part of the business – I didn't want to be in the design part. I didn't physically intend to move away, and I didn't physically intend to stay in America. That's the way life developed and opportunities arose. I think one of the things that the USA does offer is opportunities. You could settle down almost anywhere and opportunities open up. I can tell you, that is a plus point for the States and a minus here in the UK. If the job hadn't come up in the States I would probably still be here.'

I asked Bill what he thought Scotland might learn from him or adopt from where he now lives. He was once again modest and unassuming, telling me that he doesn't know what he would do to change it for the better. Yet I knew that Bill was actively involved in promoting Scottish interests, not just culturally through assisting in Tartan Day, but economically in a myriad of other ways. He is ambitious for Scotland and wants to help in its social and economic improvement. Given his business experience, he is conscious that it's a global world and some industries that were symptomatic with Scotland are lost and gone for ever. But he sees hope in other sectors. 'It is a global world. You have got to adapt. The financial community is sound. There are opportunities to build and finance some of the hi-tec knowledge-based businesses to develop it further. One of the challenges is how to do that. It is an education issue. There is no silver bullet. It's a long journey, with lots of relationships, but there are major opportunities, with Edinburgh being as high as it is in the finance side of the house. It's a relationship business – there is no quick fix.'

Where he is well-versed to comment and begins to open up is in relation to Tartan Day. He's no 'Brigadoon' Scot, but sees benefits that can be derived through using tartan imagery to draw in friends and funds. He tells me that he only recently joined the St Andrew's Society, and that was at the request of some friends. Whilst he enjoys Burns suppers, other aspects of what is portrayed as Scottish culture and heritage are not for him and he finds them uncomfortable if not unpleasant. As a businessman, he sees an opportunity to use a soft sell to promote a hard product. 'We need to get some sort of gateway; of using what's there. Tartan captures the attention. Tartan Day offers opportunities in Washington and New York and perhaps Chicago. I don't think there's such a Scottish connection in California to develop but there certainly are bases in those cities. There is an opportunity to exchange information. Just to get the Scottish thing going. This is what we are doing; this is what is going on and what you could do to help. Washington DC is an international centre that can help with that. It is a fantastic opportunity for people to discuss links further.'

Bill Sim's take on Tartan Day is a bit like my own and others' opinions on Scotland as a whole: it's doing well, but could do so much better. He clearly has a sense of frustration at what struggles to be done, as opposed to what could easily be achieved. The tartan paraphernalia and the shortbread tin image have a place, but must be balanced with a drive for economic progress and social advantage. 'You can use the tartan and historical stuff to capture people's attention but we have to get more business people involved in Scotland. I love Burns' Nights and I have been involved with them for 35 years. But businesses can provide the balance. These people can tell each other where Scotland is going to benefit – be it in financial services or otherwise.'

I can't help noticing that despite having been away for 35 years and now being an American citizen, he still talks about 'us' when referring to Scotland. It's a subconscious use that he is unaware of but it shows his genuine commitment to help his native land. All the extensive calls on his time and doubtless cost to himself and his family life, he does for nothing. It's therefore important that Scotland should listen to him when he has remarks to make and points to raise about how we are operating and performing in America. He has worked with the staff sent over by the Scottish Executive to promote Scotland, albeit working out of the British Embassy. He is unstinting in his praise for their efforts which is not something matched by press or politicians back home. He does believe that a greater secretariat is needed – too few are doing too much, and as a result not enough is getting done. The structures matter and resources are vital. A greater input from Scotland to add to the volunteer base could see not just Tartan Day celebrations but also Scotland's economic gains from its diaspora really take off.

He makes a final point, which I have seen at first-hand having been on a Tartan Day delegation, that Scottish politicians must appreciate: when abroad, they are all on the same side. The actions of some and political factionalism does a disservice to the individuals involved and is a discredit to their country. He is quite pointed if not barbed in his comments and I must say, rightly so. He is doing this for nothing and he has a right to expect better from myself and my colleagues. 'When you leave Scotland, leave Scottish politics behind. We have enough problems in DC with US politics, without worrying about Scotland's. Petty infighting and point scoring must cease. Everyone should be on the same side. Everyone is there to represent the same country.'

So a Gorgie Boy lights up Washington with its light and power. He may be settled with his family across the wide Atlantic, but he retains affection for his native land and is unstinting in his efforts to improve and promote it. The efforts of himself and his colleagues is on a voluntary basis, and must be matched by equal and greater commitment from politicians and government here. It's the least we owe him.

Interviewed by Kenny MacAskill
May 2005

Paul McAleavey

HEAD OF CLIENT RELATIONS FOR
THE EUROPEAN ENVIRONMENT
AGENCY, COPENHAGEN

Flying High from Fishcross

PAUL MCALEAVEY IS FLYING HIGH in more ways than one. Formerly a special adviser to Margot Wallström, European Environment Commissioner in the European Parliament in Brussels, he is currently heading up client relations for the European Environment Agency in Copenhagen. It's a busy schedule living with his new partner in Malmö, Sweden. He commutes daily to Copenhagen and returns fortnightly to Scotland to see his two young daughters who live in Edinburgh with their mother. Whether he remains on the continent or comes home to Scotland, he is assured a bright future.

Copenhagen is a long way from the small village of Fishcross in Clackmannanshire, where his parents still occupy the house in which he grew up. He regularly returns to Fishcross, sometimes with his children, but more often to take advantage of the family's season ticket for Celtic Football Club. The community of Fishcross has left a deep impression on Paul, perpetrating him with values and ideals which he has never forgotten.

He belonged to a mining family as well as a mining community. Whilst not a wealthy area financially, he sees it as rich in a myriad of other ways. Being safe to roam in fields and woods and to play football with friends he considers priceless. His father was an electrician in the pits, where his grandfather also worked. Following the strikes in the mid-eighties, his father was made redundant, leading him to teach in the local further education college. Paul was the youngest of five children, keeping his mother busy at home. It was, and remains, a close-knit family in a close-knit community. One of his sisters still lives in the village, and his brother resides in nearby Sauchie. He still has close friends from school living and working in the area.

Following his education in the village school, he attended Lornshill Academy in Alloa. There he recalls a young Jack McConnell – then a teacher and now First Minister. Though he was not his set teacher, Paul was occasionally tutored by him, and there are memories of Mr McConnell enforcing discipline in an adjacent unruly class. However, it is obvious that as well as discipline, the future First Minister instilled respect among staff and pupils.

Although each of his family was very smart, Paul was the first of them to enrol at university. Modestly, he puts that down to being the youngest, which brought with it not just greater attention but a single room when his brother left home to join the army.

It was not just the mining community in which he grew up, but the miners' strike that moulded him. He remembers the strike vividly. His father was out for the duration and he recalls not just the poverty occasioned by it, but the violence accompanying it in a community faced with strike breakers. The strikes rocked the whole community, including Paul's family. It was a particularly tough time for Paul as he was sitting his Higher examinations during the action. The strike helped shape his political convictions and he remains a Labour party member to this day.

Notwithstanding the difficult backdrop, his natural ability saw him through his exams. Perhaps as a result of the ongoing events, together with financial constraints, he was desperate to leave school as soon as possible, and went straight to university at the age of 17. Little thought was given initially to where to go or what to study, so he embarked on a course in Electronic and Electrical Engineering at Strathclyde University, because of the campus's proximity to Celtic Park and the working class desire for a vocational degree. But the course was, if not quite an unmitigated disaster, most certainly not for him. Unhappy, he sought to drop out, and recalls returning home with some trepidation to tell his father of his proposals, only to be given full support and encouragement to pursue whatever he wanted and to be assured of full support in whatever that may be. On the bedrock of that he returned to Strathclyde to complete an honours degree in Political Science and Economics, but recalls that as well as parental support he had government funding. 'At that time I was able to get five years' funding so I went back into first year to do Political Science and Economics and that is what I graduated in. It was a fantastic opportunity to have gone back and still get funding to do an honours degree, even though I had dropped out of my first year. I am not sure you would still be able to do that, but it was a great experience.' He also points out that he left with no debt straddling him. Current politicians, including myself, would do well to note the benefit of allowing some flexibility to students who find themselves on courses that they are clearly unsuited for and to remedy that without huge financial burdens.

Prior to graduation, Paul travelled and having enjoyed the experience so much, decided that he wished to learn and study abroad. As a result he successfully applied to do a PhD at the European University Institute in Florence, recalling with amusement that the interview had seen a shortlist drawn up detailing other candidates from Oxford, Cambridge or whatever other illustrious alma mater, while 'Fishcross' was simply recorded against his name. Four years were spent in Florence, with a year back in Scotland working for the Scottish Office. After graduation he decided he wanted a career in the public sector and applied to work in the European Commission. Out of 55,000 applicants, only 200 were recruited. He was one of them, and it saw him move from Florence to Brussels.

At the Commission he worked under and was influenced by Alan Larsson, Director General of the Employment and Labour Market section. He had been a Social Democratic Finance Minister in Sweden prior to his nomination to the Commission. Alan became a mentor to Paul, resulting in a continuing Swedish connection when he moved to working as special adviser for Margot Wallström in 1999, when she was appointed European Commissioner for the Environment. He wrote speeches for her and advised her politically for five years as they collectively clocked up the air miles debating and discussing Kyoto and other matters in Washington, Moscow and Beijing.

Domestic matters then impacted on his European career. He married a fellow Scot he had met in Florence and they moved together to Brussels. Ending in divorce, he had to decide whether to return to Scotland or move elsewhere. As a result of a new relationship, and doubtless the influence that both Larsson and Wallström had on him, he decided to move to Sweden. An opportunity arose across the Öresund Bridge at the European Environment Agency in Copenhagen, where he now works. He remains a European Commission official but on secondment. The Agency is responsible for collecting data on the European Environment and he heads up the team responsible for relations back in Brussels with both the Commission and the Parliament. At the age of 37 he's certainly flying high from Fishcross.

It's during one of his regular fortnightly trips home to see his two daughters, Ailsa and Hannah, that we arrange to meet up at the Scottish Parliament, organised around his taking them to school in the city. It's clear that he loves them dearly and takes his parental responsibilities very seriously, despite the difficulties caused by living in a different country. He is youthful, friendly and casually dressed. We tour the Parliament building because although he had been on a visit in an official capacity with the Commissioner to the temporary home on the Mound he had not yet visited the new building. He has previously been involved in parliamentary life, however, having been part of the backroom Labour team for the 2003 elections during a leave of absence. He may not know his way around the building, but he knows his way around the corridors of power both in Holyrood and in Brussels.

Fishcross and the values it instilled in him are fundamental when I ask him what Scotland gave him. 'I am unsure whether it's a peculiarly Scottish experience but in the sort of community I grew up in I had a sense of fairness drummed into me. My grandparents and my own parents gave me a tremendous opportunity and fantastic encouragement and really drummed into me the importance of education. I appreciate that as being something that came from my family and my schools. Being brought up in Scotland, I had fantastic opportunities to pursue education. That is one of the most important things which Scotland gave me.'

Scotland and Fishcross shaped not just his political values but also his sense of identity. And that identity, and his confidence in it, is something he considers to have grown and developed over recent years. Initially, he felt like many Scots do: a conflict between the need to express his national identity and not be tarred as a narrow nationalist. 'One thing I didn't like in the early days of living abroad was that if I wanted to mark the fact that I was Scottish then I had to somehow almost apologise that my national identity did not mean that I was xenophobic or that I hated English people, or anyone else for that matter, because I don't.'

He senses that not only has he changed, but Scotland and the Scots have. A growing political maturity in the country has been matched by an increase in self-confidence amongst the people. 'Leaving Scotland in 1990, with the political debate that was going on at the time, gave me a clear identity. I can say that Scots are not short on their sense of self-identity, but that it has changed over time. When I went abroad at first it was very important to me to mark the fact that I was Scottish and I was forever correcting Italians who referred to me as "inglese". I always made it clear that I was Scottish. There was a whole lot of debate going on at the time – the constitutional convention and the whole devolution/independence debate, particularly after the 1992 election result. I felt stridently Scottish and felt I had to justify it. But as I have got older and Scotland has matured it is a lot easier now to be Scottish. I don't feel I need to wear a Scottish badge to show I am Scottish. I think that the prominence that was given to Scotland across Europe at the time of the referendum and the whole debate about the new Parliament really helped it calm down and people started recognising me as a Scot without me having to press my case. I feel more relaxed in my sense of Scottishness and I think that others recognised post-devolution as a separate identity for the Scots.'

Paul McAleavey is confident in himself and in his country. He sees ongoing debates – whether on alcohol abuse or sectarianism – as a healthy aspect of a fledgling democracy. 'I have lived on and off in Italy for four or five years, worked in Belgium for ten, and now I cross the bridge every day from Sweden to Denmark, and for me the debates are the same in every country. You don't need a chip on your shoulder or a Scottish cringe. The Swedes are having the same debate on alcohol. The Belgians continue to argue about their own internal divisions and Italy has its own problems as well. It is just a recognition of the maturity of our country to actually admit "we are brilliant at this but are less good at that." Growing up in the 1980s and 1990s through Thatcherism – it is normal that we have a deep debate about what we are as a country and maybe it's more pronounced in Scotland. I lived in Italy at the time of the "clean hands" corruption scandals – you can't imagine the debate it sparked off. In Sweden too, the high profile murder of the Foreign Minister in 2003 – in a land still recovering from the assassination of the Prime Minister some years earlier – led to debates as to whether the Swedish model of the "open society" was collapsing. It is normal that nations should have such debates.'

He's confident not only about attitudes of the people but what is happening on the ground in his homeland. From his own experience in environment, he has praise for progress made. He recalls the difficulties of the 1990s, and is conscious of the time needed to see environmental change come through. 'We had a long period of under-investment – you can't turn that around overnight. I personally think that the environment is relatively high on the agenda with the Executive. I think that the renewable energy targets which have been set for Scotland are at the forefront in Europe and I am quite proud of that.' Further progress he thinks could be made by showing that environmental protection and economic growth are not mutually incompatible but essential partners to success. He sees an opportunity for Scotland to lead that debate by example.

As a high flying Eurocrat, Paul has some comments that should be listened to and acted upon, concerning both Scottish involvement in Brussels and the civil service. 'Within Brussels the Executive is doing a good job and the Scottish Parliament has profiled itself well. At civil service level though, I think it takes a bit longer for change to work through. I think that the confidence of the Executive and the Parliament to strike a different programme *vis-à-vis* London has been, in my experience, greater than the willingness of the civil servants to do so.' Details are not gone into as it would be inappropriate for him and unfair on others, but the message is clear.

He sees room for improvement in how Scotland operates in Brussels. 'Events are important – putting on the kilt, going out and promoting whisky and tourism – but events do not shape the political programme. There is now a five year political cycle, and what is becoming clearer is that you can increasingly anticipate what is coming, years down the line. That is where the Scots should be playing the game. More investment in that, advancing issues and trying to influence that agenda, with less focus on promotional events.'

Paul McAleavey has been moulded by both his small community and his native land and he has never forgotten it. He sees his self-improvement and growing self-confidence mirrored in post-devolution Scotland. He is concerned with issues and describes himself as relaxed about whether there should be further constitutional change. I can't help thinking that he is symbolic of a younger generation coming through who are much more self-confident, not just in themselves but in their Scottish identity. The Scottish cringe and the perception of the glass as half empty is being replaced by self-assurance and the view that the glass is half full.

In a few years, Paul will need to decide whether to return to Brussels, stay in Copenhagen, move elsewhere or return home. 'I have not ruled out coming back to Scotland. At some point in the future I would like to be active in Scotland in some kind of public capacity – whether that is politically or serving in the civil service – but I do see myself at some point living and working in Scotland.' It is clear to me that whilst his return home might be detrimental to the interests of my own political party, it would most certainly be beneficial to the nation as a whole.

Interviewed by Kenny MacAskill
May 2005

Fiona Hunter

INTERNATIONAL RELATIONS
DIRECTOR FOR THE UNIVERSITÀ
CARLO CATTANEO, MILAN

An Honest Lass

I HAD PREVIOUSLY NEVER MET Fiona Hunter, although I know her mother and had met her late father, who was a dentist in Musselburgh and a dignified and kindly man. Her mother is a lovely lady, still living in the 'honest toun', who had talked to me with evident pride about her daughter working in university education in Milan and of the time when she had taken her to the San Siro stadium to see AC Milan play football. So when I considered who to interview for this book, this seemed an opportunity not just to meet a high achieving Scots woman in a critical sector, but a girl after my own heart with a passion for football.

As International Relations Director for the Università Carlo Cattaneo in Castellanza near Milan she is often back in Scotland, either in that role or as Vice President of the European Association for International Education. Whether in student exchanges or placements, or through other promotional or professional work, she is a regular visitor home.

As I am to find out, Fiona has taken a rather circumventious route to her present senior offices. On this occasion she's back with a delegation from across Europe involved in international education. She meets me in the Parliament, and as it's her first visit to Holyrood we embark on a brief tour of the building. As we enter the Garden Lobby, she immediately recognises the sculptures adjacent to

Queensberry House as being created by her brother, Kenny Hunter, a world renowned sculptor. Despite them being a significant presence in the building, I had to confess that whilst I knew he was her brother, I had for some reason failed to connect the two.

After a brief tour we retire to my office for a coffee and a chat. Fiona is an attractive woman in her forties, bright and cheerful, with a distinctive Scottish accent. Although born in Norwich when her father went south for employment, from the age of two she was brought up in Musselburgh. The family lived in Bridge Street and she attended Campie School and then the Mary Erskine School in Edinburgh.

Her mother still resides in the family home, and this is where Fiona stays when she returns to Scotland. In addition to Kenny, she also has another brother, Callum, who works locally but resides in the west. Many of her friends from school, college and university are still in Scotland, few of whom live in Musselburgh, although she is still recognised locally. Fiona has fond memories of Musselburgh, particularly of walks along the esplanade. The sea is the one thing she misses most about her home town, and she relates it to a happy childhood. 'My memories of Musselburgh are of bracing it along the seafront on a cold Sunday afternoon, going for a walk up the banks of the River Esk, or going out to the lagoons to see the birds.'

Like so many others at her age, Fiona was unsure what she wanted to do when she left school. Accordingly, she ended up doing an HND in Secretarial Studies and Languages at Napier College of Commerce and Technology (as it was then). She tells me that the skills she learned there have served her well throughout her life, but having enjoyed the language aspect of the course she moved on to study French and German in the newly-started Interpreting Languages Course at Heriot Watt University. The obligatory year abroad gave her a real taste for Europe and its lifestyle. 'I loved being immersed in another culture – not just visiting a country for a holiday, but living it. Seeing the daily reality of another culture, and really getting to grips with what was going on. I knew then that I wanted to go back to Europe. I suppose I am naturally curious. I wanted to live the languages. I really wanted to learn the language and its culture.'

A twist of fate then played a part in her life. A scholarship to study in Berlin fell through but an immediate vacancy came up in France at the University of Tours which she gladly accepted. What was supposed to be a limited sojourn following her graduation in 1980 turned into four years at that institution, followed by another three years in Paris. When Parisian life began to lose its allure, an interest in Italian saw her relocate to Naples in 1987. Her boyfriend at the time had a passion for sailing and they set up a business of chartering yachts in the Bay of Naples. It was a new and unregulated area and they had to build up the business from scratch. Fiona was involved in the international marketing of the business, which saw her travel extensively across the continent in search of custom. It was a remarkably successful and innovative venture.

At the same time, she had been working in the university in Naples and after a while decided that she preferred life in higher education to business. Moving to Milan and searching for employment, she saw a poster for a new university that had opened and she enquired speculatively but ultimately successfully. The Università Carlo Cattanco Castellanza, where she is still employed, is one of few private universities in Italy, which are recognised by the state but not funded by it. Students pay fees and it is very involved with the local business community, which has been pivotal in its creation.

Fiona began by teaching English, then moved on to international affairs following a colleague's departure. Single-handedly she has since carved out her current position, through which she has become involved with the organisation of which she is Vice President – the European Association of International Education. The EAIE has a membership of 1,800 people worldwide, and is based with a full secretariat in Amsterdam. It represents all the different aspects of international education in universities, from marketing and recruitment, through to international study and exchange programmes, allowing her to return to her homeland capital. Education is clearly dear to her heart, and she is practising what she preaches about lifelong education by currently studying for a doctorate in Business Administration in Higher Education Management.

When I ask her what Scotland gave her she has no hesitation in saying that it was values: the values with which she was brought up and seeks to live by; views and attitudes that were partly passed on through her parents, but also by the very culture and ethos of the country. She recognises that they can vary depending on the era in which you grow up but believes that some are unique to Scotland and transcend generations. 'I grew up in Scotland in the 1960s and 1970s and so I think the Scotland that I grew up in gave me very strong values. I think they are still present, but perhaps not quite as strong as they once were.'

For her those values manifested themselves in a variety of ways – education, identity, equality and fairness. Given her current employment, education is pivotal and she sees Scotland as having been fundamental to that. Education is dear to her heart and it's evident that she is grateful for the opportunities provided, and the encouragement given in a myriad of ways, both directly and indirectly. 'Learning has always been important to me, and the sense of freedom that goes with education is huge. I support education programmes from the United Nations, especially specific programmes for women in the developing world, but also because I really do see education as the way to building your own future. The whole Scottish ethos of getting an education has always been fundamental to me and is something that I try to pass on. I really believe you can make a difference through education.'

Scotland has remained part of who she is. She has now lived abroad for the majority of her life and is clearly one of that new breed – a citizen of Europe. Although not a definite decision, it seems unlikely at the moment that she will return permanently to Scotland. The country is important to her, and she enjoys the regular visits home, but she appreciates the opportunities offered by living elsewhere. 'I never think of Scotland as a place to come back and live in. I do come back four or five times a year. I walk the streets of Edinburgh and feel at home. Scotland will never stop being a part of me. Edinburgh is part of me and it is very much with me. I think I will stay in international education, but I could end up somewhere else.'

Identity is important to her. As someone who travels extensively, she is conscious of a shrinking world in a global age. She thinks it is important that people and countries retain some semblance of their individuality and identity. Scotland has given her a sense of both these values, and she considers that vital. 'You really have a sense of your own identity and your own culture. This sense of belonging which today is also a value, in a world that is changing so rapidly and dramatically. We all need a sense of who we are, and a sense of belonging somewhere. There is a sense of values that you can connect with. But at the same time there must be an understanding that these values don't necessarily serve others, and that there are many ways of achieving the same objectives.'

Returning to the theme of values she mentions that Scotland has given her a sense of fairness and equality. 'The idea that we are all Jock Tamson's bairns has stood me in very good stead. The sense of having your feet on the ground and working hard – that is very much what I was brought up with. I think everything I have ever achieved has been as a result of hard work. Scotland gave me some tools and those tools I have found very useful.' These are clearly tools that she has used herself in her career when she adds, 'it is a very Scottish thing of doing what is fair, a sense of doing what is right and also very much this idea of treating others as equals. Universities typically are very hierarchic. For me, when I am speaking to students or chancellors, they have both got a job to do and I speak to them in exactly the same way – I think that is very Scottish.'

She recalls her late father as a very upright and honest man and believes that the values her parents inculcated in her were one and the same as those in the country as a whole. Ethics have become a requirement for business life, never mind government and society today, but she believes that Scots do well as a result of values that were imbibed and inherent. 'The Scottish work ethic has the ethos of being honest, transparent, accountable, fair and trustworthy. I think it is naturally of the Scottish psyche and helps you to stand firm.'

However, Scotland failed to provide her with job opportunities. That said, she freely admits that it was always her desire and intention to at least try life aboard. But she is conscious that others did so not by choice but through necessity. 'When I left Scotland in the 1980s it wasn't a conscious choice to leave – I wanted to go back and experience Europe. I didn't want to leave Scotland – it just happened that way. In the seventies and eighties there weren't a lot of opportunities in Scotland for graduates wanting to exploit their language degree. Most students on my course, who weren't all Scots, did go abroad because they had studied languages. In 1980s Scotland, you got a job, not a career.'

However, she senses things are changing, with an improvement in available opportunities which she considers a great advance. She sees the tradition of education that she benefited from as a great asset for the country and something that it should major on. At the same time she is anxious that it should not lose its sense of identity, and as a consequence, perhaps those values. As someone who lives abroad, travelling extensively and working in an international field, she is fully conscious of the consequences and effects of globalisation. She narrates a tale of being in Tallinn, Estonia where there is new-found wealth and westernisation. 'On the one hand you applaud them for their ability to move and change so quickly, but at the same time you look around Tallinn and feel there is a danger that too many international cafés, international food and drink are all flooding in, and that transformation has come too quickly. A few cafés advertise themselves as authentic Estonian cuisine. No restaurant in Italy would advertise itself as authentic Italian.'

Fiona's home is not just Scotland, but Europe. However, she is adamant that Europe must retain its constituent parts and individual identities. She is anxious that the sense of identity be retained as it underpins the values that she cherishes and holds dear. As someone who loved Scottish history she feels that it is important along with other aspects of cultural identity. These she believes must be both taught and fostered. 'You have to have a sense of where you come from and what makes you who you are. I think Europe offers an opportunity to smaller countries. But they need to hold on to their core strengths and develop them. You have to have a sense of your past, and I think that is something that is no longer very fashionable.'

There she has clear views on what needs done and it involves education. 'Are we really teaching the next generation? Do we have sense of culture with a small c? Everyone talks about Scottish music, dance and songs. Realistically, how much of that belongs to the people of Scotland, and how much of it is just ceilidh nights at major hotels? I think it is critically important to retain our own sense of identity in a global world. You can't just have knowledge about now, because that knowledge will become obsolete in the future, but you can know your history and that is fundamental. You need to have an understanding of your own culture and your own position and that naturally makes you curious and interested in the cultures and traditions of others.'

Fiona Hunter is a woman who has travelled extensively and come a long way from her home in the 'honest toun'. She believes that being Scottish has given her a great deal and in more than a material sense. It has allowed her to achieve and succeed in her chosen field. Both her parents and her native land have provided a set of values to live her life by. As a citizen of Europe, she will likely continue to reside on that continent. Scotland, though, remains embedded in her soul, even if it is not her physical residence. Appreciating what it gave to her and provided for her she is anxious that it should retain what created that unique nature and identity. Fiona Hunter believes she has learned a lot from Scotland – perhaps Scotland should learn a little from her?

Interviewed by Kenny MacAskill
May 2005

David Scrimgeour MBE

BUSINESSMAN, MUNICH

An Edinburgh Wanderer

SETTLED IN MUNICH, GERMANY, David Scrimgeour has wandered far from his Craigentinny roots. Frustrated, he left school at 16, but is now highly successful in his own consultancy business. His current achievements follow upon a multitude of jobs and careers that culminated in setting up and staffing the Scottish Enterprise Locate in Scotland operation in Germany and Austria, for which he was awarded an MBE. Now residing in Bavaria with his wife and family, business commitments ensure an ongoing connection with Scotland, and he retains his Scottish roots by bringing up his children bilingually and returning for regular family vacations. Both his travels and travails leave him eminently qualified to comment on his native land.

His participation in this book had come about as a result of his membership of the Global Scots network, something which he is extremely committed to, as I am to find out. A notice about the book, together with a request for anybody willing to participate, had been placed on the Global Friends of Scotland website, and David responded with alacrity and interest. We arrange to meet up in Edinburgh, as he is returning to collect his mother for a stay in Germany with his family, as well as carrying out some business. Though our paths had crossed when we were both solicitors in Edinburgh, our meeting at the new Scottish Parliament is our first real get-together. Not long turned 50, he's tall and thin, with greying hair adding to his character; very distinguished – even dapper; and quite the successful German businessman, yet retaining a clear Scottish accent and possessing no airs and graces. His honour for services to business is hardly touched upon, but was undoubtedly neither given lightly nor without merit.

Born in 1954 and brought up in the Craigentinny area of Edinburgh, he belongs to a very cosmopolitan family. His sister is Chief Nursing Officer in Palm Springs Hospital, California, and his brother, now a senior civil servant in the Scottish Executive, had a brief interlude in the Russian Republics with the Organisation for Economic Co-operation and Development. Sadly, his father has passed away, but his mother has moved the short distance from Craigentinny to Duddingston. From our chat, it's clear that his late father, John, has left a deep impression on him. John Scrimgeour was born in Port Glasgow, and joined the shipyards at the age of 14. When he reached 16 he successfully completed the civil service entrance exams. During the war he served in the Royal Air Force, and on demob returned to the Scottish Office, where he worked his way up the ladder until he became Director of the Scottish Prison Service. David tells me with obvious pride that his father had been the only man at that level without a university degree at the time. His mother had also been a civil servant from Glasgow, though they had met in London after the war. Memories of David's childhood include sledging on Restalrig Avenue where he stayed in the days before mass car ownership or indeed, global warming. Although he recalls his childhood as peaceful, he was clearly unsettled at school. The local Royal High Primary School at Northfield led him onto the Royal High Secondary School, and looking back, he feels he rebelled against the school as an institution, with its ancient history and what he perceived as some contemporary elitism.

Drifting out of school at 16, he wandered away from the Edinburgh of his childhood. He moved south, as many young Scots did, and still do. A sojourn of six or seven years in Bath and the West Country in the seventies saw him take on a variety of jobs, from construction, through catering as a chef, to long distance lorry driving.

None suited him and he remained restless. He lived in Holland for a year and travelled extensively in Europe, describing it as a search for the experience that had not been on offer at home. Having said that, enough of the Scottish work ethic remained to ensure that, notwithstanding the hectic day jobs, adequate qualifications were obtained at night school, allowing access into university.

On reflection, it was the travelling in Europe which was his turning point. Realising that he was heading nowhere, he headed home to study at university. A degree in History from the University of Edinburgh was followed by a truncated Law degree. A spell in a private practice with a firm in the same city followed. It was a job that he found enjoyable but having met Barbara, his German wife-to-be, at university, one that could not be maintained if they were to set up home together. One of them would have to move if they were to remain together, and although he had prospects as an Edinburgh lawyer, he still possessed a bit of the old wanderlust. Despite being unable to speak German, and with no obvious job prospects, he headed to Barbara's Bavarian home. He now finds himself fluent in German, successful in his own business and the father of two bilingual children, Anna and Alex.

Initially, he worked in Munich for a law firm, helping them to develop business in the UK. In 1992 he began work for Locate in Scotland, setting up their operation in Germany and Austria. Promoting Scotland from abroad gave him an insight into his native land which he is using successfully in his business, and is keen to pass on through the Global Scots network and other avenues. He remained in that post for eight years and received an MBE for his work there. In 2000 he decided to strike out once more on his own and now runs a highly successful consultancy firm, focusing on helping British financial service companies do business in Germany, with some blue-chip companies in his portfolio, and also offering routes into Scotland for German investors, whether in tourism or other sectors. Though successful and settled in Germany, he does not rule out a return to Scotland, with the age of his children having him consider whether a Scottish education may now be in their best interests. Whatever his own difficulties, he perceives merit in the Scottish education, and it is clearly an option. With the children being bilingual and having returned annually, it is not a world away.

When asked what Scotland gave to him, he refers to his late father, who personifies the meritocratic opportunity that was afforded, and the roots that were retained. 'My father represented the democratic situation in Scotland. It was possible from that background of working in the shipyards and living in a single-end to end up as head of the Prison Service. Scotland gave me a sense of being able to actually do anything. Though I didn't feel working class as such, I didn't feel a million miles away from it.' In addition, it gave him a sense of identity and values that he feels have served him well, and still do. 'It obviously gave me a sense of nationality, of having a place that is my home, even though I am somewhere else that I feel positively and strongly about. There aren't that many places that really provide that, in a way that is both meaningful and, to be frank, useful, from a business point of view.'

However, he also sees downsides to being Scottish. His occupation and his residence abroad have given him an insight into some aspects of our attitudes or identity that, if not flawed, at least need addressing. In perceptions of the diaspora and economic dynamism, he sees comparisons to be made with, and lessons to be learned, from our Celtic cousins, the Irish. One of the intentions of this book had been to address the corrosive nature of the 'kent yer faither' attitude that is begrudging towards the expatriate community, and if not actually jealous of it, almost resents its success. He feels strongly about that and picks up on it. 'The Irish go abroad, but they actually do come back and they are encouraged to do so, whereas in Scotland there is a strong sense, which I experienced when I left – though less so now – that that's it. It should function naturally that there is a flow back and forwards. There's a dislocation between Scots at home and abroad. I think most families have someone who has emigrated, yet there is a feeling by the ones here, especially if things are not going well, that it's unfair. Almost, "you made your choice so sod you".'

Similarly, he sees a problem in the attitude to business, and again he sees a contrast with Ireland. 'It's another thing I didn't get from

Scotland. There's a lack of entrepreneurialism. You should never slag off the competition, but when I worked with Locate in Scotland, the Irish were the competition. The Irish are in it for the money, which is a great attitude, and an attitude the Scots don't have. The whole thing about Tartan Day – yes, we want to promote ourselves, but large chunks of the population have a problem with the use of tartan. The Irish just get on with it.' Liberated from the straightjacket of the public sector, he sees not just room for improvement, but a need for change. 'I think the public sector is incredibly dominant in Scotland. Working for Locate in Scotland I was in a sort of intermediate position between private and public sector, and now with my own company I have reached the other end of the process and I am well aware of the importance of having an entrepreneurial attitude. My business is in the financial sector; I have seen an incredible change and it is so fundamental. You have a situation where you have two huge banks, never mind the insurance sector. Some companies, whether it be the Royal Bank or Standard Life, are becoming increasingly international and are very successful. Others are not. I think there is something about that fact that the economic development strategy for Scotland has been far too inward investment orientated, and has not focused, for whatever reason, on the areas of opportunity in Scotland. They have suffered from the lack of awareness of the public sector agencies. Unfortunately, all this combines with the lack of entrepreneurial thought.'

However, he does see improvement, as well as having free advice to dispense to his native land (which he would normally be able to charge handsomely for). He sees the Parliament assisting in the interaction with the diaspora, and sees real opportunity both for Scotland and Scottish business. 'My thesis of our country here is that there is a fundamental openness to interacting with the rest of the world that I think is less prevalent in little England. However, Scotland has not benefited from that openness. It hasn't really had an expression except in terms of people leaving Scotland. Financial services and tourism are big areas of opportunity for Scotland – because of the image, because of the know-how, and because of the skill of these organisations.'

He sees progress not just in the financial sector but also in tourism, experiencing this as a customer every year. 'Inward investment promotion and tourism, as the Irish show, are very linked – it's all business at the end of the day. There has been a problem with the product and the service but I think coming back to Scotland every year for a holiday – last year in Fife and this year in Arran, who knows where next year – that the quality has improved incredibly in the last 10 or 15 years. It is much easier to get good quality accommodation and good service. You have got the basic product which you can't manufacture, but you need to add value to sell it and capitalise on it.'

As well as seeking to promote Scottish links with Bavaria, which, he points out, include a twinning of over 51 years between Edinburgh (the city of his birth) and Munich (his new residence), he sees parallels with other parts of Europe. 'I actually compare Scotland to Austria. Similar population, different geography, but Austria makes its own decisions. It has been, in its past and recent history, economically very dependent on Germany, but that has now changed. When you look at what Austria has achieved in terms of their business development into central Europe and so on, and you look at their economic growth, etc., you see that. I think the change that is happening in Scotland, slowly but surely, is connected to the fact that the dependence on England is gradually reducing.'

On that aspect he still sees room for improvement, both in government and government agencies. It's not just trade opportunities available in Bavaria that are being missed, but the chance to work internationally with the country. Their economy and manufacturing base with companies such as BMW and Siemens leaves them well placed at home as well as abroad, as far as he sees it. 'I am a bit frustrated about the lack of response from Scotland to what was on offer from Bavaria. Bavaria has agencies who work with California, Quebec, France, Russia – the response from these countries is fantastic. Whereas here – no chance. It is stark. Any time I raise this with the department in the Scottish Executive, I know I am banging my head against the wall. An opportunity wasted.'

His frustration is born from a desire to see his native land improve, and an awareness that so much more could be achieved. However, he remains optimistic about his homeland's progress, and eager to participate in it, not simply to avail himself of business opportunities that may arise, but to allow others to succeed as he has. It seems to me that David Scrimgeour is as Scottish now as he ever was, and is as equally entitled to comment and participate. His comments on the size of the public sector are not an attack upon it, but simply an echo of the concerns of many Scots. Many of his comments and comparisons with Ireland are not just fair comment, but absolutely spot on.

Fundamentally, David and others in the diaspora are part of the Scottish community – the only difference being that they live abroad. Their success should be applauded not scorned, and their input welcomed not denied. We remain, like the Scrimgeours, one Scottish family, whether we reside at home or abroad.

Interviewed by Kenny MacAskill
May 2005

Maggie Morrison
HEAD OF MARKETING STRATEGY FOR CISCO SYSTEMS, CALIFORNIA

East or West, Still a Glasgow Girl and a Glasgow Gael

MAGGIE MORRISON IS A HIGHLY SUCCESSFUL and extremely busy lady, on the move upwards and onwards. Just back from a stay in the Netherlands, she is in the process of flitting to America – moving from Amsterdam, where she was Managing Director of Cisco Systems Ltd in the Netherlands, to California, where she is taking up a role defining strategy, process and structure for the Cisco sales force at a global level.

I meet her at the house in Bearsden that she and Dougie, her writer husband, have retained as their home, despite their international jet setting. It's a gloriously sunny day of which there are all too few in Scotland, the view and setting magnificent, and it's easy to see why this remains home no matter where they travel. The place is hectic with visitors from the Netherlands and more friends due in from other parts of Scotland. Despite that, she remains calm and welcoming, coping with numerous tasks simultaneously, from welcoming guests to sorting out plane tickets. Like the glass of champagne she holds in her hand, she is bright and bubbly. In her early forties with a clear Scottish accent, its obvious that whether in Amsterdam or California, she's still a Glasgow girl and Glasgow Gael at heart.

I had previously met Maggie Morrison on several occasions in her position as Operations Director for Cisco Systems Ltd in Scotland, which she held from 1997 to 2002. As well as having a high-powered job, she was actively engaged in business and community projects but still found time to advise a fledgling MSP, and indeed any others who asked, on commercial and telecommunications issues. Approachable, friendly and easygoing, she was conscious not just of her roots but the need for her company to be involved in a wider society, and to some extent epitomised the concept of corporate responsibility, never mind business in the community. Cisco Systems had a reputation for community involvement and she pursued it with zeal throughout Scotland and particularly in her native Glasgow. As well as indulging a technologically challenged MSP, I discovered that we shared a common heritage from the Isle of Lewis of which I was to find out more.

A sixties child, she has fond memories of growing up in the Glasgow of that era. Born in Rotten Row, she grew up initially in Easterhouse which she recalls as a safe and pleasant place to live, despite later social and economic problems. Her reminiscences vary from travelling on the bus to Hillhead School, to playing on the midden out the back of the close. Wandering freely about the scheme or the city, she compares it rather sadly to today's situation as we speak of the school opposite, where kids are met by their parents and movement is clearly restricted. Children are more constrained, and their parents more anxious than before. Maggie's family subsequently moved to Kelvindale, then to Bearsden, and her schooling also changed from Hillhead to Cleveden as the grant aid ended and a comprehensive period started for that institution. Her mother and father still live nearby but her brother has moved down to Maidenhead in England where he – ironically – works in IT with a major competitor to Cisco. Friendships are still retained from both school and community.

Her mother and father, Mary and Finlay, were from Lewis stock, and as with many from those parts, were a teacher and policeman respectively. Her mother was born and brought up in North Dell, coming down to Glasgow to attend university. Her father, though brought up in the city, hailed from a family that saw Habost as home. Meeting in a dance hall in Glasgow they discovered they came from villages that were only three miles apart. Maggie grew up in their image, living in Glasgow but viewing Lewis as home. Many relatives and friends were Lewis folk or from other Highland or island communities. She recalls as a young girl being intrigued by a man who had been evacuated from St Kilda and being amazed at the thought of someone being alive from an island that was no longer inhabited. Every holiday other than Christmas saw her return to Ness on the island of her forefathers. Those too were equally happy times – roaming free, collecting water from the well or bringing home the peats. The islands may have been economically poor, but they were socially rich and the memories and values have remained embedded in her soul. To this day she says she feels 'Glaswegian, but my spiritual home is Lewis.'

As someone whose father was also from that community I am aware of the lingering call that these islands hold, not just for first but for future generations. Whether it's in the gene pool or in the blood, there is something haunting that ensures these bleak and desolate islands retain a hold, no matter where you stay or are brought up. Whilst the Highlands and islands may be located physically in the north, for many Scots they are located deep within their heart.

Leaving school, she headed north again, this time to Aberdeen to study languages at the university. Unlike many from Glasgow she chose to go to a university that would see her leave home. She was encouraged to do so by her mother, for which she is eternally grateful, but conscious of the pain it must have caused her. Etched in her memory is her happiness as she prepared to leave, matched by her mother's ill temper, ending in tears as her daughter prepared to depart. She recalls chiding her mother that she would be back in ten weeks and her replying that 'you'll never really come back home again'. And she was right.

Graduating in the early eighties, jobs were not readily available and she required to ensure that she was neither too tied to a particular discipline or geographical area. As a result, like many Scots before her, she took the high road south. Despite having a degree in French and German, she moved into sales and telecommunications. Her first job was in telesales for an electronic component company in Slough. The next move was to another company that wished to utilise her linguistic skills in selling their own component products. Further moves saw her quickly climb the career ladder in the sales and telecoms field. In 1996 she joined Cisco Systems as a Regional Sales Manager in the south east of England. Although the company had a base in Ireland at the time, Scotland was covered from the south east of England, notwithstanding a foothold in the country. She voiced her opinion that more could be done and achieved if there was not just an office but an appropriate presence in the land. The firm, to their credit, took her at her word and the next year she was despatched north to locate and staff a Scottish office. There she stayed until she moved in 2002 to the European headquarters in Amsterdam. Now it's across the Atlantic with a global remit.

When asked what Scotland gave to her, Maggie's views chime with many others. 'Scotland gave me a belief in the education system. If all other things are unequal in terms of your background, then I think education can really make a difference. It also gave me a real desire to be the best I could be, with a sense of fair play and a sense of humour as well.' That has seen her achieve remarkable personal success, but at the same time has ensured a commitment to assisting others less fortunate. Whilst at Cisco in Scotland she was heavily involved not just in the Govan Initiative but the East End Partnership which covered her old home ground of Easterhouse and sought to provide skills and learning training in areas of deprivation.

Maggie Morrison is a very successful Scots woman and on reflection she feels that success is something Scotland seems to have a problem with and indeed it's accompanied by an innate pessimism. She refers to a recent incident at a Scotland rugby game to highlight it. 'I don't think we are very good at celebrating success. There is a begrudgery – I think that's an Irish word but we seem to continually put ourselves down. Up until now, Dougie and I have always gone to Scotland away games – whether in Paris, Rome or wherever. We were there in Rome when we were beaten and I was following the supporters out of the stadium. Young guys in their kilts with flags and their heads down. Singing about how bad we were and almost rejoicing in it. We almost expect to be beaten and I find that disappointing.'

As someone who follows the fortunes of the national football team, I can empathise with her. A sport is just that and accepting a loss with good grace is absolutely essential, and all part of the game. Better a bedraggled Tartan Army accepting defeat than a rioting mob rejecting it. Being good losers is one thing, but actually celebrating defeat is quite another. Taking almost a perverse pride in being defeated and how bad the team might be actually seems to affect the national character. It almost defines the nation as losers, and success as equally un-Scottish. It seems to both myself and Maggie Morrison that it must be possible to marry a sense of fair play in a sport with a competitive edge that lauds success if not at any price. Otherwise the prophecy becomes self-fulfilling and defeat not only expected but assured.

Another matter that she has noted from abroad is the difficulty many at home have in marrying a tartan image with a contemporary Scotland. As someone who works in a very high tech and modern sector her views are not what might first be assumed. 'I know that Scotland is about far more than tartan and whisky and Robert Burns for that matter, although I don't know anyone who is ashamed of Burns because I think he is fantastic. But why does it need to be one or the other? Why can't we have the tartan, bagpipes, whisky and all that stuff – why should it be an add-on? I felt when I was working here in the nineties we seemed to want to reject that because it was too corny or something. I think we should be proud of that and by all means show people there is also another side to Scotland.'

She's very proud of her Scottish identity and assured in it, which is something she thinks has been added to by being part of the diaspora. 'All the Scots I have ever met abroad are extremely proud to be Scottish. Sometimes I think that Scots outside are more proud of Scotland than Scots who live there.' The more expatriate Scots I meet the more I find that to be true. Not only are they proud of their roots but proud of their country. But are we proud of them? She says, 'I used to get the impression that some people were almost waiting on you to fall flat on your face because you were breaking the mould and you were willing to go abroad.' It seems to me that it's about time the respect was reciprocated a bit more and the diaspora applauded for what they have achieved and appreciated for what they can still contribute.

What the future holds for her and Dougie she does not know. They are looking forward to a sojourn in the USA but have retained their home in Bearsden, not knowing whether American life will be for them. She enjoyed the stint in Amsterdam and her limited contact with California has been stimulating with it being a very multiracial and multicultural environment in the office as well as the country. 'I have always said to Cisco that selling this house is not something that is negotiable for me. I don't know exactly what we will find when we go to America or how we will feel about living there. I genuinely believe that it is a good thing for Scottish people to go abroad. If they come back, then they come back with a broader perspective and a greater variety of experience of different cultures.'

Maggie Morrison is a very modest woman. She has had considerable success in an area which she had no background in and is quite male-dominated, succeeding not just on a Scottish but on an international stage. She admits the reason for leaving is job opportunity and regrets her lack of entrepreneurial talent. 'We would both love to come back to Scotland permanently. I know that I am not alone as I have talked to other people in a similar position – the difficulty is what job would you come back to do. I don't feel I am an entrepreneur. I admire the people, who are – Ann Gloag, Tom Hunter, Angus McSween and so on. These people have managed to achieve what they have and stay in Scotland.'

It seems to me that the failing is not hers for a lack of entrepreneurialism but Scottish society's for the absence of opportunity for someone as skilled and talented as her. She has done very well for herself and her native land. The lack of opportunity afforded her to do so at home is not her fault but ours. If Scotland is to be the best it can be, then we need to ensure that talents such as hers have an opportunity to flourish here as well as abroad.

Interviewed by Kenny MacAskill
June 2005

Hugh Boyle

CHAIRMAN OF ZOOM AIRLINES,
OTTAWA

The Sky's No Limit for a Lanarkshire Lad

MOST PEOPLE WOULD BE DELIGHTED to have set up one successful business in their lifetime. For one Lanarkshire lad it's not just one highly successful company he has created but three. Not just modest ventures, his firms employ many people and reward him handsomely. Indeed his latest venture into the aviation sector is continuing to soar – proving that the sky is no limit to his ambitions or talents.

Hugh Boyle was born and raised in Bellshill, and is now resident in Ottawa, Canada where he is Chairman and major shareholder in Zoom Airlines. They fly regularly from the UK to Canada and continue to ply the routes they introduced, connecting Canadian holidaymakers with the Caribbean. In addition, he operates a major Canadian travel agency, Go Travel Direct, selling seats direct to the public with a format he was highly successful with back in Scotland. Those businesses are booming and the airline, offering connections between Glasgow and Halifax, Toronto, Ottawa, Calgary and Vancouver, is used by outbound Scots, inbound expats, and native Canadians. Zoom now employs more than 300 staff and has offices in both Ottawa and Glasgow. Given the turbulent times that have faced many national carriers, it's a meteoric take-off for a lad from Lanarkshire.

These highly flourishing ventures follow on two previous businesses that proved equally successful and remunerative. Tiring of life as a chef, Hugh Boyle entered into the travel trade with his brother John, now a well known Scottish entrepreneur and Chairman of Motherwell Football Club. In the early 1980s his brother was starting up a small travel company in London, with only two employees. It was so small and strapped for cash that he couldn't afford to pay himself a salary, and was forced to work elsewhere to make a living. Undeterred, Hugh signed up. An office in Scotland followed, and from there the company grew. That company was Falcon Holidays, and it went from strength to strength, used by many both north and south of the Border. In due course, First Choice, a major UK operator, entered onto the scene and bought the firm out, changing its name in the process. The buy-out left Hugh considerably richer, but keen to continue in the business.

The Boyle brothers set up Direct Holidays in 1991, a company which became a household name for many Scottish families when considering a summer holiday. This too was cross-border, operating mainly in Scotland, but with an office in London where Hugh had based himself. They ran and operated that firm until 1997 when again they were bought out by a larger combine as the success of the venture was noted and the client base and concept sought. This time it was My Travel who acquired the business and left Hugh and his brother very wealthy men.

At this juncture Hugh considered retirement. He had started, built up and sold on two highly successful companies and yet was still only in his forties. It had, however, been at a personal and domestic cost, with long hours and restricted family time. His children were 10 and 12 at the time and he and his wife Christine decided to consider their options for both retiral and relocation. They considered moving to Australia, but felt it to be too far away. Given the children's age a major factor in relocation was an English-speaking environment, although weather, health and education also entered into the equation. Christine's sister and brother were both located in Ottawa, so that was where they eventually headed and settled. They have been there ever since, enjoying both the city and the Canadian lifestyle.

Although he had sufficient means to never have to work again, a life of idleness was not for Hugh. 'After a couple of years I just saw there was a huge opportunity in the travel industry here and I set up Go Travel Direct. I then had significant problems getting flights because nobody in Canada wants to sell direct sale seats to a holiday company, as everything is done through travel agents. So we were very much the black sheep of the travel industry – but as a Scotsman, I didn't give up, and I started the airline.' It now transpires that the airline has surpassed the travel company in size and revenue, making the most of Canadians' desire to flee their cruel winter.

As with many entrepreneurial ideas, flights to Scotland came around more by accident than design. Travelling from Heathrow to Glasgow on business, he was seated next to a Canadian who told him of his epic 19 hour journey from Halifax, Nova Scotia, changing in Montréal and London, simply to play golf in Scotland. 'Previous to Zoom flying from Halifax to Scotland there was no direct flight and never has been, yet it is the shortest point between Scotland and Canada. It takes off from Halifax and lands in Glasgow in around five hours or less. It's the same as a Tenerife flight.' He sensed an opportunity, and now the business is booming, with passenger numbers soaring in both directions.

A permanent return to Scotland is unlikely with his family now settled in Otttawa. His eldest daughter Amy has recently started university in Montréal. He does, however, return home several times a year, on business and to visit his elderly father, who still resides in Lanarkshire. He now has a Canadian passport to accompany his standard UK European one – something which is more to do with the need to be a Canadian citizen to own an airline across the Atlantic, but also allowing him easier access and less form-filling when travelling to the USA. But it's not what it says on your passport that matters, but what you feel in your heart – and he tells me that he is forever Scottish.

Brought up in Bellshill, his father was a grocer and his mother a housewife. He had a happy childhood, attending St Saviour's High School and then Motherwell College, where he trained as a chef. Two years' practical experience then followed at the Royal Stewart

Hotel, then in Jamaica Street, Glasgow. At 18 he headed for Spain, something he puts down to his Scottishness and the wanderlust it can provoke. This was in the early seventies before aviation and new technology made the world a smaller place. There was no family relationship with the Iberian Peninsula and both the language and the difficulties in communicating home were problematic, but he persevered. He worked as a chef in Javea, near Alicante, and stayed there for two years. Then he decided he had to move, or be destined to stay forever, so headed, like so many other Scots, to London. He worked there as a chef at a hotel in Tower Bridge, which he found to be a rewarding experience. A few years later, he moved on to being the private chef for Maxwell Joseph, the industrialist who, at that time, also owned Metropolitan Hotels. It was a prestigious job, with his employer hosting private dinners for the likes of Margaret Thatcher. A great deal of time was spent simply waiting about, and being a man abounding with ideas and energy to burn, it was not a job which satisfied him. So he moved into to the travel trade with his brother, and the rest is history.

I meet with Hugh in his offices in Ottawa, located in the suburbs not far from the airport. It's a modern, unpretentious block, and as is the case in much of North America, almost inaccessible without a car. A taxi takes me to the interview, and the driver is from the Lebanon. Hugh later comments that this is not just a multicultural community, but a multiethnic country. We had never met before, though I had previously been introduced to his brother. There is a clear family likeness and a Scottish accent is still evident. He's warm in his greeting and convivial in his company, and we settle down in his (far from ostentatious) office to discuss his upbringing and his views on his native land.

He has fond memories of Bellshill, both of the place and the people. It's obvious it has had a deep effect on him, describing it as 'a tough place. It was hard – and I think you saw a lot of things going on. We weren't poor, but we certainly weren't over-privileged. Lots of families were living hand to mouth.' As someone who entered into the service and hospitality sector, it's not surprising that some of his memories are contained in that sphere, but also of the darker side of Scotland. 'I always remember pubs with no windows and you couldn't see in. I was always wondering what was going on behind those doors as a child. There would be double doors all over the place and it always intrigued me as a child.' He recognises that things have changed, and that Scotland has moved on in many ways, but adds, rather humorously, 'looking back, a lot of things you did-n't actually think about because they were just there – its not until you are older when you see green vegetables and you realise the fact that peas don't come out of cans.'

When asked what Scotland gave to him, he is forthright and unambiguous. 'Scotland gave me a very good start in life, and good values and understanding. I think the people of Scotland are any-thing but mean. I never understood that phrase – Scottish folk are the most generous people around. When I was growing up, I thought people were hard-working; which they were, as I came from a min-ing town where every family had someone who worked at Ravenscraig. Those values stay with you a long time and that will never change.'

Given that most of his highly successful career has seen him located outwith Scotland, even if operating within it, I was curious on his take on the business climate. There is a great deal of discus-sion and current concern about a lack of entrepreneurial spirit in Scotland, compounded by an uncompetitive business environment. He believes it is still a good place to do business, even if a lot more could be done to assist. Banks and funding had never been a signif-icant impediment to him; there were greater opportunities available in Canada, with a larger number of entrepreneurs coming from its size and population, rather than anything ingrained or genetic. Like many of our expat community, he is modest about his own achieve-ments. I, however, tend to think that there are economic constraints that afflict business opportunities in Scotland, and a culture that, if not disdainful, is at best discouraging of the entrepreneurial spirit. That said, individuals like Hugh Boyle are a special breed in any society.

There were two areas where Scotland contrasted unfavourably with his new home: religious tolerance and immigration.

Sectarianism remains a scar on Scottish life, while Canada benefits immeasurably through immigration. He remains conscious of the sectarian divide in Lanarkshire in particular, but all of Scotland in general. Just walking around in Ottawa makes you conscious that you are in a multiracial and multicultural society. Located on the border of Ontario and Québec, it's a bilingual area, and the faces of its citizens are from every part of the globe. It is a great melting pot and that mix applies as much in schools as in the street. This is something that he thinks has benefited Canada. 'One of my sad memories of being a young child: at the time I did find it strange that children in the street were going to different schools. The difference was prevalent then between Catholic and Protestant children. There were two societies, even as a child you grew up knowing that "they" lived on the other side. Whether it was right or wrong, they were on the other side. You didn't mix because you weren't allowed to – you didn't go to school together, you didn't play together. I think it is very sad.' This contrasts with Canada, where he comments on his daughter's recent attendance at a Jewish friend's festival, and of schools where they mingle and mix with children from a variety of racial backgrounds and with a multitude of faiths. 'The sectarianism did have an enormous effect on people. Having been away from Scotland and had children who tell me about significant religious dates from throughout the world – I recall there were bigotries on both sides. But it remains very focused and very strong, certainly when I was there. Obviously that is what moulds a child.'

The sectarian baggage was carried into the workplace. 'Even when you went to get a job your religion was an issue – people asked what school you went to just to find out if it was a Catholic or non-Catholic school. No wonder children have grown up bitter and twisted.' It is something that he is deeply conscious of as being a problem in Scottish society. It's something he says more in sorrow than anger. 'When I see all the religion going on in the world and all the wars about religion it is very sad. I am a Christian and go to church occasionally and find it helpful.' His comments resonate with me. I can recall knowing the words to various so called 'party songs' long before I had any understanding or conception of what they related to and being conscious of the gulf that existed between two primary schools separated by a path but located a world apart. Separate schooling is a deep and emotive issue in Scotland, troubling society and frightening politicians. Nothing can be done to change the current situation of separate schooling without the consent of all communities, or it in itself would be seen as sectarian in itself. However, whilst it's easy to argue that denominational schools do not cause religious bigotry, they most certainly create a tribalism that scars contemporary Scotland.

As well as the social mix at school, Hugh is impressed by the racial integration in Canada and views immigration as something Scotland should welcome not fear. As an economic migrant himself he sees the benefit they bring. 'Canada is a huge country with a tiny population made up of immigrants from all over the world. I think that the influx of immigrants who see opportunities is a benefit and we should not look on it negatively. The natural tendency is to think that they are taking our jobs and all that. Actually, though, they create wealth. Every country that has been successful has been fuelled by immigrants.' He has seen the benefits in two countries, both from an emigrant's and an immigrant's perspective, giving his views additional validity. Immigration as well as emigration has always been an aspect of Scottish life. Migrants have added to our society throughout our history and will continue to do so. As Hugh states, they boost our economy, and as Canada shows, add to the diversity of our people and culture.

Hugh Boyle is one of many Scots who have been economic migrants throughout the centuries. Scotland should be proud of what he has achieved but also recognise the validity of the point he makes about economic migrants being a blessing not a curse. He may no longer reside among us but his wealth creation benefits us all, as the jobs and air routes testify to. Whatever the passport he carries, he has been moulded by his native land and remains forever a Scot.

Interviewed by Kenny MacAskill
June 2005

Jim and Isobel Bell

MEMBERS OF THE ILLINOIS ST
ANDREW'S SOCIETY

The Falkirk Bairns

SCOTS ARE RIGHTLY DISMAYED by the stereotypical image of them as tight-fisted and mean. It's an inaccurate and unfair portrayal. Some comments are humorous or whimsical, and are treated in that vein. Others, though, are simply ill-founded and met with righteous indignation.

But what of the perception that resident Scots have of the diaspora, and in particular of St Andrew's Societies? Here the impression is of a 'white heather club' – drinking whisky, toasting Scotland on St Andrew's Days, the Bard on Burns' nights, and bringing a tear to the eye of the homesick Jock. Is that image justified, or is it just as unfair?

I embarked on this book with some fixed perceptions that I soon became aware were mistaken – none more so than those I had on the St Andrew's Societies. Contact had been made with two Falkirk bairns, Jim and Isobel Bell; now resident in Illinois who, as well as having their own successful careers, were mainstays in the Illinois St Andrew's Society. I sought to meet them, out of curiosity, regarding both themselves and the society.

The Illinois St Andrew's Society was formed in 1845 at a time when Chicago was a pioneer town in the Midwest with a population of approximately 12,000 people; not the global city it is now, with seven and a half million. As the west of America opened up, there was substantial Scottish migration. Today, Scots place names abound; from Montrose, a train halt a few stations out from O'Hare Airport, to Marshall Fields, one of the city's largest department stores, which was begun by the son of a Scots immigrant in 1881.

The Illinois Society was founded to assist Scots immigrants in surviving in their new land. The organisation's purpose was not the celebration of Caledonia and the land they had left behind, but the protection of Scottish migrants in the new world, against the often difficult circumstances they met. Formed to offer succour and support rather than beer and whisky, they were more akin to a friendly society than a ceilidh club.

In his book, *How the Scots Invented the Modern World*, historian Arthur Herman details how Scots had many advantages as emigrants, especially in America. The Calvinist desire to allow everyone direct access to the word of God had provided basic education and created a highly literate people. Hence when the Scots arrived on foreign shores they were able to quickly advance, both socially and economically. Their literacy allowed them to be upwardly mobile, as opposed to remaining huddled masses at the ports of disembarkation, be it Boston, Baltimore or New York. It's no surprise, then, that the ethnic Scots are one of the richest communities in the USA today.

However, the grass was not greener for all. Many emigrant Scots faced adversity and poverty. Life in the Midwest and the west was tough, unrelenting and unforgiving. 'Relieve the Distressed' became the motto, and assistance was rendered in good times and in bad, serving many Scots well during tumultuous events like the Civil War, the Chicago Fire and the Great Depression. From the cradle to the grave, Scots who had made it in the New World sought to support those who had fallen upon hard times in the new land through St Andrew's Societies. Food and shelter was afforded, employment provided, and even burials budgeted for. In 1910, a home for the elderly was established and though now run as a commercial concern, was symbolic of the society's mission and service.

As time has passed and the nature of the Scottish immigrant community has changed, the society has evolved. It continues to hold and host Burns' nights, St Andrew's Day dinners and Highland games. And why not – these are all part of Scottish culture and heritage, and take place in Scotland as well as abroad. In America, they provide an opportunity for emigrants to meet and mingle amongst friends. The emigrant's life is not always a happy one and leaving causes difficulties and distress. Life for many in the present, as in the past, can be hard. Even if you are financially comfortable, there are other sacrifices made that can be painful. Kids grow up without grandparents and the distance can be insurmountable for many.

The society also provides a variety of contemporary benefits, not just for their members but for Scotland. There is a Scottish law society, a Scottish genealogy group, a Scottish-American history group and an arts and culture section. In addition, there is a Scottish business forum, which fulfils many roles, from providing regular input on what is happening in the Scottish public and private sectors, to helping Scots understand American business, particularly in the Midwest. Many leading Scottish politicians and businessmen have been assisted in their quests for support for Scottish interests in the USA.

That is a history which Scots all over the world should celebrate, not scorn, and those resident in Scotland should be proud of, not disparage. Like many in Scotland I had viewed St Andrew's Societies with some scepticism, if not disdain. I had a stereotypical image of a drinking club for the homesick Scot where 'Songs of Scotland' were played and sung, and the 'Auld Country' lamented. By the end of my discussion I felt ashamed of my original perceptions and saddened by the lack of awareness of their history in Scotland. I had found a past that Scots should be rightly proud of, and a present that we can surely benefit from.

The Bells collect me from my hotel in downtown Chicago and take me to a restaurant for a chat over lunch. Prior to my departure, they had been exceedingly helpful in arrangements and are equally kind in their hospitality on my arrival. They are still close to Scotland in a variety of ways even if they are now long-time residents of Chicago.

Jim Bell is Senior Vice President for the Bank of Scotland in Chicago, and Isobel Bell works with Scottish Development

International. Their central Scotland accents are still audible beneath the softer American tone. Returns home have been regular as a result of family, with Isobel's elderly mother still living in Falkirk. Jim has no siblings but Isobel has a sister still in Scotland, as well as a brother in Canada. Both have retained friends in the land they left.

Jim and Isobel Bell were both brought up within sight of Falkirk Steeple, on Wallace Street (then Camelon), and on the banks of the Forth and Clyde Canal, attending Falkirk High and Graeme High, respectively. Coincidentally, their fathers both worked in the foundry – an industry on which the town was forged. Memories of the community are warm, with Jim reminiscing about Falkirk Football Club winning the Cup in 1957, and remaining a fan to this day. Isobel fondly remembers gala days and highland dancing. Both recall, with a mixture of humour and horror, the dull and lengthy day that was a Scottish Sunday.

Jim joined the TSB in Grangemouth immediately after leaving school, later moving to Bank of Scotland in its Falkirk and Laurieston branches. Isobel was a bookkeeper in the town. Both had a hankering to travel, and a sojourn abroad encouraged them to look around at opportunities. Primarily, they decided to try Canada, as it was easier to travel back and forth, and for parents and family, that remained an important consideration. Scots banking qualifications were held in high regard then, as they are today, and openings were plentiful. Jim applied to the Royal Bank of Canada and was readily accepted. They left Scottish shores in January 1970, and within a week of arrival, Isobel had also picked up a job, in addition to the higher paid employment for Jim that had lured them there in the first place. They have been abroad ever since. He worked with RBC for 23 years, in Canada and the United States, with stays in Toronto, Buffalo, New York and Chicago, moving to the US Corporate Banking Division of one of the large Japanese banks in the early nineties, before Bank of Scotland recruited him back some three years ago, completing the circle.

American society was more to their liking than Canadian, although they are conscious of its vices as well as its virtues. So they returned to the Windy City in 1994, which they decided to make their home. They have been there ever since and are likely to remain. A permanent return to Scotland is unlikely, but regular visits for part of the year and perhaps even a home are probable. Two sons, Michael and Christopher, have now grown up and live locally. Both have served in the American forces and are American citizens, but have an affinity for the land of their parents and are keen to maintain those links for future generations. That, doubtless, partly explains the association with the St Andrew's Society. Both Jim and Isobel said that initially in Canada they had scorned such clubs as they sought to immerse themselves in a new culture and integrate in a new land. However, as time passed, absence made the heart grow fonder, and they gradually became more involved in the societies.

For them, Scotland provided a sense of history in their new home. 'A proud nation. It gives you something that others don't. It's a very eclectic mix here in the USA. Being Scottish gives you roots. Being Scottish gives you a sense of belonging, a sense of comfort and pride, as well as identity.' Anxious to avoid using clichés, Isobel could not help but comment on the work ethic. 'It came through strongly. Ethical and honest. It's genuine that getting your sleeves rolled up was part of the culture and fabric of Scottish society.'

What Scotland failed to provide was the kind of self-confidence that seems to come naturally to Americans. They had to acquire that across the Atlantic. 'We were never taught to be self-confident and we didn't really have it.' That has had to be learned over the years. North America also offered the opportunity that Scotland lacked at the time and they saw it, and experienced it from different angles. For Isobel, it was gender. 'Being female meant there was less opportunity. You didn't feel that nearly as much when you came to America.' For Jim, it was career opportunities. 'There was the lack of opportunity in banking. There were only five or so banks, and you were pretty much told you wouldn't become a manager until you were 35.'

The job opportunities take us on to contemporary Scotland. As we seek not just to make contact with the diaspora, but persuade some to return, Jim and Isobel have some points to make. Firstly, the need for a vibrant economy. 'It's the vibrance and opportunity that keeps people in America and gives them little reason to seek fame and fortune elsewhere.' That has been argued by many from a variety of viewpoints in Scotland. Jim, though, makes an additional point. 'In terms of bringing Scots back, I have never heard of a Scot in America being offered a job back home. There are, though, a lot of Scots here, some of whom might just do that. That opportunity needs to be available. There are many Scots here with an awful lot to offer.' We have a skills shortage and a demographic crisis. Perhaps, as well as fresh talent from other lands, we should recruit more actively amongst our own who have departed.

As befits a couple who are keen to promote Scotland's future as well as celebrate its past, they have much to say. They correctly point out that Scotland is now approaching the diaspora to seek assistance. But what is Scotland offering in return? 'We can't come with a begging bowl bearing golf and bagpipes. What will we give back, not just what we will take. What's the *quid pro quo*?'

As with preconceptions about the St Andrew's Society, there is a misconception about expat Scots. There is a difference between Americans of Scots descent and Scots in America. That needs to be borne in mind. However, the view that expat Scots are no longer one of us, but a different race when they live abroad must end. It extends from sniping at Sir Sean Connery's residence, to a rejection of others who have left but wish to retain Scottish identity. They may lose rights they had as residents but they will never shed their ethnicity. Being Scottish is too often an exclusive identity requiring you not simply to have been born and brought up here but continue to work and live here. For many this has never been possible and in a global world, most certainly cannot be.

This attitude is not shared by the Irish. They are very inclusive, to the extent where it has been comically implied that drinking Guinness provides honorary citizenship. But, they certainly welcome and appreciate the diaspora and are inclusive towards anyone sharing some Irish identity. It is impossible at present to imagine Tartan Day or St Andrew's Day being celebrated worldwide by one and all, as St Patrick's Day is. That is partly because they are more welcoming in their identity than the Scots.

I have seen instances of Scotland supporters at football matches challenging others' right to follow the team because of their English accent. It was not their fault they were brought up outside Scotland, but they most certainly feel Scottish, and why not?

In the past, Scots worried about losing their identity. Situated on the same island as a much larger neighbour, there were understandable reasons why assimilation was feared. However, with the restoration of the Parliament, now is the time to be inclusive rather than exclusive, and to welcome as kinfolk Scots who have left, as well as new Scots who have arrived. If we want their help we must welcome their identity.

In 35 years of returning to Scotland, Jim and Isobel have always been made to feel at home themselves. However, they are aware of others who have not. No Scot, I am sure, can be unaware of the snide comments or disparaging remarks made about expats, whether they be Sean Connery, Jackie Stewart or others. That is the point that Jim and Isobel make. 'We need to make emigrant Scots feel welcome and make them feel at home. The Irish are fully inclusive; the Scots are exclusive. We need to address that. When they go home they need to be treated as if they are at home and not just visiting. There needs to be a feeling of returning to their roots and feeling welcomed.'

It's time to treat them as our kinfolk and not as a separate race. Scots resident abroad, and people of Scottish descent, should be welcomed as part of the wider diaspora and the broader Scottish community. In the global world in which we now live, not all Scots will either wish to continue living in their native land, or be able to do so if they wish to achieve their dreams and ambitions. But they remain Scottish, albeit without the rights accorded to residents. We should welcome people who wish to identify with us, and grasp an opportunity; not view our Scottishness as a private club for residents only. As the Bells said – be inclusive, not exclusive. We are all Scots, the world over.

Interviewed by Kenny MacAskill
June 2005

Helen Maria Nugent

ASSOCIATE PROFESSOR AT THE
ART INSTITUTE OF CHICAGO

A Kirkie Girl With Designs on Chicago

CHICAGO IS A VERY IMPRESSIVE CITY, and not at all what I expected. The name alone conjured up images of the 1920s prohibition, of Elliot Ness and Al Capone, inspired by the television of my childhood. However, with a wonderful backdrop of Lake Michigan, and having the splendour of the Chicago River running through it, it is a naturally beautiful city. Like many industrial cities, it has reinvented itself and rejuvenated its centre. Public parks are plentiful and it is one of the greenest cities in the USA. Sculptures and artworks abound, not just in its many museums and galleries, but in famous statues dotted around the city, from Picasso to Henry Moore. Chicago is now thriving as one of North America's leading contemporary art and design centres.

Flourishing in that city's environment is a Scots lass at the school of the Art Institute of Chicago, acknowledged by many as the principal graduate art school in the USA, where she is Associate Professor of Architecture, Interior Architecture and Designed Objects. Given the length of that title it's no surprise to find that she originates from Kirkintilloch, one of Scotland's longer place names. Helen Maria Nugent meets me in the foyer of the hotel in which I am staying on South Michigan Avenue. As befits her profession, she asks me for my aesthetic opinion on the hotel, and I reply that the views over Millennium Park to Lake Michigan are stunning, but within it smacks of fading grandeur, as it lives on past glories and is badly in need of a makeover.

Helen Maria is small and vivacious, attractive and outgoing, confident yet considerate; almost the archetypal gallus girl that only the west of Scotland can produce. Over coffee she begins to tell me about herself and what brought her west. Knowing I am a Scottish parliamentarian, she immediately mentions the new Holyrood building. Having endured, like all members, a great deal of grief about the cost and the construction, it is interesting to hear not just her view, but the American opinion on it. She tells me it is big news, in a positive sense, in the American art and architecture scene, having been the subject of lengthy articles in the major North American technical and professional journals. She produces one such journal to prove it: sure enough, there on the front page of the leading architect's magazine is our own Scottish Parliament.

It's fascinating to hear the views of a Scot who sees the situation from afar, and in a much wider sense than those of us involved; either in the political struggle for its creation, or carrying the baggage relating to the cost of its construction. She's immensely proud, not just of the building but what it stands for. It makes me think that sometimes those of us back in Scotland, and certainly those involved in the political scene, are too close to the coalface to realise the enormity of the change it has created. 'It puts Scotland on the map as an equal. I am not talking just about the building itself, but as an institution.' The international ramifications, as well as interest, are obvious to her, even if missed by many back home.

As someone who is deeply impressed by the building within (but deferring judgement on the exterior for several years until it blends into the landscape), I am interested in the perspective of the American expert. Her comments seem to match the growing interest in it, if visitor numbers are anything to go by. 'The new building has had so much attention here. Everyone comments about the "crazy building in Scotland". People don't know what to think about it and find it shocking because it comes from a completely different mentality. When people think of Scottish architecture, they think of Charles Rennie Mackintosh and our castles. This Parliament building looks like something that could only have been built in Scotland, and it's fantastic how this guy [Enric Miralles] had such a huge vision.'

Helen Maria is a seventies child. She grew up in Kirkintilloch, where her mother, aunt and brother still stay. Her late father was an electrical engineer, and her mother started off in dressmaking, dabbled at nursing at Lennox Castle, and now works in the furnishings sector. She attended Kirkintilloch High School until she moved onto the big city; to Glasgow School of Art where she studied as an undergraduate in the department of Environmental Art, and completed a Masters in Design.

The west of Scotland is a community that she remembers fondly, and obviously still misses. She tries to return at least once a year, and next year, with a sabbatical due, she'll try and extend the stay. Being married to Ronald Kirkpatrick, an American architect, has heightened, if anything, her sense of Scottishness. As displayed by his name, he has Scottish ancestry, and their wedding took place in a Glasgow registry office with guests from both sides of the Atlantic resplendent in kilts and tartan. Ronald's interest in Scottish history and his fascination with Scottish culture mean that regular sojourns home are assured and a permanent return is not ruled out, though it is made increasingly difficult as both prosper in their careers.

Like many expats, she is torn between a love for her homeland and the benefits that are on offer in her new one through size and diversity. 'Compared to Glasgow, I have students in my class here from Korea, Israel and Bangkok. It is so diverse and I would miss that. I also like the fact that I can go to certain parts of town where I will know everyone. But then, there is also an anonymity that is fabulous. When I go back to Glasgow, where I haven't lived for 14 years, I am guaranteed to meet someone I know walking down the street. But I see lots of opportunities here in Chicago. I often think that there will be a point when I have to decide what I want to do, and I don't want to be an American. I am not an American.' Even if marriage and employment keep her in the USA, she will forever remain a Kirkie girl.

Memories of Kirkintilloch are fond, and in the main relate to its geography. Perhaps residence in a metropolis like Chicago sees her remember Kirkintilloch as a village, with the canal and the Campsie hills beyond. Its proximity to Glasgow may also have something to do with her current location, as she recalls the enjoyment of being able to meet with friends and access the big city. Encouraged by her mother and aunt, she had participated in art and design as a child, and though constrained by the school timetable, had finally managed to study it as an academic subject in her sixth year. By then she was hooked, and art school followed.

Once her course was completed, she ventured out into the wide world of work. A Prince's Trust award allowed her to stay and work in Scotland, so she and a friend started a small company of their own. It was a difficult time for all, especially for youngsters trying to break through. However, a former teacher told her of an academic art and design conference that takes place in the States each year, the largest of its kind in the world. She and her business partner decided to chance it and travelled to Seattle. Deciding to make the most of her Scottish ethnicity, the presentation materials were decorated with a tartan bow. It proved to be a masterstroke, provoking wide interest and comment. Returning to Scotland, a call was received from the University of Florida where a job was offered setting up a foundation programme establishing workshops for art research and practice. A contract, initially for a year, became a stay of four and a half years. It was a sojourn that saw her prosper in her career and meet and marry her husband. Tiring of life in a campus environment in central Florida, they decided to move. The joint requirements of her and her husband meant that only a few cities fitted the bill, but a vacancy arose in Chicago as the director of a programme. Chicago's size offered adequate options for Ronald, so they moved north. Now, with a permanent tenure at the school and an increasingly high profile, she has never looked back.

What Scotland gave to her is encapsulated in the struggle she had to make her career. 'Scotland gave me the ability to do anything. It did take effort, and it did take knowledge. You needed to know what you were talking about. It also took guts to go and make it happen.'

That was something that she felt had almost been inbred, but was also fostered at art school in Glasgow. 'The idea of the programme I was on was that art was always about the public, and all the projects we had to do had to be in the public eye. A lot of the other departments were not like that – they were working in studios. It was hard, but you were prepared. If you had a good idea, everything was possible. Almost everyone I went to art school with, in the three years we were in the programme, is still in the arts. I went to school with Douglas Gordon. We were a real go-getter crowd.' She does add a caveat to that, though. 'I was one of the last to go to school and get a grant – my fees were paid. That gave me the option of not having to work. I did work in bars eventually, but I had time to do what I loved doing.' Helen Maria is not the first to have commented on this in my interviews and I can only hope that opportunities have not been closed off to future generations.

However, there were downsides to trying to succeed in design in Scotland. Chances were few and opportunities less, especially for a young female. The nature of her work in design meant she was involved in production and a factory-type environment which added to the difficulties. 'My friend and I, when we were at art school, tried to get jobs and could not get anything because we were young girls and there were the big boys' clubs – there was no way in. We did manage to do some kind of workshops in teaching projects, but it was hard, and I have to say that I think a big part of it was that we were women and not men. We were also young. Over here, if people think that you have a chance to do it, they give you that chance, even if you don't have all the necessary experience.' She cites her own experience in obtaining the job in Chicago which, after all, on its own is prestigious and in a major institute. 'The person doing the job before me had been a professor who was much more qualified. I knew at the time it was going to be hard but on the other hand I thought "what is the worst I can do" – that kind of attitude. In Scotland, I don't think that was the case. I think it was worse because I am a woman. It was even more difficult. Working in factories was difficult because of that. It was hard work, being surrounded by men in the factories. The women were in the office doing secretarial work, so I was subjected to a lot of ridicule. A lot of patting on the head, "poor wee lassie, we'll help you" type of thing. The men treated me like their daughter or wee cousin. They didn't take me seriously.'

That said, she does think that there has been a considerable change in attitudes, and again refers to a more recent experience. 'I think there has been a big change. A few months ago a bunch of architects were over from Scotland. There were as many women as men. These women were doing amazing architectural projects. It was about equality.' However, I still can't help thinking that there remains a considerable distance for Scotland to travel, not just in attitudes towards women, but in being less risk averse and more willing to take a chance on youth. Many of these attitudes are cultural and more difficult to change – but change they must.

Our discussion of what Scotland could do takes us back to design in general, and to the Parliament building in particular. She sees great opportunities for her native land. 'In terms of art and design in Scotland there are so many artists from there who are so famous now. Probably more famous outwith Scotland than they are in it. There is a lot of talent. When I go back there are always lots of new buildings up. There is a culture of design going on, with bars, clubs and restaurants all springing up. Design is so interesting in Scotland now.' She sees comparisons between Chicago and Glasgow and comically comments on Chicago being like 'Glasgow on overdrive'.

However, she sees a need for Scots and Scotland to raise their ambitions and its horizons. Other small nations are actively involved in promoting their artists and designers through their embassies and consulates. The Dutch, she mentions, are actively pushing their craft and design. But she sees it as attitudinal as well as in tangible promotion. As well as practical steps being taken to support them, a cultural change needs to take place to compete in the first place. 'Scottish architects aren't bidding to build in the Millennium Park. I wish there was more support for these people so they can go out into the world and get something global. The new Parliament building has had so much attention here. People need to change their attitude of thinking that we are too small, or that nothing ever happens here. Of course it can happen if you try hard enough. I wish Scotland was able to expand on that. It seems that countries like the Netherlands, Sweden and Denmark think of themselves as global, yet have their own national identity, and they have respect around the world. They are part of the world and Scotland differs there – the self-belief is lacking.'

Helen Maria Nugent is a talented woman – whether she is lost as a permanent resident of Scotland, only time will tell. However, she is actively supporting other Scottish talents in the art and design world. She has travelled many miles and achieved a great deal since departing her Kirkintilloch home. That success has been aided by values forged in Scotland but equally impeded by attitudes which were prevalent there. If Scotland can retain the values they instilled in her, and adopt the drive and determination she has shown, then it will be a better land for it. She has designs on Chicago, but a vision for Scotland.

Interviewed by Kenny MacAskill
June 2005

John Higgins

DIRECTOR AND CORPORATE CHEF
AT THE GEORGE BROWN CHEF
SCHOOL, OTTAWA

Cooking for Canada

ACCORDING TO THE CANADIAN CENSUS, over four million Canadians claim either full or part Scottish heritage, out of a total population of just under 30 million. In addition, tens of thousands were born and brought up in Scotland but now reside across the Atlantic. It's not just place names but accents on every street corner that resonate of Scotland. The odds of interviewing two from the same Scottish town would appear to be low. However, I flew to Ottawa then Toronto believing that Hugh Boyle was from Hamilton and John Higgins from Glasgow. Yet it transpired that both were from Bellshill, and had both attended St Saviour's High School and Motherwell College. They didn't know each other, but as is the way in small town Scotland, they knew of each other. Our country truly is a village.

John Higgins is a world famous chef. His career has seen him cook at the top venues and finest establishments around the globe: from Gleneagles in Scotland and Buckingham Palace in England to the finest hotels in the USA and Canada. He even captained the Canadian culinary team that won the World Championships in 1997 – a victory that gave him immense satisfaction as it took place before family and friends back on Scottish soil in Glasgow.

We meet in the lobby of the King Edward Hotel in Toronto – not just a prestigious hotel but a city institution and another top venue which he has on his CV. A stocky guy with a big heart, he sounds as if he's just arrived, is friendly and very much mine host. He is greeted fondly by all staff; that may be expected as he was formerly the Chef de Cuisine and Director of Food and Beverage at the establishment; however, it's one thing to be popular when you are in a senior position, but quite another to retain that popularity when you have left. As we adjourn to a nearby restaurant, it's clear that he's not only well known but well liked within and without his former place of work. A journey of 500 yards takes quite some time as he is hailed and greeted by all on route – staff or not. In the restaurant, after he has renewed his acquaintance with the staff, we continue the discussion we commenced back in the hotel.

Like many Scots he embarked for Canada in the expectation of a brief stay. But his six month trip has turned into a stay of 25 years. Now married to Arlene, a Canadian, he has taken out Canadian citizenship. He returns home regularly and doesn't rule out a permanent return if the proper opportunity arose, but given his experience and seniority those positions are few. But he most certainly has neither renounced his Scottish roots nor given up on his Scottish identity. His parents, John and Mary, a steelworker and a nurse, who are now both retired, still live in his hometown, and his sister lives in Glasgow. They visit regularly, with Arlene going over annually and John on occasions. His roots go back to his upbringing in Bellshill where he remembers the people fondly but recalls it as a tough environment. But it was a background that moulded him and has driven him on to the heights he has reached.

Now 46 years of age, he had always wanted to be a chef and to work at the best establishments. As a 10 year old boy he caddied with his uncle at Gleneagles and was intrigued and enamoured by the prestigious hotel. Friends either sought to dissuade him or actively disparaged him for entering the hospitality sector. It was not what most working class boys in the Motherwell area were doing but it was what he wanted to be.

Leaving school, he went to Motherwell College where numerous teachers inspired him with tales of working in the big hotels like the Central in Glasgow, Turnberry and Gleneagles elsewhere in Scotland

and Buckingham Palace outwith it. If they could do it, so could he, and another benchmark and target for attainment was set. Similarly, a postcard from a family friend in Canada when he was an impressionable teenager provided a new horizon. His drive and determination have seen him fulfil those ambitions and reach those horizons.

After college he started as an apprentice at the Central Hotel in Glasgow which back then was not just a prestigious hotel but also part of the British Transport Hotel chain. That link allowed him to move initially to the Station Hotel in Aberdeen then on to Gleneagles, realising an ambition and providing an enjoyable experience. Keen to move on, and eager to sample other top-rated venues, he applied for and succeeded in obtaining a job at Buckingham Palace. He thoroughly enjoyed working not just at the Royal Palace but also at other residences such as Balmoral, Holyrood and Windsor. Like many, he has the highest regard for the Royal family, but contempt for many of the hangers-on. While at the Palace, and in his younger and fitter days, he recalls being stopped by the police in London for cycling too fast. Providing his address as Buckingham Palace resulted in an aggressive reply that he had just met 'Dixon of Dock Green'. However, a phone call later confirmed the authenticity of the young Scot's remark and he was allowed on his way, suitably chastised by a perplexed Metropolitan Officer.

From London he crossed the Atlantic to work in the equally prestigious Four Seasons Hotel in Toronto. A year in a sister hotel with the same name in Washington DC followed – where a fellow Scot was a hard taskmaster but an excellent teacher – before he returned to Canada and the Sutton Palace Hotel in Toronto. It had been another of his ambitions to be an executive chef by the time he was 30. He achieved that in 1988 at the age of 29 when he was appointed Chef de Cuisine at the King Edward. He subsequently became Head of Food and Beverage. Along the way his skills were acknowledged by both his guests and his peers. A Mouton Cadet award in 1987; a Chef of the year accolade from the Escoffier Chefs Society of Toronto in 1992; and a victory at the Great Canadian Chefs Cooking Competition in 1993 are among numerous titles and prizes he holds, as well as his captaincy of the winning Canadian team at the World Championships in Glasgow in 1997. Having a reputation for a creative approach to cuisine, he also gained a name for innovation in hotel food service operations, but credits his wife Arlene for creating haggis pizza!

Ever since his time at Motherwell College he had a hankering to teach. Throughout his career he had been influenced by others and, having enjoyed a successful career, he wished to both enable and encourage others to succeed as he had. As a result, in 2002 he became Director and Corporate Chef at the George Brown Chef School, one of the most prestigious academies in the hospitality sector in North America and one of the top chef schools. He remains there now, with 1,600 students on a variety of programmes.

John Higgins is someone who has not only been highly motivated but equally determined to reach the numerous goals he has set for himself throughout his career. No surprise then that he credits Scotland with providing that tenacity. 'Scotland gave me an attitude that you never give in. You never say no. I remember a teacher at school telling me the story about Robert the Bruce and the spider. That is the attitude I have.' In addition it provided 'good grounding, good values and gave a great opportunity.'

However, he recalls his tenacity at being hindered by a limitation on his expectations. 'People used to dampen down my ambitions, and thought I saw myself as a big shot. Working class guy turning out to be a chef. Some folk even denigrated me because of my ambitions. There was an expectation you would just stay and get on with your life like everyone else. They have turned around now but it is a trait with some in Scotland.' But, he adds, 'Scotland gave me an opportunity. If you harness the opportunity that's good, but I think some people could never do that for themselves. That's why, when I had the opportunity to move away from Bellshill, I took it. Not because I wanted to, it was because I couldn't fulfil my ambitions there. I used to look at people and then look at myself and think I must be strange because I had ambition to go places. That's sad.'

I can't help thinking that what he has said is all too common and all too tragic. It's the curse and blessing of municipal socialism in our land. It nurtures and allows success that otherwise would be unavailable for many but places a ceiling on their aspirations and a limit on their success, rearing and educating, but only to go so far and no further. To advance beyond a certain level or to even just seek to do so breaks an unwritten code. Hence why so many often succeed abroad rather than at home. This barrier needs to be broken, or the cycle will simply continue and the John Higgins of this world will continue to be born in Scotland, but destined for success abroad.

He remains proud of his roots and confident for the country of his birth. Comparing it with his new home in Canada, he sees opportunities for Scotland to learn from it and improve both herself and the chances for her people by copying aspects of it. 'I am proud of being Scottish. I think Scottish people are genuine and proud, albeit sometimes too hard on themselves. There is no need to be so down in the dumps as many people are. The Scots are very self-conscious. The expectation for kids here in Canada is very high compared to Scotland.' That is not said as a criticism, but as a matter of fact, and it's something those of us resident in Scotland need to address.

'There are a lot of good things happening with the arts, tourism, technology and culinary at the moment. The world is changing at such a rapid pace and, as we all know, change is inevitable. People need to view and consider both the negative and positive outlook. I look at things from a different angle. When you are there and living it, you accept it. Now I am outside looking in, it allows me to view both environments. I don't think people in Scotland realise just what they have. They don't tell other people either. We need to get out of our shells a bit. Other countries are making noises. Americans are full of it. They talk the talk. We need to do a bit more of it.' John Higgins is a confident guy who has every right to be given his personal and career achievements. While younger Scots may be less reticent than preceding generations, there is still a considerable distance to travel. Scotland is a beautiful country with a lot going for it: too often the glass is seen as half empty not half full. Those who disparage Carol Craig and the establishment of a Centre for Confidence and Well Being would do well to heed his comments.

This discussion takes us into his own hospitality sector where he sees great improvements in quality on offer, but still sees a need for a change in attitudes towards service provided. 'There is a change across the board, but a lot could still be done as far as customer service is concerned. Here in North America people get a great welcome and manners are excellent. Scottish people are also polite and there is a genuine thank you. It is about harnessing the natural.'

Change is something he thinks cannot simply be restricted to those working in the hospitality sector but must also occur in people's attitudes towards service. 'Customer service needs to be improved. When people travel they expect a lot of things. We need to ask how can we make it better, how can we get a better attitude. That's not just in this business but any business. Ask people, "How is your meal, how was your stay?"'

It's something I recall my brother commenting and indeed acting upon when he returned from a spell working in North America. I was initially surprised and indeed mildly shocked. But he was right. Being reticent and simply accepting bad service is unhelpful, ill serving both the customer and the company. If we don't tell them they won't know. There is nothing wrong in sending back a cup of coffee because it's cold or raising some other aspect of service that is inadequate. Until this preference to suffer in silence – as it's the Scottish way and to do otherwise is un-Scottish and rude – is overcome there are limits to changes that can happen in the sector. Just as a natural politeness can be added to by a question or statement, good manners can be maintained but poor service still challenged.

Constitutional change has been long overdue in Scotland but a cultural change is equally needed if we are to be the nation we aspire to be. Service is not servility. Reticence is not respect. Good manners do not mean meek acceptance. Equally, self-confidence is not arrogance. Talking up your country is not boasting. Believing in yourself is not conceit. John Higgins uses the attitudes and values instilled by his native land to overcome the barriers set by it. If we can do likewise then many more can emulate his success without leaving our fair land.

Interviewed by Kenny MacAskill
June 2005

Professor Andrew Ross

PROFESSOR OF AMERICAN
STUDIES, NEW YORK UNIVERSITY

The Scottish American

A SCOTS LAD FROM ALLOA, whose father was an Eastern European refugee, ends up as Professor of American Studies at New York University. Truth, as they say, is often stranger than fiction. Professor Andrew Ross may now lecture and write on a variety of other topics, in particular labour studies, but his title remains that of Professor of American Studies. He is, as I am to discover, an extremely interesting character and a very talented individual.

He presents as almost the archetypal east coast liberal academic so despised by the Bush administration. Longish hair and casually dressed, his room at the university is papered with books from floor to ceiling. His accent was by far the most American of the exiles that I had met, and indeed he says that when in Scotland, it's easier to describe himself as American than explain the truth. But he is proud of his Scottish identity, and keen to help Scotland prosper in the modern world.

He grew up in Alloa with his sister and four brothers. His father was a Polish Jew who had fought in the Polish Free Army in World War II. Returning to his native land was impossible, and romance with a local lass followed, as did the Scottification of his name. He describes his mother, Mary Jean, as a respectable working class lady. Both his parents have passed away now, but it's a romantic background for an altogether intriguing man.

His father worked in Alloa's famed brewing industry. He remembers his childhood fondly; proud of his community, though tinged with sadness at a town that was down on its luck. He recalls a Sunday morning paper delivery that did as much for the experience as for the money, an outlook which doubtless continues in much of his work to this day. 'I delivered papers at the "bottom end" which were notorious slums – the Bowhouse. They have all been cleared now. It was the most desirable route of all because the tips were the best, yet these were the poorest people in town. Even though many of them were unemployed, they were by far the most generous.'

They were a high achieving family. He and his younger brother went to Alloa Academy, with his other siblings attending Dollar Academy on scholarships. All graduated from Scottish universities. The brothers encompass a research scientist, an engineer, an accountant and an academic. But all, except his eldest brother who now lives in Auchterarder, have emigrated. They are scattered to the wind, with his sister (an accountant) in Sydney, one brother in San Francisco, and another in North Carolina.

Alloa changed during his life there, not just through the decline of heavy industry, but also in the political mood. 'I grew up breathing socialist air. By the time I was in my youth, that was nationalist air.' It has remained a marginal seat to this day, contested hotly by SNP and Labour. He departed after the failed devolution vote in 1979, 'vowing, vaingloriously, to return to Scotland only when it had its own Parliament. The referendum gave me an excuse to leave Scotland at the time. I felt a sense of betrayal.' He seems almost the embodiment of much of the spirit that ebbed, if not flowed, out of Scotland as the aspirations of the seventies were crushed by the Thatcherism of the eighties. The defeat, albeit by default, in the referendum came shortly after the debacle of Argentina on the football field, and a crisis of national self-confidence occurred.

Whether or not he needed an excuse to leave, he certainly made the most of it. Graduating in English Literature from the University of Aberdeen, he spent some time as a roustabout in the North Sea oil industry, before completing a postgraduate degree south of the border at the University of Kent. With no desire to stay in England, and with little opportunity as he saw it under the Thatcher regime, he took off for California. Further postgraduate work at Berkeley followed before he obtained a position at Princeton, which he describes as the most Scottish (historically speaking) of all the American universities. The directorship of the American Studies programme at New York University subsequently followed, though his direction and course of study has veered towards the labour market and globalisation. He has written extensively for papers and periodicals, and authored or edited 15 books. They include: *No Respect: Intellectuals and Popular Culture* in 1989; *Strange Weather: Culture, Science and Technology in the Age of Limits* in 1991; *No Sweat: Fashion, Free Trade, and the Rights of Garment Workers* in 1997; *The Celebration Chronicles: Life, Liberty and The Pursuit of Property Value in Disney's New Town* in 1999; and *Low Pay, High Profile: The Global Push for Fair Labor* in 2004. His latest work saw him live in China and learn Mandarin, as he researched the basis for *The Fast Boat to China: Corporate Flight and the Human Consequences of Free Trade*. Clearly, he is not only prodigious in his output, but hardworking in his input.

I had met first met Professor Ross when a mutual friend asked if I could give a tour of the Parliament building to a visiting exiled Scottish academic. I was delighted to do so and became curious about this soft-spoken but highly thoughtful Scottish American. He happily agreed to participate in the book and arrangements were made to meet him at his university office in Greenwich Village, New York. Situated near Washington Square, it's not only a student area but a very bohemian environment, in sharp contrast to the financial district just a few blocks away.

Before I can even begin the interview, he is explaining in detail his views on the Scots in America. 'No Scot that I know has suffered any discrimination living here, unless you were a Loyalist years ago in the Revolutionary period. Scots have had a fairly plain sailing in the United States. I think that's one of the reasons why they are not particularly clannish, other than the societies. They are not as clannish to the same degree as other nationalities.' He accepts the Arthur Herman doctrine that literacy allowed the Scots who landed in

America to immediately adapt to the terrain and make their mark, unlike other ethnic groups who huddled together for mutual protection. However, he adds an additional view that the 'Protestant work ethic' inculcated in them drove them on to success in a land geared towards – if not created for – that doctrine, allowing them to prosper.

The exceptions were the Scotch-Irish, and he moves on to tell me of recent research. Their activities, especially in the south of the United States, raises the darker side of the Scottish migrant's legacy and the more dangerous aspects of the *Braveheart* phenomenon. 'They have been associated with a lot of white supremacist movements in the south. Some of it is coming back to haunt the political scene, particularly with *Braveheart*. They campaigned very hard for the establishment of Tartan Day. It goes back a long way to the founding of the Ku Klux Klan. You could find *Braveheart* on the shelf of every southern right-wing politician. A lot of it is to do with the "lost cause": the Civil War was the lost cause in the south. There is now an ideological undercurrent to it here. It doesn't help that they are Anglophobic in the lost south. It's not entirely ethnic. It's anti-Washington, anti-federal and anti-establishment.'

I find this history of Scots in America that I have heard about on my travels and interviews fascinating, from the darker side in the south to the aspects to be proud of in the north. It's something that is little known in Scotland, rarely taught, and mentioned usually in sensationalist terms in the media. The teaching of the history of his native country and his people is something that Andrew Ross feels was not provided by Scotland. 'When I went to school there was not much about Scotland or Scottish history. I remember a lesson on Skara Brae. We learned about British history in the nineteenth century, Napoleonic wars and so on. No pre-Union history was taught. There was no stimulation towards anything Scottish. We got Highlander stories and tartan, but nothing more profound that would stimulate curiosity. I imagine some of that has been remedied over the years, but I think it's a big issue in schools.' I couldn't agree more, and only wish it were true that it had been remedied. Scottish history needs to be taught to allow the Scottish people to understand who they are. It did not simply start in 1314 or end in 1707. There is a rich journal, some of which is unpleasant, but all of which we should know, to be confident in who we are, proud of our achievements, and take responsibility for our failings.

Asking him about the journey from American Studies to Labour Studies, he provides a fascinating answer, not just because of the transition, but for his latest conclusions. 'We are always trying to internationalise American Studies and to deparochialise it. The last thing America needs is more insularity. Scholars need to play a role in that. What I do is Labour Studies. I have written a great deal about low wage labour and companies offshoring. I worked in China for a long time. I spent a year learning Mandarin. I took my family to Shanghai and decided the most useful thing I could do was to interview Chinese employees working in foreign-invested companies in technology driven sectors. The Chinese economy is rapidly moving up the technology chain. I think mine will be the first study of skilled Chinese employment in these sectors. It's an interesting experience with regard again to the Scottish example – because what I came across was that the mainland Chinese employees faced exactly the same job pressures as their counterparts in other countries, such as the US, who are losing many of these jobs. The job pressures in China are exactly the same as everywhere else. They knew their position in the labour market – there is always a danger of being undercut by foreign investors.'

Not necessarily much comfort to a worker threatened by offshoring here, but illuminating all the same. The lessons for Scotland are hard to extrapolate. However, as someone who has argued for a lower tax regime, he is quick to point out the downside of pursuing the neo-liberal agenda. His ambitions for Scotland are genuine, if somewhat utopian. 'I would love to see the development of an economy and culture that had an option other than to sign on to the terms of neo-liberalism, that demand an investment climate, where the labour force is dispensable and comes at the right price. Ideally, I would like to see Scotland as a model nation in that regard and one that preserves a degree of social partnership and cohesion. Certainly the Scottish tradition is there, and the ingenuity of the Scots is hardly in short supply.'

What Scotland provided for him he sees as a very mixed heritage and legacy. 'I have a sense of humour which is very Scottish. That is a scourge as well as a blessing. In general I am happy about it. I think the sense of commitment as well as community is very strongly ingrained, involving certain codes of egalitarianism and endless reserves of emotional repression which can be destructive. But Scots are not the only ones who bottle up their problems.' That sense of pride in many aspects, but cursed by others, is known to all Scots, and certainly to myself.

Married for the third time, to an American academic from Long Island, with a young daughter, means a permanent return to Scotland is unlikely. With a loft apartment in the fashionable TriBeCa area of Lower Manhattan and a house in upstate New York, would any of us want to return? However, he is keen to contribute to his homeland's progress and has a fascinating idea. Explaining to me that he meets numerous expatriate Scottish intellectuals and academics on his travels, both within America and across the world, he wonders why we do not make more use of their talents. I point out to him that steps are being taken to network in the diaspora for and amongst the business community, but he correctly challenges why that does not equally apply to the intelligentsia. 'After a century and a half of exporting intellectuals, Scotland ought to be able to extract some of the benefits and rewards from those exports and has certainly earned the right to do so. It would take a certain amount of outreach, together with people willing to co-ordinate a network from Scotland itself. We need some sort of Scottish Academy with some international brains trust, with economic, cultural, political and social links. It could be very interesting.'

That, to me, seems a blindingly obvious concept, even if (to my shame) I hadn't previously considered it. Efforts have been made most recently by the Labour MSP Wendy Alexander in the Fraser of Allander lectures to involve expat and other economists in advising Scotland on fiscal options. She deserves enormous credit for that.

But with a Parliament now restored and an executive *in situ*, the ability to co-ordinate nationally, and internationally, now exists and must not be passed up. Other nations have benefited from their diaspora throughout the years, and still do. In some instances it has been kinfolk abroad who have maintained the national identity, whether as a result of military occupation, or economic devastation. Armenia, the Baltic States and Poland are nations that have done so over the years, and to an extent still do. Scotland is right to pursue economic advantage from amongst its expatriate community. It is equally correct, though, to pursue intellectual input. The two are not mutually exclusive, but equally essential. If I could gather this from just one conversation, what could a structured situation over a number of years achieve? Having already contributed that gem, he adds, 'I think you would be surprised at the number of intellectuals-in-exile who might be willing to assist. You get a different quality of conversation every time. Maybe it's because they have never been asked. But it's still cheaper than a consultant.'

I find my conversation with Professor Andrew Ross to have been a privilege. He may be a Scottish American, but he still has Scotland's interest at heart. The creation of an academy, or whatever structure is considered best, is a stroke of genius that we should be eternally grateful for. Departing from our interview he offers me a copy of his book, *The Celebration Chronicles: Life, Liberty, and the Pursuit of Property Values in Disney New Town*. I start reading it on the journey home. It's a fascinating account of how he spent a year as a resident of a town founded on the Disney name, and created as a throwback to the halcyon days of baby boomers youth, or even earlier golden ages. Safe, synthetic and sanitised. Situated in central Florida, he exposes the flaws and falsehoods that underpinned and oversold it. To some extent, it is a condemnation of the Walt Disney empire and all it stands for. No doubt that earlier interviewee Andy Mooney, Chairman of Walt Disney Consumer Products, would disagree.

It's ironic that I should have interviewed two expatriate Scots, in Professor Andrew Ross and Andy Mooney, diametrically opposed on such an issue. But has this not always been the case? Scots fought for the armies of Gustavus Adolphus, and battled against him for Imperial Russia. They served with the French legions, and fought for the Dutch republics. Rebelled with the continental states, and stayed loyal to the Crown. *Plus ça change, plus c'est la même chose.*

Interviewed by Kenny MacAskill
July 2005

Barry Potter

DIRECTOR OF BUDGET AND
PLANNING AT THE IMF,
WASHINGTON DC

Walking in the Corridors of Power

BARRY POTTER IS ONE OF THREE SCOTS featured in this book who all work within five hundred yards of each other and just a stone's throw from the White House in Washington DC. Together with Alison Duncan and Gerry Rice, he forms part of a small but highly influential group of expatriate Scots in Washington. Perhaps a quirk of fate, or alternatively a sign of Scottish influence, that three highly successful Scots should live in such close proximity to each other in the most political city in the world. Each of them also have one of their children attending a university back in Scotland, certainly putting their money where their pride is.

When Barry Potter was at Wardie Primary School in Edinburgh, a teacher said he was 'quite smart' and should try for one of the capital's fee-paying schools. He recalls, 'I don't think my parents had much money then. The only school available was the Royal High in Edinburgh where the fees were cheap and it was a school where you were selected on the basis of academic record.' It was one of those life-changing decisions that has taken him to his present position as Director of Budget and Planning at the International Monetary Fund in Washington.

An extremely interesting and intelligent man, he is unassuming and I would be unaware that, as one of 20 directors in the IMF, he holds such a prestigious position of global power. I meet him for lunch in a great power-broking restaurant in Washington, where each diner is a person of influence. On walking out, we are asked if we are brothers – only then do I realise how similar we look. Over lunch he tells me about his life, and I am given the impression that there are numerous doors along his corridor of life which could be opened, with a tale lurking behind each one, but many remain shut, and I am left wondering. Lucky for me, as I have to write only a chapter on him – I am conscious that I could write a whole book!

Now 56, Barry's career as an economist has been a succession of key positions and pace-setting work in Scotland, the UK and on an international level. Following work at the Scottish Office, he was Economic Private Secretary to two Tory Prime Ministers, Margaret Thatcher and John Major, and then played a role in assisting IMF member countries to manage their budgets. 'I was the first of my family to go to university,' he says. 'I was also the first not to be in the army by the age of 14, which had happened to my father, his brothers, and his father and his brothers before that.'

He points to one of those coincidences that says a great deal about Scottish education and the tradition of the 'lad o' pairts' who makes his way in the world: 'Recently, there were three of us in senior positions in the IMF – all educated at the Royal High School. There were no other instances of professionals at that level in the organisation all coming from the same school. That tells you something about the Scottish education system.'

Like many young Scots, Barry was initially unsure of what he wanted to study at university. He recalls that Gordon Brown was a member of his history class at Edinburgh University. 'I eventually decided I would go for the economics side and came out with an honours degree. I wasn't quite sure what I wanted to do, except that I wanted to work immediately and relieve the financial burden on my family. I could have gone into the financial and insurance sector in Edinburgh, but thought the newly-advertised job of Economist at the Scottish Office sounded more interesting.'

Barry was conscious of the issue of class in Scottish society. 'My family had become fairly middle-class – my father was by then an engineer with the Health Service and was doing quite well. My mother couldn't wait to get me into my Royal High uniform when we were invited to a wedding, as it was so much better than a state school. Once, my grandmother told us of some friends who bought their council house "so they'll be able to vote Conservative now"!'

He says his career was shaped by an early awareness of the limits to the economics he practised at the Scottish Office. 'It was dominated by regional and social policies and I was determined I wanted to do something more. I surprised myself by applying for and getting a job in the UK Treasury. After a couple of years there I moved on to work on the first devolution exercise and in particular the mechanics of how you assess expenditure needs and taxation capacity, an issue which I have been interested in all my professional life.' Later moved to the Cabinet Office, he found himself working on some of the more controversial projects of the Thatcher government. One was on contingency plans for protecting the financial markets in the case of emergencies, including the outbreak of war. Another was with a Ministerial Group preparing to cope with large scale strikes, in particular the miners. But he needed change and, for the first time, he actively sought a job in the private sector and a return to Edinburgh with the then Coopers & Lybrand.

Because of his background, he found himself back working on regional and social policy, local government finance and other initiatives which he confesses he didn't enjoy. 'I was doing nitty-gritty stuff where I felt to some extent the consultancy was exploiting the public sector. I have to confess that I did have an ethos where I would have preferred working for the greater good rather than just for private gain.' At financial cost to himself, he returned to the Treasury and was immediately involved in the Thatcher government's ill-fated Poll Tax plan. 'It's no secret anymore,' he says. 'The Treasury was trying to show, not on the grounds of local government finance, but on taxation principles, that it just could not be made to work. If we had had the gumption back in the Treasury in the mid to late eighties to research more carefully what had happened to types of poll taxes in other governments in other situations, we might have been more effective in presenting the counter-argument to Mrs Thatcher.' For the last nine months of Mrs Thatcher's premiership, Barry was her

Economic Private Secretary. 'They told me, "we thought you might like the job as Private Secretary to the Prime Minister." It was not the top job – which was actually less top than you might imagine – as its holder then dealt with running the office, intelligence matters and the Queen. The people who were doing the day-to-day work were those on the economics, which was me, and the foreign affairs and parliamentary sides.'

After working for John Major at Number Ten, Barry admits that he 'felt physically exhausted' by the time he left. 'The job was enormously demanding and, again, I felt that I had taken time out from my children's and my wife's lives. By the time you have left that job, you have also made enemies right across Whitehall; it is inevitable. So it was fortunate that I was loaned to the IMF in 1992, initially as a consultant. I then decided to make it permanent and in 1996 I became Division Chief – once again dealing with budgeting for public expenditure, helping countries to manage budgets, set them up, to control them. Apart from the importance of a shift for the family, there was a growing awareness of a terrible inwardness about the British Civil Service. It might be summed up in the phrase "if it isn't invented here, then it doesn't exist". At the IMF, I could get the broadest possible understanding of how these things are done in different parts of the world.'

He finds the American work ethic preferable to that in Scotland. 'I very much love the "can do" ethos and the positive outlook in the United States. The political setup is very different and I may not always agree with what the administration of the day is doing. But I still find the American society very attractive. I may retire early from the IMF to go back to Scotland. But I would never take a full-time position anywhere else than here.'

Barry believes there has been a lack of confidence when he reflects on Scotland. 'I can still remember the pain of my first couple of years in the Treasury. I was this relatively young guy with a strange accent; that was still in the days when they asked what Oxbridge college you had gone to, not university; and a time when the traditional civil servants could respond to a complex point one made on exchange rates, with: "And I thought Hegel was difficult."

I found the atmosphere quite forbidding. There were some Scots around but their accents had been cleaned up and the Scottishness buried. Still, above all the Treasury taught me how to think: there is a disciplined approach there which I have not seen matched, even here, on how to analyse a particular issue.'

He believes that Scottish society still remains 'a little insular' and 'surprisingly stratified'. He considered devolution important, but acknowledges that ideas need to flow more. 'I supported it for 20 odd years – I thought it had to enliven the political process. Irrespective of your political viewpoint, one of the troubles was that the Scots had one party which dominated. So there wasn't much exchange of ideas, rather, too much of a continuity from one generation to another, and a failure to absorb new ideas and see where you might take things.'

Like many others in this book, Barry is impressed by the Irish example. 'What shocked me when I first came to the US is how well organised the Irish lobbying group is and how amateurish the Scots are. The Irish have been successful in bringing in ideas; but whilst I would say the Scots are better educated, they don't bring ideas in and they should. It has become very clear that, unless your private sector is healthy, the country is going nowhere. You cannot expect the public sector to do it on its own. There are not the leaders there and never can be. The national image of tartan, golf, haggis, whisky isn't enough. The one thing I would emphasise is the education in Scotland and the quality of it. A group of us are working on making more out of Tartan Day, trying to boost the image of Scotland.'

He believes that while the country has enormous intellectual and financial assets, we simply don't make enough of them. 'The financial services industry in Scotland is very highly respected worldwide. It could do so much more to attract money from other places but you have to have drive behind it. I remember doing a straw poll of 16 of my class from university who qualified the year I did and found that only one was still in Scotland. That is a problem – and "insufficient opportunities" sums it up.'

Interviewed by Henry McLeish
July 2005

Alison Duncan

CORPORATE LAWYER,
WASHINGTON DC

From Fish-packing to a Federal Courtroom

AT THE AGE OF 16, Alison Duncan was suspended by the nuns at her Scottish Catholic school for marching in a pro-abortion rally and announcing at confession that she had nothing to confess. That teenage streak of rebellious determination and independent thinking has taken her from Dundee to her present high-flying post as equity partner in one of Washington's most prestigious law firms – the 150 year old Porter, Wright, Morris and Arthur.

Alison became known to me as a stalwart in Tartan Day organisations in Washington DC. An exemplary internationalist, passionate and enormously proud of Scotland, she has been flying the flag for Scotland in America as a labour of love, for no reward. Lively, attractive, tough and determined, she is the epitome of the strong Dundee woman – immortalised in song as the backbone of the community.

Born in Alyth, Perthshire, Alison is one of a family of three boys and three girls. Like many Scots, she pays tribute to the example set by her parents – Ian, who rose from police constable to Chief Superintendent, and primary school teacher Esther: 'A brilliant woman, first in her family to go to Lawside Academy, which was unheard of, and during the war, the first to go as far as Glasgow. In any other country in another life she would be Prime Minister.' But, she adds wryly, 'Six children born in nine years to a very Highland Jacobite Catholic mother. I lapsed at the age of nine!' Her fondest childhood memories are of growing up in what was still-rural Downfield in Dundee. 'My grandfather was the village poacher and my father was a good hunter. When we stayed in my grandad's tiny but-and-ben we fished in the River Ericht, which was rich in salmon, and he taught us how to guddle fish. My grandparents were not formally educated, but they were incredibly smart. My grandfather could have written books on birds, and his idea of going for a walk was pointing out every bird and every nest and would educate us along the way. My grandmother would tell us about local history and was part of a very old tradition of storytelling.'

Despite her brush with authority at school, Alison remembers training which has stood her in good stead. 'What was great about the nuns and the teachers was that they were always pointing out ways you could argue or debate in certain situations. That inspired you to talk your way out of difficulty. I look back on that fondly.'

While she was sent on holiday to Rome with 'a very Catholic family', her parents decided she was not ready for university and were tempted to cancel her applications but her sister arranged for Alison to follow her to Aberdeen. She recalls: 'I still have nightmares about the cold, of sliding down the streets in Aberdeen and being unable to stop and going right into traffic. I would wake up crying with the cold. We were poor students then and didn't have toilets inside. I was against fur until I went to Aberdeen!'

Her 'biggest leap forward' was to apply for a fellowship to study abroad and, as the only woman in the finals, overhearing the judges. 'They thought I would sell well in America because I was articulate and funny. I heard them saying, "She is an educated Scot." I don't think they meant it as an insult but I have to say I smarted at being referred to as "an educated Scot", because in my view there was nothing else but!

'They told me I could go anywhere in the world. Because we were poor I thought "I will go as far as I can in the world", and decided on America. I turned down Harvard, Smith and Stanford, decided to go big and picked the University of Maryland in DC. By doing a Masters degree in American Studies and American History,

I became fascinated by the American Revolution, the role of the royalists and patriots and especially the role of the Scots.'

After returning to Scotland and teaching at the American School of Edinburgh, she applied to the Foreign Office and was warned by her mother that being Scottish, female, Catholic and a nationalist that her days would be numbered. While awaiting word from the Foreign Office, she met her husband-to-be – from whom she is now divorced – who was an American lawyer, staying in London for negotiations. She compares her position in America favourably to that in Scotland. 'Everything that worked against me in Scotland worked for me in America,' she says. 'I always thought everything in life was location – real estate, love, career – and I knew that having a Scottish accent was a minus in Scotland and the UK but a huge plus in America. I was able to access positions and people and realised doors were opening. I came out whilst engaged and then a position opened up with the British Embassy. My boss Fred Pearson was Welsh and said he was surrounded by Oxbridge types. He was looking for a lawyer and an accountant and I told him I was neither but he said "No, you are a worker." The most important thing on my CV was the fact I had been a fish-packer in Aberdeen. He knew I had never had any money, I had been waitressing and doing other jobs. Fish-packing was money; it was dirty, smelly and it was good money. Sometimes it was a conversation starter. Fred said I wasn't what he expected, but anyone who packs fish is a worker and I was smart. He basically made me as his right hand and we negotiated contracts for the British Embassy, buying things like Chinook helicopters and electronic equipment. I learned so much about the American legal system and government contracts that he suggested that I go to American law school, because he didn't think I would go any further in the British Embassy. To my absolute astonishment, I passed the law exams and, although I was pregnant, specialised in government contracts, an important area of expertise in Washington DC.'

With the Thatcher government in power, she decided to stay in the US. 'I thought then it would be a five-year Tory administration. I thought then, and think now, that I was being more effective being a Scot in Washington that I would have been back home. I was selling

Scotland every single day, wherever I was – even travelling on the metro, and socially, when people would ask me about Scotland and confused it with Ireland. Americans have come a long way in the past 25 years – at one point, many of them thought we were part of Iceland!' Alison regularly visits her homeland, but is somewhat disturbed that friends and family tell her not to make her return permanent. 'Of all my close friends from Aberdeen, one is in London, one in Johannesburg, one in Germany. None of them are in Scotland,' she points out. 'Americans today think the real Scots left 200 years ago. Because I live here, I am American and my children are American – but we count as real Scots, just like the Scots at home. I think nationality is a state of mind; it is not about geography. As far as I am concerned my law partner – although an African American – is a native Scot because through me, I have made him suffer, absorb and like Scottish things. If you love Scotland, you are Scottish.' She admits: 'I would go back permanently. I don't see why one of the international companies I work with should not think about locating north of the border. If they have an office in Brussels, why can't they have an office in Edinburgh or Perth – and relocate me to Scotland?'

Alison is passionate about her native country, and has no doubts as to what Scotland gave her. 'A morbid fear of midgies but love for the land, an appreciation for eccentricity, adventure and wit (thanks to Aberdonian winters, Glaswegian pubs, and Dundonian friends and family); an endless thirst for its history (fuelled by Ted Cowan, TC Smout and Tom Devine); its brilliant contemporary actors and writers, and an odd sense of dislocation every time I return. My license plate says "PICT" (which in Washington DC gets thumbs up from fellow-Celts and the occasional thump on the bumper during the World Cup or Six Nations games). I also have a tendency to develop a twitch when someone says I am "Irish", so I'm really proud of where I am from and for all the gifts that the country gave me. That's not a recent development, or one brought on by living the past 20-plus years in DC.' As testimony to this, her first daughter, Alyth, was named after Alison's place of birth. She also has a second daughter, Isla, and a son, Ian.

Although she acknowledges the lack of Scottish history taught to her, she values what she would learn outside class time. 'I used to do walking tours in Edinburgh for tour groups (even if my mother would sniff that it was not the "real capital" like Perth) and was always impressed by how many tourists seemed to know more about Scotland than most Scots. Although Scottish history was not taught in schools or universities when I was growing up, my parents were determined to educate me – my mother for history and my father in wildlife, hiking and travel around the Highlands and Islands.'

In the typical Scottish tradition of being proud of a harsh upbringing, she remarks, 'Thanks to my upbringing, I like to think I'm one of the few attorneys in DC that can guddle and gut fish (I am not making this up), pick berries at the speed of light, happily eat wild mushrooms and assorted forest shrubbery (my granny was really into homeopathic remedies, and we still don't talk about the foxglove incident). I can survive quite happily when we lose power during the occasional tornado or hurricane because Scotland taught me how to rely upon myself and think fast. Above all – it may sound horribly clichéd – it gave me a deep and abiding love for Scotland, its potential and its people. I'm one of "Thatcher's refugees" as we all left in the late seventies and early eighties for jobs. I'd love that to change for the present generation so we can keep that intellectual capital working for Scotland.'

On the other hand, like many other interviewees in this book, Alison considers Scotland to be negative in its outlook and confidence. 'It's hard to talk about what Scotland did not give me. The expatriate lament is that everyone cares about Scotland except for the Scots. One of my high school teachers at Lawside told me that that the most important asset I had (which was not, to my disappointment, my long red hair, green eyes, winsomely crooked teeth and devastating wit) was my determination to climb to the mountain-top. He told me that it didn't matter if I didn't make it. What was most important was that in trying so hard, I would get further than anyone expected. As I was hardly the smartest person in the class, I never forgot what he said. I just wish he had educated a lot more folk. When I go back home, I call it "negative rain", as that's all I seem to hear or see or feel from everyone there, and it saddens me. The contrast to other nationalities could not be more stark. With that teacher an exception, my background and education did not give me a sense of optimism for a future in Scotland.'

Alison finds the Scottish attitude to America disappointing. She has three points to make about lessons Scotland should learn. 'My American friends or family (including my American daughters who have worked or studied there) have the same three questions. And these questions really go out to the public, as it happens in pubs, in cafés, in street corners, newsagents, everywhere. First, why are the Scots so rude to visiting Americans who are studying or visiting there? Don't the Scots want the money, the business, the international setting? It can't surely be political; after all, 55 million people voted against Bush and Americans certainly don't hold every Scot responsible for Blair's re-election. The personal nature of the grievance is troubling and it seems so churlish to make visitors feel unwelcome. Second, many Scots still distance themselves from the Highland games or Tartan Day celebrations in the States. Yet American descendants have carried the cultural and familial traditions forward into the New World and kept them alive. No one remotely thinks that St Patrick's Day in Chicago is quite what Dublin had in mind, but my heavens, look at the industry, tourism and business links they make as a result of these American celebrations. Third, when expatriates like myself come home, we are always treated as foreigners and certainly not as Scots. It's a collective "shunning" that affects us all when we return.'

She believes full-heartedly that Scots should adopt a broader view of nationality, as other European and Nordic nations have. 'Isn't it good for Scotland to have "transnationals" like myself – or anyone who is interested in Scotland – promoting Scotland? Of all nations, it seems ironic in the extreme that the Scots have such a parochial attitude to nationality. Now – thanks to the Parliament, the Congressional Resolutions enacting Tartan Day, formal Congressional visits to Scotland in 2005 (the first ever!), Scotland at the Smithsonian Institute, Craig Ferguson on CBS nightly – these are contemporary developments showcasing modern Scotland. They have built upon those cultural connections and we are beginning to become visible again.'

She is optimistic about Scotland's future in the international arena. 'One of the things I really look forward to seeing is Scotland stepping up its game on the international scene, joining the world, and it's already happening. Up until a few years ago, you could spend thirty minutes on Capitol Hill or in watering holes in Foggy Bottom talking about Scotland and the response would be, "So, what part of Ireland *are* you from?" with a vague reference to some Brigadoon backwater. From the guide to European law firms that sits on my desk (listing London firms for all of the UK and no mention of Scottish law firms) to American almanacs and maps that don't even mention us, we have a way to go.'

Despite this, Alison is convinced that Scotland has made her an optimist. 'One lesson I have learned from a classroom in Dundee to a federal courtroom in DC, is that if you don't speak up and use your voice, you really don't exist.' The same goes for Scotland: we have to speak up with pride, if we are to be heard at any level in today's global world.

Interviewed by Henry McLeish
July 2005

Gerry Rice

DIRECTOR OF COMMUNICATIONS
AT THE WORLD BANK,
WASHINGTON DC

A Glasgow Boy with the World at his Feet

GERRY RICE MIGHT HAVE BECOME a professional football player or pop musician. Instead, one of the most unconventional career paths in public life – from one of Glasgow's grittier neighbourhoods, via a PhD and a Kennedy Scholarship at Harvard, coaching American high school kids in soccer and playing guitar in clubs – has taken him to his present high-status job as Communications Director at the World Bank in Washington DC. Born in 1955, Gerry is another Glasgow East End boy made good. The son of a second-generation Irish family, his father was a lorry driver for the local Tennents brewery before becoming a school janitor.

I meet him in Washington DC, not long after the G8 summit in Gleneagles. He has an extremely informed perspective on the future of Scotland. 'I read a slogan at the recent G8 summit that said Scotland is "the world's best small country". I like that.' He has travelled widely, and is an extremely cultured man, accomplished in so many different areas, yet is completely unassuming and down to earth.

Gerry spent his childhood and teenage years in the Calton district which was then notorious: 'It was renowned as being one of the roughest parts of Glasgow. I remember the newspapers saying it was one of the most deprived areas of Europe. It had a lot of gangs, the infamous one being the Calton Tongs which featured in some films later on.'

Despite the background, he looks back very positively on his childhood. 'My parents did a great job in bringing up my two sisters and myself. I never felt deprived of anything, quite the contrary as a matter of fact. Despite growing up in poor circumstances in a tough area – although I never thought of it that way at the time – I was still able to get a world-class education.' As with many boys in that area then and since, football – and a certain club – dominated his life. Gerry's father ran a youth club at the school where he was janitor and managed several teams. He grins, 'Football was my life and I stayed within a stone's throw of Celtic Park. You don't need to ask who I supported! I spent many happy hours kicking a ball around in what we used to call "brokies" – vacant lots where houses and factories had been torn down – playing five-a-sides on broken glass. I moved up to playing and captaining school teams and I was 12 when Celtic won the European Cup. The whole Lisbon Lions episode was very special; my dad had a Morris Mini Minor and we drove for three days to the game in Portugal. It was tremendous to be there when they won the Cup. It put Glasgow and Scotland on the world stage – at least in football terms – and that had an influence on me.'

Despite his passion for football and the fact that the Catholic Church was also a 'huge part' of his young life, Gerry did not experience the bigotry that blighted the city. 'I think that's a tribute to my parents who were very honest, fair, working class, Labour people. They took people as they found them and weren't interested in their religion or politics.'

He admits his father would have wanted him to be a professional footballer and, at the age of 16, he was offered a youth apprenticeship at Coventry City which he declined because he was homesick. Instead, he opted for a short period of part-time football with Greenock Morton, a highlight being a game against Rangers reserves at Ibrox. He admits, 'I didn't stick it very long. Looking back now, I didn't have the passion that you need to go the whole way, and, anyway, by then university was encroaching, which was an intellectual awakening for me.'

His first class honours degree from Glasgow University led to a PhD in modern American history and a study of the US Peace Corps – subsequently published as what would become known as the definitive book on the Peace Corps, *The Bold Experiment*. Gerry points out that the Peace Corps was an idea that, in some ways, anticipated today's world events. 'It was John F Kennedy's idea to send young Americans to the third world with the aim of America learning more about the developing countries and they, in turn, would learn more about America. He predicted the next big wave of history would be shaped by these countries and, seeing what is happening today with China and India, for example, he wasn't far wrong.' Slipping into the Glasgow vernacular, Gerry says trying to work on the US Peace Corps from Glasgow University was 'murder polis' and in 1977, aged 22, he applied for one of 10 Kennedy Scholarships to the prestigious Harvard University. 'It was another awakening, being exposed to some of the best minds in the world. It was amazing and Massachusetts was a revelation. I also found that being a Kennedy scholar opened up all sorts of doors for me. I was able to get interviews with all sorts of people like Sargent Shriver and Ted Kennedy himself.'

After a year at Harvard, and a summer which he spent travelling around 40 states in America, he returned to Glasgow to complete his dissertation and to lecture part-time. Still thinking that he would be an academic, he tells me of the day this changed. 'One day, completely out of the blue, I got a telegram from the Peace Corps in Washington saying they had read my dissertation and they would like me to come over and work with them for a while. It was their twentieth anniversary at that point and they asked me to come and write their history because "you know more about the Peace Corps than anyone else alive" – typical American style!'

A three month contract with the Peace Corps was extended to nine months and, during that period, Gerry became absorbed by development and developing countries, and the problem of global poverty. He applied for a job with the World Bank in Washington – the biggest development organisation in the world, with a mission to fight poverty with experts from all over the world. In between times, he made ends meet by coaching soccer in high schools in the Washington area, playing guitar in various clubs, and writing occasional articles. In late 1981, the World Bank offered him a position. 'My first job was as a writer for the Board of the Bank. The Bank has a board of executive directors representing the 184 countries which own the institution. I was hired as a writer to help them with their statements and minutes of meetings – for a young kid at the time who didn't know very much about development it was fantastic. I learned a tremendous amount.'

He then joined the Bank's Africa Region, working on Sub Saharan Africa for six years. 'I continued to prove myself as a writer and communicator and, at the end of that period, the President of the Bank, Lew Preston (who had previously headed up JP Morgan, the biggest commercial bank in the world) asked me to be his speechwriter.' Since then, he has worked directly for three World Bank presidents. 'In my current position as Director of Communications I handle all the bank's internal and external communications across the world and I am immersed in all the development issues facing the Bank. I feel strongly that global poverty is the biggest issue facing the world today and it is a privilege to come to work every day to make a contribution, however modest, to that cause.'

Gerry's wife Eilish is also from Glasgow and they have four children: two boys, Kieran and Daniel, still at school in Washington; Maura at St Andrews University in Scotland; and Johnathan, an up-and-coming singer-songwriter who has inherited the family talent for music, and appears as Roy Orbison in the new Johnny Cash biopic, *Walk the Line*. Five years ago, Gerry returned to his homeland for a year on secondment from the World Bank at the invitation of Scotland's first First Minister, Donald Dewar. 'Donald was over visiting the White House and his press secretary, David Whitton, who is an old buddy of mine from Saturday morning football on Glasgow Green, organised lunch together,' Gerry reveals. 'Part way through the lunch, Donald said, "You should come back and help us with devolution". I am passionate about Scotland and Scotland's potential, so we did go back for a year – the whole family.' He was seconded to Scottish Enterprise, working with Donald Dewar, myself and others on Scotland's international and global role. This was when I first met Gerry, and we have remained good friends since. He was also Visiting Professor at Glasgow University's Business School and during that year he wrote a small book about Scotland's opportunity in the new global economy.

Without any trace of self-satisfaction, Gerry says, 'It's a long way from Calton in the east end of Glasgow, of that there is no doubt. A big facet of my education at home was what I would now describe as social justice. My father had a strong sense of fairness, typical of the old Labour party, and those values were ingrained in me. I did serve as a community councillor in the Calton area and, although I was never really politically awakened, a strong sense of social justice was there. Looking back, I can see how those strengths have come together, from the east end of Glasgow to the world stage.' He admits that when he was younger he would find it hard to believe he was in a new country or at a major conference, but that awe has now gone. 'Now it is more about the issue, what I can contribute and how I can help move the issues forward. One of the best things about a Scottish upbringing is you keep your feet on the ground and if at any point you are in danger of losing perspective, a visit back home brings you back down to earth.'

Like many of the interviewees in this book, Gerry believes that the most important thing Scotland gave him was a world class education, even though he was working class, which he is extremely grateful for. 'That is the dream to which people all over the world aspire. I have seen poor kids over many years in Africa and other countries and all they want is a decent education. All they want is a chance. As far as I am concerned, Scotland achieved that in the sixties.'

He also acknowledges the importance of values in Scottish life. 'Looking out for other people, the fairness in how you deal with people and how people deal with you; people being straightforward, being direct, not aspiring to having airs and graces or being above other people. A sense of community. That's a really good grounding. Core Scottish values that have served me very well.'

Although Gerry has an overall extremely positive view of Scotland, he is aware of the lack of drive for ambition and confidence in the country. 'Ambition in Scotland can carry negative connotations. You breathe that in with a lot of other things. In my own case, my career growth was more subconscious, the next thing to do. Growing up in a working class family, you would never be told, "you are talented, son". That conversation never took place. So in terms of what I would like to see Scotland give people today, I think it would be more of a sense of ambition and more of a self-confidence that Scots and Scotland could achieve more, can do great things. History bears that out of course. Not in a high falutin' way of pumping ourselves up – but to push and channel our great energies.'

He believes Scots are too cautious and should take more risks. 'In Scotland, if you take a risk and you fail, there is a stigma attached. In the US, by contrast, it is hard to get a loan here unless you fail in business: they actually reckon that, unless you are someone prepared to try and fail, you are not a good risk. It's in the genes in the US – they are big risk-takers. Scotland can learn from that.'

Quiet and thoughtful, he doesn't waste words when I question him on his views on Scotland. 'I sometimes find there is a tendency to think too small. We say "this is ok", "this will do", and that is because you are in a small country that is not in the centre of Europe or the world, geographically. I think there is this tendency to think smaller than we really should.' Again, he compares this to the American mindset. 'They will immediately think "Why do two when we can do two hundred?", whereas Scots would be content just doing the two. Scotland also tends to be a wee bit inward-looking, the word "parochial" comes to mind. We tend to just look at what is happening in Scotland, maybe England – but not the rest of the world.'

However, he does see change ahead, and is convinced of the country's untapped potential. 'Scotland is connecting more with the world and is playing a larger role in the global economy. Scotland has a lot to learn from the world but it also has a lot to give to the world, too. I would still say we are not great at learning lessons from other countries, other experiences. There is an attitude of "Wha's like us?", "These things are not relevant to us".'

He is eager to do more for his country. 'I think there is a lot to learn from Ireland, for example, its dynamic economy and how Ireland has branded itself in the world. There is also a lot that we could learn from the Nordic countries. Ironically, for a country that really values education and values knowledge, we are not good at looking above the parapet and learning from what we see. Yet there is nothing wrong with taking someone else's good idea; modify or customise it by all means, but use those ideas.'

He admits that he is a fan of America and its democratic ideal. 'The notion that this country was originally founded by people who were discriminated against, people who were politically or religiously oppressed. I like the fact your accent doesn't matter – whereas in the UK it still does and they can pick out where you are from. In the US, you put your talent and ideas on the table and work hard and you are accepted for that.' He adds that 'this is a country that by and large confronts problems and doesn't sweep them under the carpet. By contrast, sectarianism in Scotland was a skeleton kept in the cupboard for a very long time. Nobody talked about it because Scotland sometimes doesn't address issues the way it should – a "don't rock the boat" attitude. Poverty is another issue that I believe is not being dealt with head-on in Scotland.'

Coming from humble origins, Gerry Rice has certainly ended up at the top of his game. Amazingly optimistic about Scotland, he would 'return to stay in a minute' if given the right opportunity. 'My mother is still in Glasgow, so are my sisters and most of my relatives. I still have friends that I keep in touch with – guys that I used to play football with and my best friend I met on the first day of primary school in the Calton. I have been back half a dozen times this year alone. Scotland will always be my home.'

Interviewed by Henry McLeish
July 2005

Dario Franchitti

INDY RACING DRIVER, NASHVILLE

A Big Star in the Big Country

AMERICA IS THE BIG COUNTRY and Dario Franchitti is big in America. I am to discover just how big both are when interviewing him in Nashville, Tennessee, where he now resides, and where a motor race in which he is competing is taking place. A Bangour bairn like most from West Lothian – before its replacement by St John's – he has hit the big time in motor sports across the Atlantic, driving Indy cars with the Andretti Green racing team.

Indy cars are to America what Formula One is to Europe. The cars are of a similar weight and, to the untrained eye, look much the same. The difference lies in the tracks: Indy racing uses more purpose-built oval circuits with cambers, while FI is laid out on a variety of more diverse and flatter courses. The nature of the tracks and the different regulations make Indy racing different, but just as fast as the European variety.

I arranged to meet Dario a few days before the race at the Nashville circuit. It was a long time since I had been taken as a boy to Ingliston racetrack, so I went with much curiosity and little knowledge (which would show). My first mistake was to forget that America is the big country and the land where the automobile is king. I naively anticipated a short taxi ride to the racetrack. How wrong I was. It might be the Nashville track but it was located in deepest Tennessee. The driver came with a route map downloaded from the Internet and the journey took us through scenic country-side reminiscent of the *Dukes of Hazzard* film and television shows. Even then, the driver was required to stop and get instructions in a rural store from a man who looked like he should have been an extra in one of the shows. The taxi journey to the racetrack ultimately cost more than my flight from Nashville to Washington DC. The driver did not even return to the city, merely waited in the shade for me to conclude the interview.

I was collected by Dario's manager, Mickey Ryan. An affable American who had just jetted in from a sports awards dinner in Los Angeles, he picked me up in his hired car and headed for the track, saying that he had to collect Dario on route. My bemusement as to where that could be as we drove to an open field was answered as Mickey explained that Dario didn't like traffic jams and came in his own private helicopter. Sure enough, down he came, piloting his own machine and landing as if parking his car.

He emerged looking tanned and fit, wearing jeans and a T–shirt, and adorned with sunglasses pushed high up on his head. In his early thirties, he's in the prime of his life, as well as at the top of his sport. Notwithstanding his mode of arrival, I could have been meeting him off the train from Bathgate at Waverley station. The accent was still the same and he was open and friendly from the outset. Mickey took us all into the centre of the track where not only the vehicles and the pit stops were located, but also the driver's mobile homes. That term is somewhat of a misnomer (or certainly vastly different from what it implies here in Scotland). The mobile home would struggle to fit on a Scottish road, never mind being fitted out with everything a superstar could possibly want, down to the plasma screen behind the driving area, where we sat across from each other to chat.

Later, we take a stroll to the pits and I am shown the car he drives. It is brought home to me just how fit he has to be and how talented he must be to be so successful. The car is so fast that if you got it onto the ceiling, it could be driven upside down without falling to earth. The G forces can make breathing impossible when corner-ing and on other manoeuvres. The car looks smaller but more pow-erful when seen close up. The noise from vehicles driving around the track is much louder than it sounds on television. Fitness is vital as well as supremely quick reactions and undoubted courage. The mental and physical effort required to race at a very high speed for two to three hours must be incredibly sapping.

He may be a sporting superstar, comfortable in the air as well as on the ground, but there was not even a hint of any affections or arrogance that is sometimes perceived as striking those with that status. Dario Franchitti remains the Bangour bairn done good. He was brought up in West Lothian, where his parents still stay and where many friends continue to reside. It's obviously a close family, with his parents over with him for the forthcoming race. They initially lived in Bathgate but moved to Whitburn when he was eight years old. He stayed there until he left to pursue his racing career. His father was in the family ice cream business, but is now retired. His mother, originally from Inverness, worked with the Tourist Board but has now embarked upon a Law degree at Edinburgh University. His brother, Marino, is also pursuing a racing career in the USA, but his sister, Carla, remains in Scotland.

His helmet, displaying both the Scottish saltire and the Italian tricolour, demonstrates how proud he is of his Scottish identity and Italian ancestry. It was his great-great-grandparents who made their way from Italy, but three grandparents were of Italian origin and he is proud to be an Italian Scot. He attended Stewart's Melville in Edinburgh, but cars and racing were always to the fore. He tells me, 'both my grandfathers were interested in cars. My dad was the same, and he raced too, but just as a hobby. He raced go-karts and cars at Ingliston. I had a go-kart when I was three, with a little Honda engine on the back.'

From that initial start the racing took off. 'I started racing and went to the West of Scotland Kart Club in Larkhall and another couple of circuits up in the north of Scotland. That was the foundation. Then I started competing in England and Europe for more competition. I started racing cars at 17. David Coulthard and Allan McNish, two other Scottish boys, had gone to race with David Leslie and his dad, David senior, who were running a very successful racing team. The Leslies put together a deal for me to race before the season started. I did that for a year for them. Mum and Dad re-mortgaged the house to allow me to do it.'

Dario justified their faith when he won the championship that year. Then another expatriate Scot, former FI champion Jackie Stewart, intervened by assisting in funding and sponsorship. It is a debt that he has not forgotten, praising Stewart, and replicating him by sponsoring another up-and-coming Scottish driver. He drove for Mercedes in Germany and they brought him over to the USA in 1997, where he had an impressive career on the CART racing circuit, vying with the likes of Juan Pablo Montoya, now an FI star. In a short career he managed to post 10 wins, and in the 1999 season he tied on points with Montoya, only losing out when the winner was determined by back-calculating the season's wins, and Montoya just edged it. From there he moved on to the Indy Racing League in 2003 but his first season was curtailed by a back injury. In 2004 he earned his first victories, winning at Pikes Peak and Milwaukee, having five top five finishes and ending the season ranked sixth. Not bad going for a first full season.

His memories of growing up in Scotland are fond and relate in the main to cars and racing. He remembers the long drive up the old A9 to his mother's family in Inverness, and attending races as a youngster when first his father and then he himself were participating. He credits his mixed Italian and Scots heritage with providing different things: one providing passion, and the other a very analytical side. Whilst throughout his career he has been assisted by his parents, and latterly by Jackie Stewart, he feels Scotland lacked facilities, and worries about future stars, even though he tries to help them himself.

'There was Ingliston years ago but that has gone and now there is only Knockhill, who do a great job. For someone who wants to do what I do, you have to progress. Given Scotland's size and population, I wasn't able to do that there. That meant I had to go to England and further abroad to race at a higher level. It wasn't so much choice as circumstance. I was lucky in the fact that we got a lot of support from Scottish companies, whether it be Marshall's at Newbridge or all those types of companies. Unfortunately, I don't think a lot of the other Scottish drivers now get that support, certainly not from Scotland.' It's a problem he sees that's not restricted to his own field but also afflicts other sports. It's something he would like to see changed. 'More could be done. Equipment is expensive. Safety gear is expensive. In racing even from the first level of cars you spend tens of thousands of pounds a year. If there was a system where successful people could pay back the money that was invested in the first place, that could work. I sponsor a young driver because I believe in him and I think it is important to give something back. I got help myself, so I find it important to help others.'

Dario Franchitti remains firmly rooted in Scotland, even if now resident in the United States. He's married to the American actress Ashley Judd, famous in her own right, and that, together with his racing career, means a great deal of time has to be spent across the Atlantic. However, both he and Ashley come over often, and indeed own a house in Scotland. He remains in touch with friends from school and home, and mingles with other expat Scots, whether watching Celtic or Scotland games in the States. Success has not changed him, and neither has it changed his views of Scotland. 'I am known here as a Scot. I am proud of that. You are always welcomed wherever you go.'

The race takes place the Saturday after I leave and whilst I miss the action on television, it's widely reported and I read all about it in the *Washington Post*. With the lead having gone back and forth, with seven laps to go Dario dipped inside to go in front and held on for his third victory. With the 2005 Indy car race season only just over halfway he is in fourth place overall, only a handful of points behind the second and third placed drivers – with one win and six top five finishes out of 11 races, and winnings that amount to only a fistful of dollars short of a million.

The tragedy from a Scottish perspective is that we neither hear nor know enough of his success. Whilst live on television in the States and in all the papers, including that august journal the *Washington Post*, coverage in Scotland was muted. Viewing was available on limited satellite channels but denied to those with terrestrial channels and unavailable on prime networks. The column inches in the papers were few, if any at all. Yet this is a Scot competing and winning at the highest level.

Scotland does not have a multitude of sporting stars to choose from and many of our national teams are currently in the doldrums. Yet Scots are keen to celebrate the success of sporting compatriots. This has been done through the years, and not just with successful football sides or grand slam winning rugby teams. No matter what the sport, a successful Scot is taken to the nation's heart and supported. Boxers such as Ken Buchanan and Jim Watt, swimmers like Bobby McGregor or David Wilkie, athletes like Allan Wells and Liz McColgan, darts player Jocky Wilson or even the Olympic gold-winning women's curling team – all have seen the nation tune in, hoping for a Scottish victory.

Sport matters and adds to the collective 'feel good factor' as much in Scotland as it does elsewhere. Greece went wild when their football team won the European Championship. Finns avidly watch races for Kimi Raikkonen and Formula One success. Indy car racing may not be a major spectator sport in Scotland, but neither was curling nor even darts before some Scottish success was scented. The rooting for Andrew Murray in tennis at Wimbledon in 2005 shows the appetite that Scotland has for a sporting winner even in a sport that is not universally watched, never mind played. Scotland was fortunate to be able to watch him as a London-centric media pursued the holy grail of a British winner at Wimbledon. Similar good fortune was had with the Olympic curling success that saw a potential British win and the BBC change it's scheduling. The current diet of television sport is scheduled for an audience south of the border, with coverage of English county cricket or northern English Rugby League, never mind the Oxford Cambridge boat race. They may be fillers for the schedule but should surely not be to the preclusion of the following of a major Scottish sporting star or other such events.

Other small nations come to a halt when one of their citizens is competing, as Scotland has done in the past with the football team or individual stars like Watt, Wells or McColgan. When the national team played Brazil in the World Cup the whole nation watched. Memories are etched in all of the individual successes, whether the explosive run of Wells or the power of Wilkie's strokes. Scots followed Jim Clark, Jackie Stewart and David Coulthard in FI motor racing. Scots cheered their success, commiserated with their defeats, and grieved Clark's death.

Scotland would follow the exploits and endeavours of Dario Franchitti with the same zeal, if only they were able to do so, and could read about him and watch him perform. Our media have to take some responsibility for reporting on him and fostering support for Scottish international success. It's not simply that we want to support our compatriots and are desperate for their sporting success. He is also an excellent role model. Highly successful in a highly competitive environment. A clean-cut young man, he's highly presentable with little vanity and no obvious bad habits. As we seek to tackle delinquency and anti-social behaviour, Scotland should be promoting not ignoring him.

Dario Franchitti deserves Scotland's support and Scotland is entitled to follow his success. The time has come for Scotland to be able to watch his exploits in its own media. He is big in the big country. It's time he was big in his own country.

Interviewed by Kenny MacAskill
July 2005

Dr Jill Savege Scharff

MD AND PSYCHOTHERAPIST,
WASHINGTON DC

A Scots Quine

CONSCIOUS THAT SCOTSWOMEN have gone abroad, as well as Scotsmen, I am anxious to maintain some form of gender balance in the interviews. Although they are obviously out there, locating them is far more difficult than it is for men. When I put the word out to friends and contacts, the information forthcoming is less and the leads are shorter than for males. The list provided by the Global Scots network is very male-dominated – that is not meant as a criticism, but as a matter of fact. Enquiries with female friends who have worked abroad leads me to believe that it is more than simply the gender inequalities and difficulties they faced at home in Scotland. There is a greater tendency it seems, albeit anecdotally, to return for family reasons, parents or children, or to assimilate, through marriage and family circumstances.

An additional difficulty faced in tracking them down is if the name is changed on marriage. It may no longer be evident of a claim to Scottish roots or ethnicity. Dr Jill Scharff, who I meet in Washington DC, is a case in point. Highly qualified, with a glowing CV to her career in medicine, specialising in psychoanalysis, her surname masks her maiden name of Savege, obscuring her deep roots as a quine from the north east of Scotland. But Scottish she is – and proud of it.

We meet in Washington DC when the USA is in the grip of a heat-wave and the natural tendency for the city on the Potomac to endure extreme humidity is exacerbated. Thankfully, the hotel in which we meet is air-conditioned; moreover, it's a morning meeting, allowing us to escape the full extent of the midday heat. Tracking Jill down has seen us pass like ships in the night, constantly missing each other's phone calls; she is evidently a very busy and hard-working woman. Times for potential interviews are limited to early hours over the weekend. Not only is her diary busy but her work rate prodigious. Mention is made of that when we chat.

She welcomes what Scotland provided for her, but recognises that her efforts had to increase in the United States. 'People in Scotland have tremendous motivation but some don't see themselves getting ahead. I remember the structured nine to five jobs with strict coffee breaks and lunch hours. I wouldn't get away with that here. I start at 7:15.' The information leaflet that she gives me about the medical practice which she runs with her husband confirms this, offering appointments between 7:15am and 6:30pm, Monday to Thursday, plus some on Fridays. In addition to work; appointments, lecturing, book writing and a family life provide Jill with a grinding diary. The archetypal 'Scottish work ethic' mentioned by others in this book that allowed them and their compatriots to prosper, has been a factor in her progress. It's an ethos Henry and I have a great deal of empathy with, and one we would do well to remember back in Scotland.

Jill Scharff is slim, feminine, petite and well-mannered, resembling the southern belle. She is good company and very kindly, offering to entertain myself and my family at her own home, but time and distance constrain that. Possessing a happy and natural smile, she puts you at ease and listens in a manner doubtless honed from years of listening to clients. She has a lot to say about her affection for her native land and views on how to improve it. She is a woman who, through her innate talents and hard work, has achieved a great deal, rising to the top of her chosen profession while bringing up three children, and still having time to participate in her love for theatre and the arts. She has faced the glass ceiling and broken through it.

She is proud to tell me that she was born in Arbroath – taking care to remind me that it is the town where the Scottish Declaration of Independence was signed – and raised in Aberdeen from the age of five. Her father was an accountant and company secretary with a textile firm in the city, and her mother was a housewife. Her brother still resides in Aberdeen, working as a fish merchant. She returns at least twice a year. Her father died many years ago but her mother is still alive. Jill details the difficulties that Scots abroad face as life's great circle turns. It's not simply kids growing up without grandparents, but the difficulties faced with ageing parents. 'My mother is still alive and in the same house, aged 90. It is a worry and I call her every day. When your parents get old it is very stressful. I can't do enough. She is very independent and it is extremely difficult to get her to seek help, even from a doctor.' Having experienced the difficulties with my own mother who only lived in a nearby town I can only imagine the stress, and indeed, guilt, that must be felt by the distance, as well as the absence, in a foreign land.

She detects a gender difference in attitude towards Scotland from her children. She has two daughters and a son. 'The girls are fond of Scotland but don't have Celtic connections. My son loves Scotland. I think it's a male/female difference in terms of identification, maybe because of the kilt.' Perhaps: there has certainly been a major change at home in perception and use of our national dress, certainly generationally if not in gender. My generation, who would have been horrified at the very thought of wearing a kilt, has been supplanted by a generation that adores dressing up in full Scottish attire, whether for parties or sport. It's moved from 'kailyard kitsch' to cult fashion within my lifetime. Such is her son's love for the land that he has worked here and served as an intern for George Reid, Presiding Officer of the Scottish Parliament.

Her memories of the granite city are of school. 'I remember walking to school every day in Aberdeen – something my kids haven't done here. In all weathers. I remember coming home with my thick wool coat covered in snow. I loved the independence of being able to walk anywhere. It was great.' She also recalls fun with her friends. 'I remember as a teenager going to dances. You had to go to a year of classes first, then to dances at the age of 14. By college I'd sometimes be going four times a week. It was good exercise and so much fun socially.' Some things don't change. A thick coat is still required in winter and the Beach Ballroom remains a landmark in the town. Other facets of Scottish life have stayed with her, shaping her attitudes as well as her actions. 'I don't like wasting food. I don't like wasting money. My kids tease me about it.' That's surely another inherited Scottish trait and one not just from the north east. I can almost hear my late mother speaking when Jill says this.

Studying medicine at Aberdeen University she graduated in 1967 and remains grateful for a free and Scottish education to this day, as have others interviewed for this book. Too many to be a coincidence, it is something we should be proud of, but must consistently strive to maintain. Local work followed, initially at Woodend Hospital, then at the Ross Clinic. A move to Dingleton, down in the Borders at Melrose was next. Thereafter it was on to the Royal Edinburgh Hospital where she had a joint position with the city, working as community psychiatrist in Craigmillar, an area she recalls fondly, which, then, as now, did not have its troubles to seek, praising the unstinting efforts of Helen Crummy and her colleagues in the Craigmillar Festival Society.

Her work there was to play a significant role in her future direction, as she worked for Jock Sutherland who taught her psychotherapy. She is unstinting in her praise for him and indeed has published a book celebrating his and another Scottish psychoanalyst, Ronald Fairbairn, life and works. Far from being an in-house journal, this book was one she was to be speaking on at the Edinburgh International Book Festival a few months later. 'Jock was a huge influence. After three years with him in Edinburgh I went down to the Tavistock clinic in London where he had been Medical Director. He was a Scot and his career was in London. Then he returned to Scotland in his so-called retirement. He co-founded an institute in Scotland for psychotherapy. Given the Scots' reluctance to admit to psychological problems or ask for help, it was a miracle, and people thought that was excellent. A terrific medical education and psychotherapy training – that was what Scotland gave me, and it was a tremendous gift. But here's what Scotland couldn't give me: there was no advanced psychoanalytic training, which was what I needed. So, like Jock before me, I had to go and live in London, a stay which was interrupted when I met my husband and came to the States for my further training. I have been in Washington ever since.'

Her husband David was in Washington DC as a consequence of the Vietnam War. Care for returning veterans, with all their emotional trauma and psychological needs, was centred there. Psychoanalytical skills were badly needed. Passing the American medical licensing exams, she has travelled far in her chosen field. She and her husband established a private practice dealing with psychoanalysis and psychotherapy and 12 years ago established an organisation for teaching psychoanalytic concepts, many of them imported from Britain. American in location, it is international in orientation. As well as the private practice and institute, she is still a Clinical Professor of Psychiatry at Georgetown University, and lectures there and elsewhere.

Though it was romance that took her to the States, it was with a heavy heart that she left Scotland. However, she was aware that to progress in her field, she would have to work in London or in the States, the opportunities simply being unavailable in her native land, for her and others in this book and beyond. Progress has been made, but not as much as she would like. 'There is a Scottish institute now that certainly provides quality advanced psychotherapy training, but not analysis. That upsets me.' She is grateful for the start it afforded her and the values it engendered – even those acknowledged with a wry smile, such as being wasteful with money or food. She has remained in touch with her homeland, though a permanent return is unimaginable, with family and business commitments. Holidays with American friends are taken here, Scottish history and the arts supported, and I get the impression she is an excellent ambassador for Scotland. Something that she feels is sometimes lacking in those paid to and charged with that duty. 'The British Embassy Players have get-togethers, and put on an annual music hall, but they rarely play Scottish songs – it is very much English.' That's not the first time

I have heard that complaint. But she is eager and willing to assist in whatever way she can.

Unsure of exactly what it meant, I obtained a definition of psychotherapy from the pamphlet she provided me: 'An intensive form of talking therapy designed to get at the source of emotional problems and change them fundamentally. It's not about the temporary relief of symptoms of tension. It's about knowing fully our upsetting impulses and conflicts and mastering them. It about recognizing the way that early relationships affect our current relationships and modifying them. Understanding at this level is what fosters growth and personality change.'

Given the expertise that she has, I decide to probe her a little on her take on Scotland and some of our inherent psychological problems. Others interviewed for the book have mentioned the repressive culture and I am keen to explore it. She traces it back, as would be expected, to our roots, and to some extent sees the solution in education. 'The method of teaching may have to change. It is important that pupils don't hear negative stuff all the time with a focus on mistakes, and must be encouraged to speak out and be confident in themselves. In America they encourage participation. Everyone's comments are valued.' Dr Carol Craig has written about *The Scots Crisis of Confidence* and opened her Centre for Confidence and Well Being. This has been mocked by some, but no one who experiences bright and interested primary school kids transmogrify into reticent and almost sullen high school kids can be unaware of a deeper problem. We have a fine academic record in attainment, but a poor track record in self-confidence, and it needs to be addressed.

At the same time, we touch upon the drink culture and her reply sees them partly entwined. 'Scotland has a culture that alcohol is a big part of. People take a drink to feel better, to feel freer, but alcohol creates depression, and then there is a vicious circle. Health boards need to look at that. A lot of that is educating children too. So do the boards of education. I can't remember getting taught anything about alcohol or social culture, even in high school.' It seems to me that must mean not just education, but encouraging good behaviour. Affordable and accessible sports and the arts, as other expats have commented, would be a start.

Many in Scotland might be quick to mock psychotherapy as 'psychobabble', suited to rich Americans but not working class Scots, and viewed at best as effeminate, and at worst down right unnecessary. But if it worked for Vietnam veterans, might it not be better than dispensing valium or drinking yourself into a stupor, as happens in so many Scottish housing schemes? Rather than bottling it up or hitting the bottle, maybe we should work for a solution. A psychiatric nurse who is a friend of mine, working in Craigmillar, where Jill once practised, told me that employment was needed, not prescription. Getting them up for work, not calming them down, was his solution.

Jill tells me 'psychotherapy, if offered at a crisis, results in fewer emergency visits and fewer hospitalisations.' Presumably at other stages, similar advantages and savings are offered. Scotland has to take a long hard look at itself. There is no one simple solution to drug addiction or alcohol dependency. It is not just a criminal justice problem but a social malaise. Scots need to take responsibility for their own behaviour, recognising that actions have consequences and excuses are not always acceptable, as well as Scotland taking responsibility for all its communities throughout the land, including those marginalised and neglected by social and economic decline. However, given that we educated Dr Jill Scharff, maybe it's time to learn from her in taking that long hard look at ourselves and working towards a solution. I am sure she would be happy to help.

Interviewed by Kenny MacAskill
July 2005

Onnie McIntyre

GUITARIST WITH THE AVERAGE
WHITE BAND, NEW YORK

Scottish Soul

DOES EVERYONE IN SCOTLAND have their own Average White Band tale? A Scottish band that took soul music back to America, their hits such as *Pick up the Pieces*, *Cut the Cake* and *Let's Go Round Again* are immediately recognisable. Before I left for the USA I mentioned them to a friend and he instantly said he had seen them live at the Odeon in Edinburgh. While in Nashville I told Dario Franchitti who I would be meeting in New York, and he said he listened to them in his car. Growing up in the seventies, they were an institution for my generation and having stood the test of time, live on to a younger generation (including my music-loving and rock aficionado teenage son).

When I was told about the possibility of meeting founding member and guitarist Onnie McIntyre, I was intrigued. A Scottish folk band doing well in America is understandable. A Scottish rock band doing likewise is equally admirable. But a Scottish band playing soul music, viewed not just as American but quintessentially 'Black American', is quite outstanding. How did they manage that? I was intrigued, and wanted to find out more.

The band and their music were known to me when I was younger but truth be told I had lost track of their whereabouts. For all I knew, they were out there lost to the great jukebox in the sky. But I was to find out that their music lives on and they are playing regularly to a solid fanbase, both back home in Scotland and across America. Having been given a telephone number in New York, I phoned with some trepidation. Rock stars' reputations go before them: I had no idea what to expect. Fortunately, a distinctive Scottish voice answered, friendly and inviting, happy to meet and chat, but rather rushed at that precise moment, aiming to catch a flight to Cleveland for a gig. Arrangements were made to meet in New York, when I would be in that city.

Arriving in the Big Apple, I was given directions to meet in an Italian café on Roosevelt Island. A hidden gem in New York City, it's situated in the East Hudson River between Manhattan Island and Queens, accessed by road from Queens, and by cable car from Manhattan. That latter journey was a trip well worth taking. A walk up to 60th Street accesses the cable car near the Queensboro Bridge and swings you out across the river, affording a panoramic view of midtown Manhattan, and up and down the river. Leaving the constant motion and near mayhem of Manhattan behind, Roosevelt Island is an oasis of tranquillity.

A heatwave in the city sees Onnie McIntyre enter the café in shorts and T-shirt, and is as relaxed and casual in person as he is dressed. Cheery and chatty – with no pretensions of star status – he is good-natured and pleasant company, quite the man I would be delighted to go for a pint with (as I subsequently do). At the outset he tells me about the island, and it seems a suitable place for an egalitarian Scot to live – in the heart of the big city. Once home to a fever hospital, it was developed in the 1970s to provide affordable housing for New Yorkers, and the concrete developments are a testimony to that era. Its residents are diverse in race and income, varying from UN Diplomat families to what are described as 'Chapter Eight' – social housing. Friendlier and less frenetic than the main island across the water, it is a place that he is very much at home in.

I find out more about how a group of Scottish lads took soul to America. Born in Lennoxtown, Onnie grew up as an only child in nearby Bishopbriggs. His parents both came from the Parkhead area of Glasgow. His father was a Master of Works for several hospitals in the area, having started his apprenticeship as a joiner. The musical input came from his mother – both grandfathers were musicians, one playing jigs and reels, the other being Music Master at Dollar Academy. She grew up playing organ in the church, as well as the piano in the house. It was a happy childhood for him, growing up where music was part of the fabric of his home. 'I'd arrive home from school and the living room would be jumpin' to the likes of Deil Among the Tailors or Kate Dalrymple – great dance music.' With such a variety of influences, a general love of music was developed.

His parents were very supportive. He acquired and toyed with a harmonica, before progressing to guitars. Friends from school were in and out of the house: a bungalow with open ground at the back meant that group music practice was not a problem. His first gig was with a band he formed with a friend from Springburn at The Maryland in Scott Street, Glasgow – a venue which later became synonymous with the Glasgow gang violence prevalent at that time. He recalls seeing many nasty incidents when playing around the Glasgow club scene.

Leaving school and doing his apprenticeship as an electrician, he joined a band run by some Glasgow University students called The In Crowd, an experience which he describes as a 'great leveller'. It was the mid sixties and soul music was at its peak; the Picasso Club in Buchanan Street opened its doors for live music until 4am, and quickly became a haven for musicians. It also afforded influences of what would later become part of the Average White Band.

In the days before low cost travel, when transatlantic journeys were affordable only to the few, American soul artists touring Europe recruited local backing bands. Aware of this, bands were formed from a pool of musicians via the Picasso Club, and moved to London in search of work. Asked to join 'The Scots of St James', Onnie was implored by his father to complete his trade first and 'at least have something to fall back on'. Sound – and typically Scottish – advice, he finished the apprenticeship and joined the band six months later.

Within days of arriving in London their agent called with news of a break. He had travel arrangements for them. They were to fly to

Germany, as backing band to the original Drifters. A UK tour quickly followed, hitting every soul club in London, and every 'Northern soul club south of Hadrian's Wall,' as he put it.

By the seventies, however, the scene had changed. A common interest in soul music brought the members of the Average White Band together. 'We would all turn up at the same gigs. We spoke the same language, so would go for a pint and discuss the music, so it became obvious we should at least form a band and play the music we liked.'

The band members on that first session were Alan Gorrie on vocals and bass, Onnie McIntyre on guitar, Roger Ball on alto sax and piano, Malcolm 'Molly' Duncan on tenor, Mike Rosen on trumpet and Robbie McIntosh on drums. Rosen later quit, and the obvious replacement was another exile, Hamish Stuart. The name of the band came about by chance. A throwaway remark made in jest by a Scottish diplomat friend Rab Wyper about certain things being 'too much for the average white man' struck a chord (so to speak), and the name was chosen.

They wanted to go to the United States, not simply because it was the spiritual home of the music they played, but it was a market they had to crack if they were to succeed. They first toured America in 1973, and moved there permanently in 1974. There are fond memories of the early days, with a bunch of Scotsmen making their way in a black American world. Though the Average White Band played American-influenced soul music, he believes there was a distinctive Scottish element to it and sound from it. 'Having started in a pipe band, Robbie somehow managed to incorporate particular rolls into his technique that were unmistakably Scottish. I spoke to a Pipe Major once about *Pick up the Pieces*: he loved it, and recognised those aspects.' We discuss common strands between Scottish and soul music. 'Most of the soul music we listened to came from the church. Aretha Franklin, Otis Redding etc. So you had rhythm and blues with the passion of gospel mixed in there too.' Almost back to his own roots.

'The first tour we did was with BB King. When we turned up, people were confused. A black artist, a black audience and a white support band with Scottish accents?' On occasion, people assumed them to be the crew and not the band, but as soon as they started to play audiences were won over and they still retain a large chunk of that fanbase across America. One of many highlights was playing the Hollywood Palladium in Los Angeles. Marvin Gaye, the soul star who personified *Heard it Through the Grapevine*, was in the audience and joined them on stage for the encore of their version of the song.

It was an eventful time and much happened along the way. Robbie McIntosh tragically died of a drug overdose in 1974 and was replaced by his friend, Anglo-African drummer, Steve Ferrone. In January 1975 the single *Pick up the Pieces* and the album *AWB* hit the charts. Hit tracks such as *Person to Person* and many others followed. In 1980 the dance single *Lets Go Round Again* enjoyed the longest UK chart run of the year. The band stayed together until 1982. As their biography narrates, 'ten albums, three Grammy nominations, and a large multiracial following were their legacy.' One of the most 'sampled' bands ever (over 250 and counting), their songs have appeared either in their original form or have been adapted by others, including Janet Jackson, P Diddy, Lena Conquest and Phil Collins. Their music has been heard at major sporting events, on television adverts for Revlon and Mitsubishi, and in movies such as *Superman 2*, *Swingers* and *Starsky and Hutch*.

The band's break-up was an opportunity for a lifestyle change. Married and with a young son, his wife (Scottish journalist and author Marion Collins) went back to work and he swapped the touring and music star life for parenthood, writing, playing and producing jingles. That was a culture shock, with humorous tales of heading into the city, guitar in hand, with the rush hour commuters, but also one he clearly relished for the time it allowed him with his son. In 1987 he and Alan Gorrie started talking about reforming and in 1989 they got back on the road. The membership of the band has changed, and the pace of life is less hectic, but he's happy to be back doing what he loves.

Our conversation drifts on to Scotland, and it's evident he's retained a Scottish soul. Though he has leave to stay and work, he has never taken out US citizenship. His son visited annually and he still returns at least once a year. 'There is a huge pull to going back but because I have family here it would be very difficult. It would be nice to be able to live in both places, but that's not possible.' He has retained the accent, and other trappings of Scottish identity. Despite – or perhaps because – of living in one of the most multicultural and diverse cities in the world, his nationality matters to him. 'I like to be recognised as being Scottish. Identity is important, everyone can't be the same. Globalisation is all very well, and if people want to go and live in another country, that's fine, just remember where you're from.'

As with others, he feels that Scotland gave him core values, chief of which was a sense of humility, and he tells a personal anecdote as an example. 'People are not easily impressed in Scotland. There are certain things you don't get away with if you are true to your roots. That connection is still there. My parents had retired to the Borders, where my mother's family was originally from. They had just moved into their new house. We had watched both the single and album go to number one in the US charts. The first day I was back, we celebrated and I took them for a posh meal with all the trimmings. Next morning I got up, and had just finished breakfast when my Dad sticks a hammer and chisel in my hands and says "Your Mum wants a serving hatch!". That summed it up.' Soul star or electrician, you were treated the same in your parents' house, or back in the community.

He's conscious of the opportunities and freedom that he had as child in Bishopbriggs, with a happy home life, and the chance to just make music with his friends. It's something he has ensured was available to his own son, who is now through college and working as a sports journalist with a national sports network. As the conversation veers on to the contrasts between life in Scotland and America, he has no illusions. The absence of free health care appals him but the opportunities and facilities for kids in sport impress him. As we lament the decline of the Scottish football team and the difficulties for the game at grassroots level, he points to opportunities and facilities that youngsters have here in the New York area. 'Kids have any number of things to do after school. If you want to play soccer, facilities are made available. Parents put in a lot of time and effort because they know it's going to be worth it in the long run. Busy kids are too tired when they get home to go and hang out, drink, smoke whatever or chat up the lassies. If they put in the work, they will make a team. Schoolwork is kept up too, it's an incentive, if not you'll miss a game, or worse still, be off the team.'

He has a self-confessed 'passion for Scotland', and left not because it failed him, but because it could never provide the opportunities that he sought. As with others, his dreams could only be achieved first in London and subsequently in the States, though he remains optimistic for his country. 'AWB couldn't possibly have done it from Scotland back then. You had to go to London. That has now changed. Bruce Findlay proved it in the eighties by managing Simple Minds from Edinburgh. Franz Ferdinand CDs are currently in every record store in North America.

'Scotland is full of talented people who are smart enough to find a way to make their passion work. Scotland's challenge is to make sure that the possibilities and facilities are made available for everyone, that way, its talent can be developed and nurtured for success at home without having to leave the country.

'If we can retain the egalitarianism that forged us, be confident of our talents and abilities; be proud of our identity without being aggressive or negative with it, then it will happen.'

Seems sound advice to me from a guy who in the music industry has made it, played it and is even printed on the T-shirt. His desires for Scotland seem a reflection of himself; confident in his abilities without bragging about his achievements, proud of his identity but happy living in a diverse community.

Interviewed by Kenny MacAskill
July 2005

David Speedie

SPECIAL ADVISER TO THE
PRESIDENT OF THE CARNEGIE
CORPORATION OF NEW YORK

Carnegie's Man of Peace

MOST SCOTS KNOW THE STORY OF Andrew Carnegie, but most are
unaware of his involvement and ongoing legacy in peace and international relations. Yet it's substantial, as I am to find out, and a Scot
is at the heart of it to this day.

Wanting to meet this Scotsman and find out more about his mentor, I head for the headquarters of the Carnegie Corporation of New
York, on Madison Avenue in midtown Manhattan. In the reception
area I read an information pamphlet that narrates the known tale.

'Andrew Carnegie was born in Dunfermline, Scotland on
November 25, 1835. The son of a weaver, he came with his family
to the United States in 1848 and settled in Allegheny, Pennsylvania.
At the age of 13, Carnegie went to work as a bobbin boy in a cot-
ton mill. He then moved rapidly through a succession of jobs with
Western Union and the Pennsylvania Railroad. In 1865 he resigned
to establish his own business enterprises and eventually organized
the Carnegie Steel Company, which launched the steel industry in
Pittsburgh. At the age of 65, he sold the company to JP Morgan for
£400 million and devoted the rest of his life to his philanthropic
activities and writing, including his biography.'

The legacy of Carnegie's famous philanthropy to Dunfermline in
the shape of a hall and a public park are well known, as are other
buildings in New York, and equally his support for education, liter-

acy and public libraries. Far less known was his support for international peace and how the legacy operates. The *Carnegie Reporter* has an introduction from the President of the Corporation, who states, 'Ninety years ago, in 1913, during a lull between wars, Andrew Carnegie opened the Place of Peace at The Hague, which today houses the Permanent Court of Arbitration, the UN's International Court of Justice, The Hague Academy of International Law and one of the most prestigious international law libraries in the world. At the opening, he spoke about his ardent belief that war could be vanquished by the transformative power of knowledge, learning and understanding. He believed that war is wasteful and avoidable, that diplomacy and international organisations can resolve disputes peacefully and, when necessary, help national members to act collectively in prosecuting cases involving injustice.'

Powerful sentiments and, given some of the trials and tribulations the world has recently faced, as sensible and necessary now as then. The substantial legacy left by Carnegie means that it is more than empty rhetoric and mere sentiment. The Carnegie Corporation of New York was created in 1911 to promote knowledge and understanding with an initial capital fund valued at approximately $135 million, which as of 2003 had grown to a market value of $1.8 billion. This organisation is not only dedicated towards peace and understanding but well enough resourced to be able to make a genuine contribution to this goal. It operates in a way that does not court publicity – and allows others to take their ideas as their own, befitting an organisation engaged in international diplomacy.

The Scot at the centre of this work is David Speedie. Previously Chair of the corporation's International Peace and Security programme he is now Director of the Project on Islam and special adviser to the President of the Corporation. As diplomacy has moved from the Cold War and the arms race to fundamentalism and terrorism, so has the focus of his work.

He entertains me to lunch in his office on the 26th floor, which offers incredible views of Manhattan. He's short and stocky, friendly and garrulous, retaining a Scottish accent and sense of humour, but with an American edge to both. He's altogether good company, leading a fascinating life, mixing with the great, yet having neither pretensions nor airs and graces. A very learned and deeply intellectual man, he retains a common touch that doubtless serves him well in his work. Very well connected, given the nature of his work, names spring forth matter of factly (he is most certainly not name dropping, but my ears prick up all the same). A close personal friend and colleague was McGeorge Bundy, former Special Adviser to President Kennedy and Johnson, and forever associated with the Vietnam War. An acquaintance is Senator John McCain (a possible future President) as are other serving Congress members.

Born in Stirling, brought up in Bridge of Allan and attending Stirling High School, he was not just one of the first in his family to go to university, but indeed one of the first in the housing scheme he was brought up in. Modest and unassuming, he recalls that there was no greater sin than showing off: 'That was awful – lying, cheating, all of that was bearable, but showing off was terrible.'

His parents held to those Scottish beliefs in education and self-improvement evident throughout this book. When his grandfather – who had been a Sergeant Major in the Argylls – died, his father had to give up an apprenticeship as a solicitor. His mother was from a working class family in Hamilton and though without a formal education, was smart and hard-working. His parents ensured that the opportunities that had been unavailable to them would be open to their children. He is yet another from a high-achieving family with humble origins. One of his brothers is Deputy Principal at a secondary school in Dundee, another is a senior official with a local authority in central Scotland.

From there it was on to St Andrews and a first class honours degree in English Language and Literature. A postgraduate degree was obtained at the same time as lecturing there, followed by a Kennedy Scholarship at Harvard. Mervyn King, the current Governor of the Bank of England, was a fellow scholar at the time and the selection panel was chaired by the great philosopher Sir Isaiah Berlin.

While on the programme he met an American girl who he subsequently married. He and Eveline moved back to Scotland for a while where a variety of work was undertaken, including lecturing at Telford College by day and at Saughton Prison by night. He hankered for something different, and for a return to the USA.

Initially working with the British Embassy in Washington dealing with the Bicentennial celebrations he moved into a variety of positions in the arts, including Director of Cultural Affairs for the City of Philadelphia as well as President of the Jacksonville Art Museum, before joining The Carnegie Corporation. At first a Program Officer in the Co-operative Security program, he moved on to being Program Chair. 'It began in the dark days of the Cold War. I came in 1992 at an interesting time, at the end of the Cold War and beginning of a new relationship with Moscow which was really developed by Gorbachev and, to his credit, Reagan. So for 10 years I worked on this interesting mission with US and Russian relations. Arms control and weapons of mass destruction; nuclear and chemical weapons; and then the other area of post-Cold War and Civil War. I was ready for a new challenge and the President of the Corporation, Vartan Gregorian, had written an important book on understanding Islam. So he asked me to work with him in developing an initiative at the foundation that might involve research and convening meetings, to follow up on the book, *Islam: A Mosaic, Not a Monolith.*' And that's where he is today, as Project Director on Islam and Special Advisor to the President.

He has both amusing tales to narrate as well as waspish comments to make about his work. On his work on the Cold War and the non-proliferation of weapons of mass destruction, he cuttingly says, 'where they did exist, unlike in Iraq in 2003.' He tells a tale that happened during Carnegie-funded meetings in The Hague on the Chechnya conflict. Learning that he was from Scotland the Chechen delegation, in full battle regalia, tells him that Maskhadov, the recently assassinated leader, had 'seen *Braveheart* 10 times'. Not the example to follow, said he – not simply because of the outcome, but being no fan of the film, as a result of its historical inaccuracies among other factors.

He's still deeply attached to his homeland and grateful for what it provided him. 'What Scotland gave me? A world class education.

I remember every one of my high school teachers. The quality of teaching is immense. Expectations were high, the bar was set high. There was a sense of obligation that you had to live up to.' It also provided a core set of values, a commitment to them and a real sense of history. 'The strong sense that a small country had done remarkable things. Scots should take pride in their diaspora – look what the contributions in the world have been. It's remarkable.'

As with others, it was a search for further opportunities that spurred him on and led him away from Scotland. That he feels was not just in terms of employment prospect but an innate drive. 'There is a restlessness in the Scottish people. Scots want to explore.' That said, he remains well informed and deeply committed. 'Scotland is not just the place where I grew up. I check newspapers three or four times a week, *The Herald* and *Scotsman* online everyday.' He demonstrates this by challenging me about an article in a recent paper. He returns to Scotland at least once a year and his son, who has been several times, has a sense of Scottishness (notwithstanding his mother's Polish Jewish heritage), even to the extent of being a Celtic supporter – a result of being given a team scarf by their friend George O'Neil, another exiled Scot who once played for them, before moving to the USA – much to the chagrin of his lifelong Rangers supporting father!

Humorously describing himself as a 'recovering academic' he tells me he's been reviewing a book by a Muslim scholar critical of the age of Enlightenment. This is an area he feels that Scotland should almost patent and protect, conscious that it was Scotland that gave it to the world and that it was an age which saw so much achieved and is recognised especially in the USA, where he mentions Madison and Jefferson as being deeply influenced by it. I am certain that he's right. Along with ideas such as an academy for the diaspora, making more of our intellectual contribution is long overdue. Not just in how it might benefit us, but in how we see ourselves. It is an aspect we have almost let drift yet it is pivotal to the modern world and Scots were at the heart of it. More must be done to capitalise on that contribution.

His take on what Scotland should do is interesting and insightful. No romantic nationalist, he is analytical and hard-headed and discloses a firebrand past as a young Labour Agent in West Perthshire and Kinross when Sir Alex Douglas Home was the Tory candidate. He is keen for Scotland to progress and participate. 'I think Scotland has, and it's no secret, an identity problem. In my day there was a very emotional sense of nationalism: Scotland the Brave, Scots Wha Hae. To those of us who regarded ourselves as socialist, it was sentimental. Now we have a Parliament and I think it's a question of establishing where Scotland wants to be in a globalised world.'

He tries to downplay his qualifications to comment by stating that he is not resident but is aware of the opprobrium heaped on the Parliament as an institution, through conversations with his mother and a tour of the building with George Reid. That said, his take is clear from experience elsewhere. 'There is a missing link: why, for example, is there a much stronger business climate in Ireland? The Irish have been more strategic and amended tax laws. Hard choices but it's how they have done business in the world.'

He then uses a phrase that I have seen but never heard raised in connection with Scotland. 'The idea of Westphalian nationalism – it's changing. Scotland is trying to catch up with changing times.' I understand where he is coming from. The nation state is changing and evolving before our very eyes. The days of 'One Crown, One Faith, One Flag' being requirements for nationhood have long gone. No nation is entirely independent and all nations are interdependent in this globalised world. Other more mundane matters once viewed as sacrosanct to statehood have also gone in more recent times. Given the fate of Sabena and the plight of others, who believes that a national airline is needed to be an independent state? Scotland, in a modern world, often seems to be seeking the model that has just been updated or withdrawn, and that's the point he makes next, referring both to Scotland's relations with England and the world.

'The EU is changing and Scotland is trying to catch up with that. Look at Scandinavia for example. Their arrangements are sensible in Scandinavia. We need to look beyond our relationship with London.

We have Brussels; we have Geneva, Washington and perhaps even Beijing. This is where we should be going. It's good that we have a Parliament, but it must also look to build Scotland's international credentials and presence.' He sees George Reid, the Presiding Officer, who previously worked with the International Red Cross, as having given the Parliament an outward focus and pursuing that agenda.

Keen for Scotland to progress and its Parliament to evolve, he is aware that this requires a change in attitude by the Scots. 'We have to become less self-conscious and lose the perceived inferiority complex. The anti-English sentiments: get over it or live with it. We need to do more as Scots in the modern world than wear a kilt or sing songs about past grievances. We have to be proud of being Scots and confident in being Scottish. The future of the nation state is changing and its relevance comes into sharper focus. But if others can, so can Scotland. There is a sense that it's time to move on.'

I can't help but agree. It's a changing world and whether Scotland becomes an independent nation or not is for the Scots to ultimately decide in a referendum. However, it's certain that the Parliament needs more powers and Scots need more self-confidence. I used to dispute the claim that Scotland had to come to terms with devolution before it could move on, seeing it as an insult or, at best, simply another delaying tactic. Now, though, I realise that it was a correct analysis and it's a stage in our development that we had to pass through. Scotland needs to come to terms with itself, to be confident in itself and comfortable in its role in the modern world. Scots must take responsibility and participate, not spectate and complain. The 'whingeing Jock' must be replaced by the confident and responsible Scot. Addressing our flaws and failings, as well as maximising the opportunities our natural talents and innate advantages have given us. The time has come to move to whatever the next stage on our journey happens to be. David Speedie, never mind his mentor Andrew Carnegie, have shown what Scots with confidence in themselves and their identity can achieve. Time for the rest of us to do so.

Interviewed by Kenny MacAskill
July 2005

Harry Benson

PHOTOGRAPHER, NEW YORK

The World Through a Scottish Lens

LONG BEFORE THE SCOTTISH PARLIAMENT was restored and Scottish politicians could network at Tartan Day in New York or pay a visit to Malawi, when Scottish representation in the Westminster corridors of power was often confined to a Secretary of State and backbench MPs, there was one Scotsman strutting on a global stage, covering the issues that mattered and meeting the movers that made them happen.

He walked the walk, talked the talk and snapped the shots. His name may not be familiar to all in Scotland, but his photographs are recognised all over the world. Through a Scottish lens he has captured every American President since Eisenhower, he has walked with Martin Luther King, and was at Bobby Kennedy's side when he was assassinated. From the Beatles to Hollywood stars; from riots in the streets of the USA through terrorism in Ireland to peacekeeping in the Balkans, he has covered the burning issues and the people making the news. He worked in Fleet Street before heading to the States, where his CV is a resume of all the major magazines and journals from *Life* through to *Vanity Fair*, to whom he is still contracted.

He has had many books published, including profiles of the Beatles and anthologies of America's First Families. His accolades run from twice being Magazine Photographer of the Year with the National Press Photographers Association in the USA, to first place as the British Photographer of the Year, with a multitude of other ribbons and recognitions in between. Outstanding achievement awards have been bestowed for photographic genres from fashion and fine art, to sports and portraits. His photographs are iconic, but he is a standout himself in his profession. Before digital cameras were invented and photographs could be e-mailed from a laptop, he was ahead of the game. Harry Benson is that man.

I contact him through the Scottish network that operates abroad. The Scottish diaspora may not have the formal structures which many other countries do, particularly Ireland, but an informal network exists all the same, which doubtlessly results in business deals being concluded and doors being opened. But it also exists on a more mundane basis, of forwarding e-mails with snippets and jokes from home, and possessing each other's phone numbers. What matters is that it is effective. While in New York interviewing Onnie McIntyre, it is suggested that I should approach Harry Benson. After only two phone calls I speak to Harry Benson himself, who has already been informed of what I am doing. He's open and welcoming, and immediately invites me to his home for an interview.

I travel up to his apartment on the Upper East Side in New York, just across from Central Park. The doorman tells me it's the 18th floor, flat A or B. I assume he's new and unsure of the residents, but it transpires that Harry's flat consists of A *and* B, with both flats being knocked together. It's a beautiful apartment in a highly desirable area. Harry's Texan wife Gigi welcomes me and invites me in, then Harry takes me out onto the roof garden, which boasts a stunning view down Third Avenue.

It would be hard to find a friendlier, more hospitable couple. They insist on pouring me a malt whisky and Harry begins to tell me about himself and his views on Scotland. His accent, though softened by years in America, is still distinctively Scottish. For all his success and riches he remains a humble man of Scottish roots – proud of his Scottish identity and fond of his kinfolk. I sense a longing in his voice for the land he has left, even though he is now long settled in the USA. Returning to Scotland regularly, he tells me he invariably drives through the Glasgow suburb of Clarkston in which he was brought up, as well as paying a pilgrimage to his mother's grave in Troon, Ayrshire; a part of the country he loves, and where he frequently stays when back in Scotland. 'There are certain places in Scotland I love, with special memories – Hampden Park and walking along the prom in Troon in the rain. I play golf and basically talk away to myself. I meet friends or go for a fish supper.'

Part of what he misses about Scotland is simply having a conversation about nothing. 'Americans talk in subjects and their conversation has to be about something. But Scots just talk words and don't necessarily have a conversation. I can do that easily in Glasgow. We can just chat and then not remember what we said. But it's a laugh and I miss that. I love the banter in Glasgow.'

As if on cue, our chat ambles across his views on American presidents – from the lack of recognition given to Lyndon B Johnson for his civil rights drive, to his personal fondness for Richard Nixon, who he photographed shortly after his resignation from office – to his love of football, playing with Coltness United and recalling the Rangers team that played Moscow Dynamo in 1945. Similarly, we range from magazines such as *Life* and *Vanity Fair* to his time with the *Hamilton Advertiser*.

Now in his seventies, Harry is a Glaswegian, born in Knightswood but brought up in Clarkston. His mother's family were from Troon, where a lot of time was spent as a boy. His father was a zoologist who founded Calderpark Zoo. He had a brother who became a director with a major PLC in England, and two sisters who remained in Scotland. Childhood encompassed the war years, and memories are of his father in the Home Guard and German bombers flying overhead. He recalls the Rudolph Hess landing, where, despite strictures from his school, he and some friends stole a piece of corrugated iron from the plane.

His memories of school are not so happy. Skipping class one day to watch a Rangers training session, he was captured in a photograph in the evening papers and taken to task by his irate father. He describes himself as a dunce though he is obviously a very intelligent man. Today, educationalists would doubtless be able to address the underlying problem, but in those days classification and rejection followed. The headmaster advised him that he was holding everyone back, so he left school at 13. A job with Ilford Film, as a message boy pushing a barrow, followed. A couple of years were spent completing a course at Glasgow School of Art as his father sought to improve his son's lot, but he describes them as a 'waste of time'.

Photography had been an interest, if not a passion. His first love was football and like so many Scottish boys his ambition was to pull on the dark blue jersey of the national team. Never to reach that goal, he did play junior football until he left to go to Fleet Street. During national service with the RAF he had auditioned for a position with the camera club but his photos were rejected as not being up to standard. Discharged from the forces, he worked as a photographer at Butlin's holiday camp in Ayr, which allowed him to meet a good few girls. Wedding photos and agency work followed before he landed a job with the *Hamilton Advertiser*. In the days before mass car ownership, that meant journeys by bus from Leadhills to Lesmahagow. Eager to progress, he pestered Fleet Street editors – travelling up and down on the night train to London eight times before being recruited by the *Daily Sketch*. A move to the *Daily Express* followed.

It was there that his big break came. Preparing to depart for an assignment in Africa, he received a call from the night picture editor to go to Paris to cover the Beatles. 'They were just starting to take off at the time. I thought I had talked him out of sending me but I got a call back from him saying the editor was giving me no choice, and that I had to go. I was really downhearted. Then I got to Paris and heard the music. I knew they were really special. I was there with them in Paris when they were told that they were at number one in America. I knew then that I had a chance and that I was not coming back.'

Moving to America with them in 1964, he has been there ever since. He would have liked to have stayed in Scotland but knew that the opportunity to do what he wanted and to achieve what he wished could not be delivered there – so he took the chance. The rest, as they say, is history. Those who doubted him, from his headmaster to the RAF, have had to repent.

His favourite picture is 'the pillow fight' – a shot of four youthful and innocent Beatles fooling around in their hotel room in Paris on the night they made number one in the USA. It's a photo which has stood the test of time and will be recalled by many people, whether fans of the Fab Four or not. That's just one of his countless pictures that are a snapshot of world figures and historic events as seen through a Scottish lens.

He's proud of his family and patriotic about his native country. 'I am very glad to be Scottish and it has meant a lot to me. It's not like being Welsh, Irish, or English – there is something special about Scotland and it has been a help to me in what I do. Nobody has a negative thought about Scotland, which they certainly do about England or Ireland.'

'Being Scottish carries no baggage, which made it much easier for me. Telling people that you are Scottish, rather than English, softens them up. I need to get as close to people as I can, and this wouldn't have happened if I had been Irish, with all the talk of the IRA at that time.' He then narrates how it enabled him to also get close to Martin Luther King and the racist Governor of Alabama, George Wallace.

As well as the identity, he feels he received tangible benefits. 'Scotland gave me a hardness, a determination and I came out of it well. You don't want to be a failure to your friends or your family.' At the same time he feels that drive to succeed is balanced by a recognition as to how you behave when you get there. 'Scots always have their feet on the ground and never get carried away with themselves. That is definitely a Scottish thing. You don't get above yourself.' He also believes it fostered values that he appreciates and believes are recognised elsewhere. 'There is a decency about Scotland, the Scottish values are there. For example I photographed Billy Graham last week, whose ancestors came from Scotland. He said the Scottish people had the best values, over and above anybody else in the world. I agree with that.'

That said, he is conscious that in other matters, Scotland could not provide for him. Humorously, he recalls Scottish Sundays. 'Hideous. I had an Italian friend and his house was full of happiness

– spaghetti and laughter. Whereas in our house, it was just depressing.' Who in Scotland doesn't have an equally dour memory of the Sabbath?

In his chosen profession, career options in his native land were highly limited. He recalls this more in sorrow than in anger. 'There weren't enough places to work in Scotland. I had to leave because the opportunities weren't there. There was nowhere to show your work. There wasn't a magazine like *Life*. There weren't any newspapers like there were in Fleet Street.' This is less a criticism and more a fact of life in a small country such as ours. The international acclaim that he has achieved would have been impossible to come by in Scotland, and as he describes in his own words, 'I could only go so far'.

But far he has gone. Scotland can enjoy his reminiscences, and benefit from his reflection on matters and points he has to make. On education, he, like most of the Scots abroad that I have interviewed, appreciates the benefits of the Scottish education system – though in his case it clearly failed him. He is conscious of its deficiencies as well as its virtues. 'I remember the headmaster coming and telling my parents that I was a waste of space. I failed but I came out of it okay. Even though it failed me I still believe it was a good educational system.' That, to me, seems a remarkably magnanimous view. The treatment of him or any child in that fashion was, and is, shameful. Recently there has been a change in methods and provision, but there is never any room for complacency. Our education system is something to be proud of, and times have changed, but the picture is still far short of being bright and beautiful. Harry Benson's experience is a salutary lesson to us all.

On Scotland's image abroad he is scathing about the tartan image so often portrayed, and what he sees as its falseness. 'When Scots come over here, I sometimes find it embarrassing, with all the bagpipes and so on. These are people who in my life I would never go near, a crooked bunch, dancing and singing about Scotland, but a Scotland I never saw. Tartan Week, for example, is on television here, and they talk about Scots as "cute". You couldn't call Celtic fans cute, or many other people I know.'

What he does want is for those like him who live abroad to be recognised as Scots. 'I think Scotland should make expats feel that they are still one of us. We still love you. You can come home whenever you want.' Although he himself has always felt welcomed, the sentiments are ones I have heard from others. Their view is we need to 'lighten' up back home. It is still possible to be Scottish, even if you live elsewhere and when you return home you are treated as such.

Interviewing Harry Benson was not just a pleasure but a privilege. He was engaging company – humorous yet incisive, knowledgeable and kindly, determined and talented, yet equally self-deprecating and humble. His works are iconic and have been front pages on the major magazines of the world. Whilst his name is known in Scotland, it does not resonate nearly as loudly as it should. He tells me that there is to be a display of his work at the National Portrait Gallery next year. Long overdue, I think, for someone whose work is internationally recognised. Having captured the world with his camera, it is time Scotland properly acknowledged his achievements.

His experiences and contacts are broader and better than the combined membership of the Scottish Parliament. He knows more people in power than any Scottish elected representative. It is saddening, if not staggering, that he has neither been given the recognition that he is due, nor asked for his reflection and guidance. Harry Benson is not simply a Scot who should be recognised for his achievements, but one who should be asked for his thoughts and counsel. He has seen the world through a Scottish lens and it is time Scotland benefited from that view.

Interviewed by Kenny MacAskill
July 2005

Veronica McWatt

WORKS WITH SCOTLAND EUROPA,
BRUSSELS

The Gourock Girl with Get Up and Go

HAVING GRADUATED WITH AN HONOURS degree in European Business Studies with Spanish, and then obtaining an MSc in Energy and Environmental Systems, Veronica McWatt was enjoying a well-earned rest at her Gourock home. Her parents, though, had other ideas. Her father, a self-employed builder and joiner, and her mother, the bookkeeper in the family firm, had fully supported her throughout her years of study – which included an Erasmus exchange in Spain – and had watched her graduate with pride. However, in inimical Scottish style, they lectured her about now entering into the real world and the need to get a proper job.

Heeding her parental guidance but having given little real thought to what she wanted to do, she headed down to the jobcentre in Greenock. During the late summer of 1996, the Clyde was not abounding with job opportunities. However, amongst the adverts for catering staff and roustabouts in the offshore oil industry, she spied a card offering employment as a Spanish/English translator in Brussels. Intrigued by this, thinking it would be ideal and confident in her ability and qualifications she headed to a desk seeking further information, only to be met by a response symptomatic of a malaise in some parts of Scotland. 'You have to speak Spanish' was the welcome from the jobcentre staff. 'Yes, I can' she replied. 'You have to speak French,' they continued in equally encouraging vein. 'Fine, I can do that as well,' she said. 'The job is in Brussels, you have to move away,' was presumably their clinching gambit in dealing with this time-wasting girl. 'Okay, not a problem,' she persevered. Doubtless frustrated by her persistence they conceded and the information was provided.

Telephoning what turned out to be a Spanish law firm based in Brussels, she arranged an interview. With her parents on holiday at the time, she phoned them to let them know she was heading off. And off she went to a city that she had never been to before and into a job as a Spanish/English translator that she clinched on arrival. Norman Tebbit would be proud, but what an indictment of Scottish society. The story is heartening in its outcome but demoralising in its tale. Though her account is unique, I fear that her experience is not unusual.

Her name had been mentioned to me by the Head of the European Parliament Office in Edinburgh, when I asked for some suggestions of Scots to meet. Whilst I had been given an outline of going from the jobcentre in Greenock to a top job in Brussels, I had been unaware of her travails in doing so. The story intrigued me, and it offered an opportunity to meet a young Scot working in the heart of Europe. I contacted her by e-mail and then by telephone. Initially surprised to be asked, she ultimately agreed to participate and came to meet me in the Parliament when she was back over on one of her regular trips home from Brussels, in her current job with Scotland Europa. A pretty woman, slim and with black hair, I can understand why she said she was often mistaken for Spanish when she had it grown long. Confident – if slightly apprehensive – about the meeting, she's easygoing, good company and quite 'the girl next door' you'd be delighted to meet. Articulate, with a softened west of Scotland accent, it's clear that though she may be slight of build, she's strong in character.

Born in Port Glasgow, she was brought up in nearby Gourock. Her parents still live there as does her brother, who works at IBM. She attended St Ninian's Primary School and then St Columba's Secondary School in Gourock, emphasising the location to differentiate it from the private school up the road in Kilmacolm. A state school lass and proud of it – and why not, as I and others can testify, they have served us well. She's generous in spirit, seeing herself as fortunate in her childhood and in the era she was brought up in. That's something that makes me immediately warm to her. She's not a Thatcher child but someone who has done well for herself, almost all under her own volition; but appreciates the start given and the help received along the road.

Her memories of growing up as a child in the seventies and eighties have been recently jogged, she tells me, by e-mails that have been flying about concerning children being allowed out to play (or rather, not, as it seems now). As with my own childhood almost two decades before hers, she was allowed to roam free. 'We lived in a cul-de-sac. The back of the garden joined onto the moor. There were lots of young families the same age. We could walk to school and back. We would come home, change out of our uniform and go outside to play until dinner was ready. It was so carefree. Looking back on my childhood, we really were lucky. We made our own fun. We used to go down the front to get ice cream. When I was older I could go into Glasgow on the train on a Saturday afternoon to do some shopping.' I am sure it brings back memories for all adult Scots.

It's a pleasure to hear her views. As the father of two teenage children it seems to me that life is harder for youngsters nowadays with childhood freedoms curtailed and a lot of innocence lost. The overwhelming majority of Scots kids are a credit to themselves, their families and their communities, though you would sometimes struggle to know it while stories of 'ned culture' prevail. An ageing society seems to cut less slack to youngsters as a 'no ball games here' culture permeates down. This is not to excuse the appalling behaviour of a small minority who are seriously out of control. It is important, though, to remember that in many instances, their behaviour begins at home with parental failures from my own generation. 'I always went to my gran's on a Saturday for afternoon tea. Then on Sundays we would go to my Dad's mum's house for bacon rolls.' It was refreshing to simply sit and listen. Globalisation and constant emigration come at a social cost.

Her university career came about more by accident than design. Having completed her fifth year and embarking on a sixth, she attended an open day at Glasgow Caledonian. Holidays in Tenerife and summer exchanges with a family in Spain had given her a desire to speak the Spanish language. She was also keen to do a business orientated degree, and when she was told that there was an opportunity to do both combined, she took it, there and then. She returned from her outing to tell her parents she was leaving school and going to university in the big city; the first in her immediate family to do so. The honours degree included an Erasmus exchange where she ventured off to Spain to improve her Spanish, only to find that she had been sent to Catalonia and the language was Catalan. It might have deterred others, but not her; she just got on with it.

The job she managed to prise out of the Greenock jobcentre was as a translator. It soon became evident that whilst they did not require a translator, she had an aptitude for more demanding work and she moved on to working in consultancy with a related Spanish consultancy firm. That involved providing Spanish and Latin American clients with advice on EU affairs. She was the only non-Spaniard, and tiring of that she moved on to work for a Scottish consultancy firm with contracts in Eastern Europe. After a year, she moved to Scotland Europa, and has been with them since November 2000, co-ordinating the environment working group. The organisation is membership based, including both public and private sector bodies from the Scottish Environmental Protection Agency through to the Federation of Small Businesses. Information is disseminated down, contacts made, and advice given on all aspects of EU affairs.

Discussing her views on Scotland was illuminating. She is from a generation that does not carry the baggage of defeat, or possess the fear of failure that afflicts those that endured the late seventies and early eighties, in particular. There is a confidence in her identity, though no illusions about certain aspects of Scottish society. It's a pride in being Scottish, not a resentment of the English. However she does narrate, with some pride and obvious satisfaction, the behaviour of the Tartan Army in contrast to English hooligans when they visited Brussels. 'The contrast between the two sets of fans was unbelievable. I was proud to be Scottish at that point.

'There is a sense of belonging. When you are abroad you are always asked where you are from. People have stories to tell about Scotland and they want to know so much more. You are welcomed when they find out you are from Scotland. I will always be Scottish and I am very proud to be Scottish. That sometimes takes a lot of explaining when people ask about the UK. I make it clear I am not English. My boss in the law firm used to wind me up by saying Scotland is not a country. That caused a lot of arguments. He said if Scotland ever gets a Parliament, I will concede that it is a country.' Well, we have, and it's up to us now to make it the land we want it to be. And in that regard she has clear views and an upbeat and confident air. 'I think Scots should have a much more positive attitude. We do become negative on ourselves. A classic example was the jobcentre – you get no encouragement, everything is negative. Try to be more positive, more encouraging, you can do well. Go for it.'

As well as the get up and go which she possesses and feels we must acquire, there is a self-belief that she possesses but Scotland lacks. She mentions that she had initially wondered why I had asked her to participate and what she could contribute, asking 'why me?'. Having considered it, though, she thought 'why not?'. That almost encapsulates her attitude. 'What would give Scotland a bit of get up and go – if we could just publicise it and blow our own trumpet. So often we talk about Scotland and the Scots of the past – Alexander Graham Bell, Fleming etc. – the great inventors – fine, but we have moved on and we are doing all these fantastic things. We have the potential to be world leaders but we don't tell anybody about it. Shout louder. Do people know the great things we are doing? We are not giving ourselves credit. We need to highlight the good things we are doing. There are some good things going on in Scotland where no one has any idea what is going on – that needs to change. We need to have more confidence in ourselves as a nation.'

That's not to say that she has any illusions about some other aspects of Scottish life and society. As with others, she laments the lack of her own nation's history taught at school. That seems to be a common thread running through all these interviews. Too many to be random. However, she also touches upon the politically taboo subject of separate schooling, but does so in a thoughtful and non-confrontational way. 'Growing up in the west coast of Scotland until I left I didn't realise Scotland wasn't a Catholic country. I never had any negative experiences. I was simply oblivious to the fact there were issues with any other culture. The non-Catholic primary was near our house so I was aware of it but I never understood what the religious tensions were all about.' That would almost be comic if it wasn't tragic.

Meeting Veronica McWatt is a great tonic from the daily grind of Scottish politics. She is positive and upbeat, seeking much more forward thinking from her political leaders and self-belief in her compatriots, but retaining a confidence of things improving. 'I think Scotland has a great future ahead. It didn't collapse because the ships stopped being built. Look at what is happening with renewable energy. What are we trying to do about increasing our population? The economy is booming in some towns but I worry about other parts of the country. The stabbings that I read about and the levels of crime are quite scary. But Scotland has a great future. We are developing new technologies, industries, sectors – go for it.'

Listening to her, I am a believer. The future for Scotland can be bright if not golden, but only if we rear people like Veronica McWatt and ensure that they return. By all means study and work abroad – it broadens minds, raises horizons and benefits us on return. Not all will want to, or be able to do so, as other interviewees have shown. But, they must be able to return, and given the opportunity to do so. Veronica has shown what can be achieved. We need to make sure that jobs and opportunities exist for her to return, and seek out and encourage her and others to bring their talents back home. Ireland has done it, with its diaspora now returning. Scotland must do likewise. It's time to encourage the Scottish diaspora to come home.

Interviewed by Kenny MacAskill
August 2005

John MacGregor

BAR AND RESTAURANT MANAGER,
TALLINN

A Scottish Soldier

'THERE WAS A SOLDIER, a Scottish soldier, who wandered far away, and soldiered far away.' Ulster, Africa and the Falklands to be precise. A mountain of a man. Well over six foot tall and built in proportion, with forearms like tree trunks. Enlisting in the Scots Guards straight from school he served in Northern Ireland. Going AWOL he headed for Paris and joined the Foreign Legion, earning his paratrooper wings and performing anti-terrorist duties in Central Africa. The thought of a four year posting to The Horn of Africa saw him escape from Corsica and the clutches of the Foreign Legion, only to return to the British Army, and active service in the Falklands War. Now he's doing extremely well for himself in Estonia, managing successful bars and restaurants. John MacGregor is not a story but a living legend.

Scotland has a proud martial history and John MacGregor is yet another in that line, albeit with a unique, if somewhat bizarre story to tell. John MacGregor is not even his real name. Having set up a pipe band in Helsinki he found he was not taken seriously as his surname, Hardie, was not perceived as Scottish. Accordingly, he took to calling himself MacGregor. Even that has not been without incident; a friend booked a plane ticket for him without realising that his passport remains in his original surname, resulting in him facing arrest in these times of heightened tension in security and air travel.

Throughout the centuries our young men have joined historic Scottish regiments and served in the forces of other nations. They have fought in our own Wars of Independence, for the creation of the British Empire and in world wars against fascism and tyranny, as well as serving the needs of other states. John MacGregor's service in the Foreign Legion is part of a noble tradition. Whilst in Tallinn I take Henry up to the Lutheran Cathedral in the historic Old Town. Buried there in a mausoleum is Samuel Greig who died there in 1788. Born on St Andrew's Day in 1735 in Inverkeithing, he is credited as being the father of the Russian Navy. Many Scots are aware of John Paul Jones from Kirkcudbright, who turned from privateer to being the father of the American Navy during the American Revolution. Fewer though are aware that – in typical Scottish style – we balanced that out by being pivotal in the creation of the other side's fleet more than 150 years before the Cold War commenced.

That's yet another example of Scotland not knowing its own history, Henry and I agree as we saunter back. But John MacGregor and his tale we are to learn about. He meets us in the Olympia Hotel. I am over six feet in height but he towers above me and dwarfs Henry. Chain smoking, he's a rough diamond, who swears like a trooper but is altogether good company with an incredible tale to tell. Many years have passed since he enlisted as a boy of 16 but that has not lessened his broad Scots brogue. Born in Caldercruix in Lanarkshire he moved to Bishopbriggs then Rutherglen with his police officer father before returning to Plains in 1972. His mother had worked at Hoover but ceased on returning to the Caldercruix/Plains area. He has two younger sisters who still live in the village and his parents have recently moved back after a spell south of the border.

With his father being the local policeman, John MacGregor had a hard upbringing in what was and remains both a tight-knit and tough community. Attending a primary school in the village and high school in Airdrie, he left home at 16. As a result, memories of school are vague, but those he does have are a reminder of the hard upbringing. 'Walking to school, freezing in the winter, drinking buckfast at the age of 13 and getting myself into trouble. I had a lot of hassle with my dad being a policeman. I remember, even as young as five, being mocked because of it.'

Keen to enlist, he joined the Scots Guards in 1977. Service in Northern Ireland followed; the troubles were ongoing and trouble continued to follow him. An altercation with his company commander saw him placed in a platoon with soldiers considerably older than him. Unhappy about that he went absent without leave and headed for Paris. As he says, 'I walked up to a door and knocked. A slat opened and a guy mumbled something in French. I said "Legion, Legion" and the door opened. That was it. I was away for a year and a half.' He was sent to Corsica where the Foreign Legion is based. Not only was he inducted into that legendary unit but he also obtained his parachutist wings. Service in Benin in Central Africa followed, on what he describes as counter terrorism duties. He doesn't talk about it in detail, and Henry and I deem it best not to ask. A parachuting accident resulted in him being hospitalised and unable to jump anymore. Returning to Corsica, a four year posting to Djibouti in the Horn of Africa was to follow. Little time was needed to decide that was not for him. 'I thought to myself, if I am getting sent there I want out. So the last night I did a bunk from hospital with two other Scots boys. There was a wee boy from Blackridge and another older guy who had done five years in Barlinnie Prison.' Henry and I are left to contemplate just how many other Jocks are in the Foreign Legion – 'You'd be surprised,' was his response.

The Foreign Legion is less benign than the British army towards deserters. 'It took us three weeks to get off the island of Corsica. We had to hide. We broke into a beach shack and found a dinghy and a crate of Johnnie Walker. We loaded the dinghy with the whisky – we couldn't find any water but plenty of whisky was available. About a kilometre out, something in the back of my head said "this isn't going to work" and I jumped off the dinghy and swam back to shore. I eventually got picked up by a German, who put me on his yacht. He ran a sailing school and he took me to Elbe. From there it was to Florence, where I handed myself into the British Consulate and they sent me back. I heard later on that the other two boys had been blown out to sea in the dinghy, had spent weeks there and looked as if they had sent a month in the Gobi desert, all burnt to a crisp.' Two Jocks afloat in a boat in the Mediterranean with only a case of whisky? Truth is stranger than fiction.

Returning to the UK, he faced punishment by the army for his desertion. However, the tale impressed them as much as it did Henry and me. They even let him keep his 'Legionnaires Parachute Wings'. A spell in a military jail was the normal outcome. 'However, looking back I suppose I had the wow factor. Normally if you are court-martialled you are sent to Colchester, but they gave me the option to soldier on.' But it didn't prove as simple or painless as that, and he was marched in before the Regimental Commanding Officer. 'He looked at my file. Said that he didn't like my sense of humour as when I had went away I had sent him a postcard of a camel from the desert. The Commanding Officer gave me two months in the regimental jail.'

After that it was off to the Falklands. The Argentineans had invaded and the task force was mustering. Volunteers for a reconnaissance squad were sought. Forgetting the military dictum that you never volunteer for anything, John MacGregor did so. He had recollections of Germany where reconnaissance was about being out front in vehicles sheltered from the elements. When it was pointed out that there were few roads on the islands, he sought to withdraw his offer but that was declined. He says little about the conflict, other than that the soldiers he and his colleagues faced were not young conscripts in the regular army but battle-hardened Argentinean marines.

Returning from the war, he bought himself out of the army, went to college to study Hotel Management, and has been doing that ever since. A holiday romance in Spain with a Finnish girl saw him move to Helsinki. Eight years and three children later, he moved across the Gulf of Finland to Tallinn. Whilst in Finland he had set up his own pipe band. 'Five pipers, three drummers and two dancers. This is where the MacGregor came from. I played the pipes and was dressed in a kilt. The Finnish mentality was "your name is Hardie, you can't be Scottish". So it was a marketing gimmick. The advertising I did was in the name MacGregor. I never got asked if I was Scottish again.'

And now he's in Tallinn, settled in a new relationship with a Russian girl with whom he has two children. He also manages four bars and a restaurant in the city, including many of the most popular ones that Henry and I sample later on. His views on Scotland are blunt and to the point. He comments on the points made by John Ross, who we interviewed with him, lamenting the collapse in manufacturing. 'It's happening in every country in the world. I think if more people's eyes were opened in entrepreneurial ways and if people thought "I don't need to sit on my arse and feel sorry for myself", things would be better.'

He sees correlations between Scotland and Estonia. 'There are obvious differences but a lot of similarities. If they can do it here, it can work anywhere. Let's just get on and do it. Maybe it's because for hundreds of years Scotland has never had to. What does annoy me is Scottish people who I see complain about Scotland. I look at them and think, "if you don't like it, do something about it". I think Scots are more successful abroad than they are at home because they are not getting brought down with the rest of them. In Scotland the glass is always half empty not half full.'

Relaxing in one of his successful bars, Henry and I agree with a lot of his sentiments. It's time to stop the whingeing Jock syndrome. Scotland has a great future if it we take responsibility for it. With our own Parliament restored, there is no one to blame but ourselves if we don't, and every reason to believe that we can. John MacGregor epitomises that attitude. 'Wha's like us?'

Interviewed by Kenny MacAskill and Henry McLeish
August 2005

John Ross

ENTREPRENEUR, TALLINN

Making it in the Baltics

JOHN ROSS IS A PORT GLASGOW BOY, born and bred. His earliest memories of the town are a portrait of the area's industrial past: 'At 5pm every night the gates would open and 4,000 men would come out and you would be trampled on if you got in their way. Everyone's lives surrounded the shipyards. Then along came silicon glen after the shipyards closed – all operating up the valley. That lasted for 10 years; they're now gone, and now there is nothing.'

His father was a Stores Manager at Webster's Garage in the town and his mother also worked locally, as a French polisher. Attending a local primary school, he went on to Port Glasgow High School. Leaving there he worked for AMP, an electronics company in the town, going through college and serving his four year apprenticeship in mechanical production with them. In 1996, growing restless after 17 years with the company, he requested a transfer to China, only to be told that there was a better opportunity for him in Estonia. He accepted, comically admitting that he initially thought it was in Spain until a friend put him right. Hardly surprising, though, as it is only really known to people in Scotland through football – a nation Scotland are habitually drawn to play in international competitions – or politically, through its progress in the EU and elsewhere over recent years. He tells myself and Henry that he's not particularly interested in either, hence it wasn't on his radar screen. Rather than the Far East, it was Eastern Europe that beckoned – and he has never looked back since.

As is self-evident, he is making it in Estonia – appearing carefree and prosperous, and as he goes on to tell us, 'making it' matters to him. We meet him in the reception area of one of Tallinn's top hotels. The Olympia was built when Estonia was still part of the Soviet Empire, when Moscow hosted the Olympic Games in 1980. The yachting events took place in Tallinn with the hotel being constructed for the competition – though in typical soviet concrete modernist style. It has since been taken over by a major hotel chain in the Baltics, and been given a suitable makeover. Smart and pristine in a Scandinavian fashion, the walls are adorned with famous guests from Hillary Clinton through to the Scottish band Big Country.

Forty-one years old, lean and of average height, John Ross's glasses give him a learned and determined look. His accent is still distinctively west of Scotland, and he is friendly and easygoing. It's Henry's first visit to the area but I have been many times before. John Ross and I have mutual friends and acquaintances in the town. There is a significant Scottish expatriate community here, founded on business as well as football. The numerous trails through Tallinn by the Tartan Army have left foot soldiers behind, working in pubs and doing other odds and ends. Despite having no interest in football, he does see the Tartan Army as great ambassadors for the country, and I am glad to hear it. I have fond memories of trips there, even when the game did not take place, as in 1996, and Henry tells us that his son has enlisted in that illustrious regiment.

He still returns regularly to the Port Glasgow area. Business takes him back, and his mother still lives there, though she has moved along the banks of the Clyde to Kilmacolm since his father passed away. His brother, who works for a defence company, and his sister, a nurse, have both emigrated to Australia and it is indicative of the demographic problem facing the Inverclyde community, as the young and the skilled move away in search of jobs and opportunities. He still has fond memories of the area that go beyond the wistful recollection of its industrial heritage, though its current plight as the social effects of deindustrialisation bite grieves him. 'I have good memories of growing up. It was a nice environment with nice people. Latterly, it has gone downhill. There is huge unemployment in the area with drugs being a depressing problem.'

He might have ventured into the unknown when he came to Estonia but he has certainly done well for himself. When he came over a little under a decade ago, he was still on the AMF payroll. His job was to start up a manufacturing plant for them in the Baltic State, which itself had only a few years previously liberated itself from Soviet occupation that had existed since the Second World War. Ironically, the interview with Henry and I occurred on the 14th anniversary of its secession from the USSR. Photographs in the morning papers from the time showed tense and nervous young soldiers, armed and fearfully awaiting the actions of the dying and fragmenting USSR. Thankfully, the Red Army in Estonia stayed in barracks and the transition to independence was bloodless as Moscow was otherwise engaged with attempted coups by hardliners and ongoing political intrigue between Mikhail Gorbachev and Boris Yeltsin. Other Baltic states were not as fortunate, though none suffered the agony of either Hungary or Czechoslovakia decades before. Prior to the meeting, Henry and I had strolled through the town and visited the Museum of Occupations, which narrates the sad and difficult times faced by this fledgling Baltic state. Invaded by the Red Army in 1940, it suffered under the blitzkrieg of the Nazis, only to endure liberation by the Soviet Union that turned into nigh on 50 years of occupation. They were difficult times indeed and John Ross arrived when the nation was not even five years back on the international arena.

Difficult times they may have been, but both Estonia and John Ross faced up to them. The manufacturing plant was started for AMP and employed 300 people. In 1999, though, the company was bought over by TYCO who wanted to close the factory. He and three of his colleagues decided to start up on their own. Admitting to some good fortune, with the redundancy payment being sufficient to finance it, and TYCO giving work at the outset, it was still a big risk for him to put all his worldly cash into a venture in a foreign country, and especially one so young and whose future was still so uncertain. EU and NATO membership was a long way off at that time and the Russian Federation was neither stable nor friendly towards its neighbours. But, mirroring the country, he took a risk and has reaped the rewards. 'The company make electrical harnesses and cable assemblies and in the past six years we have grown and now employ 260 people. We have business in Scotland and elsewhere in the UK but most of our business is in Sweden. Ericsson is one of our biggest customers.' As well as success in the business, he's blossomed out of it. There are other business interests and he's obviously doing very well for himself, leaving us to check up on a new house that he is building for himself and his Russian-Estonian girlfriend on the outskirts of the city.

As well as making it on an individual basis in the Baltics, he is continuing to make it in manufacturing. He considers manufacturing to be very important, and thinks that Scotland neglects it at its peril. 'When I return to Scotland, I see new fitness centres and sports centres, but countries need manufacturing. I don't understand how we are going to survive without it.' Call us old-fashioned, but Henry and I can't help but agree. Growing up in Fife and West Lothian we have seen the demise of much of our industrial base. It is a global world now and Scotland is doing very well in financial services and other softer skills areas. Certainly, many of the old heavy industries are lost and gone never to return. However, we are not seeking nostalgia, but a solid economic base – and for that, manufacturing does matter.

John Ross is proud to be Scottish and still loves the country dearly. As with others interviewed before him, he sees his nationality as an asset. 'Being Scottish and working abroad is a brilliant thing. Scottish people have a great reputation around the world. We are seen as being friendly, approachable, good fun, and that works in our favour. This works particularly well to our advantage in Estonia, a small country with a big bad neighbour.' At that Henry looks at me and we can't help but smile. As well as returning for business or for family reasons, he takes his clients and his girlfriend on occasions. 'She has been to Scotland a few times and really enjoys it. Apart from the weather, of course. I have taken 20 customers or so over at different times for training. They love it, they love the scenery. We Scots take it for granted. Scots abroad are much more nationalistic and more proud of their country than those that remain.' I am struck that although he goes on to say that it's unlikely he will ever return and makes some points that are critical of Scotland, he never ceases talking about 'we' or 'us'. Estonia may be his new residence but Scotland will forever be his home.

As well as the natural beauty of the landscape, he feels that Scotland provides other things that he is conscious of. 'The resilience of the Scottish people is very evident. When Estonians here get a problem or a setback they are not quite sure how to handle it, whereas a Scot would be used to it and get on with it. What you find here is that people work very well up to a point. When the pressure comes, it just hits them and they collapse. Whereas in Scotland there is a different attitude. In poorer areas of Scotland in particular, people are very strong.' Some of that may be explained away by years of Soviet rule with risk aversion and almost robotic behaviour but there is still something about Scots that gets them back up when they have been knocked down. John Ross is one of them. Redundancy was a blow that was faced and overcome.

There is an area though where he thinks that Scotland has lost its attitude and previously instilled values. The work ethic is something that has been commented on by many interviewed for this book. It's clear that it has been a driving force for their individual success and for many of their compatriots. But it's an attitude he thinks has been lost by many. 'My memory of the area I was brought up in was that the work ethic was poor. People probably won't want to speak to me after they read this – people believed that the company they worked for owed them something, or if the company wasn't there then the government owed them something. They didn't want to work. Over here my job is so much easier because the work ethic is here – they desperately want to work. There is no social system like Scotland to fall back on. I am a production manager and was doing that job back in Scotland, and it was a grind getting people to work at weekends. It's different here.'

John Ross may worry what people think but Henry and I both think he has a point. Relaxing after the interviews over a drink, we chat matters through. Both of us have been brought up in a welfare state and still passionately believe in it. After all, we were born in it, treated, reared and educated by it, as were our parents before us, and our children after us. We are conscious, though, that a dependency culture has grown up over recent years and needs to be addressed. In believing this, we do not see ourselves as being heretical to our left-of-centre beliefs, but addressing a clear social problem. Individuals have rights in our society but they also have responsibilities. Working is one of them, as is accepting responsibility for your society and showing respect to others within it. In some areas of Scotland, working is abjured at best and scorned at worst. Expecting the council or the government to do everything is seen as an individual's right with no consequent duties upon themselves. It is seen in idleness and manifests itself in anti-social behaviour. We both think John Ross was right to point it out, and Scotland would do well to take it on board and recover the work ethic that drove us to past success.

What also concerns him is not just the attitude of some towards work but the obstacles he sees put in place that impede business. 'I think that running a business in the UK is very difficult as the government is always penalising people – taxing them enormously, whether on buildings, or water supply. If I reinvest in another company here in Estonia I don't pay tax. It's a brilliant thing to develop businesses. I don't understand why other countries don't do it. It's too expensive to run a business in Scotland. I think 40 per cent of the profit would go back to the government. In Estonia the flat rate of tax is 24 per cent. Where is the incentive? Back in the UK, accountants set up purely to advise on tax avoidance. In Estonia there is no way of avoiding it and its simple, so why bother.'

A competitive economy is sought by all. Politicians, political parties and economists are divided on the best way of achieving it, but achieve it we must. Henry and I don't have time to discuss it in detail and neither do we agree on everything nor even share all of John Ross's sentiments. However, we do recognise that as well as ensuring a change in culture from dependency to responsibility for individuals, we must seek to create an economic climate that builds a competitive base for Scotland and its businesses as a nation. Estonia is a small nation like Scotland, located on the periphery of Europe. It has not been blessed with many of the natural advantages given to Scotland. Yet it has not just made the best of its circumstances, but done exceptionally well despite the lack of them.

John Ross is almost the personification of that land. Despite the adversity of redundancy in a foreign land, he simply made the best of it and has done spectacularly well as a result of it. A permanent return for him might not be possible, but surely we can heed the points he makes and create an environment where he can expand his successful business back into his native land? He's making it in the Baltics – we need to 'make it' in Scotland by keeping a manufacturing base.

Interviewed by Kenny MacAskill and Henry McLeish
August 2005

Bob Creighton

PRESIDENT OF MENTORSHOP INC.,
CONNECTICUT

Networking in North America

BOB CREIGHTON IS A MAN TO KNOW. A mover and shaker, you get the impression that he knows everyone, and everyone knows him. Indeed, he was one of our first points of contact for compiling this book, and he provided us with many contacts. A highly personable man, he's pivotal in the Scottish-American community.

I meet this networker par excellence in a hotel in Edinburgh, where he tells me about his life. He grew up in the south side of Glasgow and smiles at the recollection. 'I think I was about 19 when I first met somebody who had a front garden. The only buildings I had known were tenements but I have many happy memories of a great family life. With five brothers and sisters it was lots of fun but never quiet.' Now, he lives on a five-acre estate in Connecticut and as President of MentorShop Inc., an international consultancy, he is a well-known and respected figure in the Scottish-American development arena. Becoming a US citizen in 1999 has not diminished his 'Scottishness' and he feels his native country should make more use of members of the Scottish diaspora. He says, 'My experience is that people flourish when they leave Scotland. It is probably something to do with environment but there are other factors at play. Whatever the reasons, I think it is a positive thing and it has helped create in the Scottish community overseas our country's greatest international asset. My three brothers and two sisters still live in west central

Scotland and they are very happy there. They have occasionally talked about moving overseas but by the time they came round to thinking about the possibility seriously they had other ties and were reluctant to uproot their families. The reality is that there are opportunities for people everywhere but for me – and this still strikes me as an odd thing really – it wasn't until I left Scotland that I was able to start appreciating them or feel confident enough in myself that I had something particular to offer.'

For Bob Creighton, the world started to open up in his own home city when a friend suggested he should go to university. 'I would have been quite happy as a youngster of 16 or 17 to leave school and enter the civil service as a clerk. To be honest, I had no great ambitions as a youngster and I think my family would have seen that as a good job for me at the time.

'When my pal said, "Why don't you go to university?" I don't think I knew what a university was and that's the truth. I ended up doing a degree in economics and history at Strathclyde. I had no real idea of what I was going to do with it; it was just two subjects I enjoyed. Many of my classmates went into teaching but in those days it wasn't a career that held any great appeal to me.' After a first job doing market research for the Weir Group, his career path was decided by an approach in his mid-twenties to join the Scottish Council (Development and Industry). 'The Council is a marvellous organisation; it is extraordinarily well connected and I enjoyed my time there immensely. That experience whetted my appetite to work internationally and I eventually transferred to Chicago in the mid 1980s to help the North of England's inward investment efforts. A couple of years later the then Scottish Development Agency asked me to join their office in Connecticut, again doing inward investment. It was an exciting time to be with the organisation, working on major projects with companies like Sun Microsystems and Compaq.' Despite the quality of the work and the exposure he was getting to business leaders from many different walks of life, he was becoming frustrated. 'I am not the most patient person in the world and on these big projects in the 1980s there was a long gap between the first meeting in the US and a successful company launch in

Scotland. In that sort of environment it is often difficult to measure your progress or your contribution. After five years in the field I felt it was time to move on. I had a notion to set up my own business even before I left Scotland but I was short on ideas and confidence and it really wasn't until I came to America that people started to encourage me. That re-enforcement helped give me the belief in myself and take the first step, something I haven't forgotten. At that time, I felt there was a lack of marketing support for Scottish companies in America and that was the initial direction I took – but it must be said this all pre-dated Scottish Development International."

Setting up his own business in the US to provide support, research, marketing and other services for Scottish interests, including occasionally for his old university, he quickly found that the opportunities for Scotland in America extended far beyond the immediate corporate world. 'Increasingly, we were being asked to create strategies for employment in Scotland and our focus gradually shifted from helping develop corporate links into the much wider realm of public policy. The fact is that Scotland has many challenges and whether you are working in education, community development, tourism, government or elsewhere, there are always opportunities to learn from others in helping shape your thinking. Today the thrust of our business is based on the conviction that by helping support and extend international linkages between different sectors of our two countries, we are playing a small part in helping establish Scotland as a genuine global player.'

With his work, he is constantly seeking to improve Scotland's place in the modern world by looking at what other communities have done to address particular issues. The elements that work are then packaged into a uniquely Scottish solution. 'We have also been working with others in Scotland and the US for the past few years on a students' leadership programme. The aim of that particular initiative – and it is something we would hope to see replicated in other sectors – is to improve employment skills and help create a new generation of globally connected leaders in Scotland.'

Bob specifically states that Scotland gave him values, which he has carried with him throughout his life. 'I remember there being a marvellous sense of "family" when I was a youngster. You are not aware of this at the time and only appreciate it when you look back. I believe Scotland also gave me a sound academic education; a good work ethic – an understanding that you don't get anything for nothing; and good values shaped by that basic Scottish sense of common decency. I think I would put these at the top of the list of skills that I took with me to the US.'

Although now an American citizen, will he ever return to Scotland? 'You never know, life is full of the unexpected. For the moment though I feel I have the best of both worlds since my work allows me the opportunity to travel between the US and Scotland every few weeks. Despite the great numbers who leave, Scots are not particularly footloose and when they put down roots somewhere they tend to stay. That certainly has been my experience of fellow Scots in the US. I think what you are seeing today – helped by greatly improved communications – is a truly global community of Scots who are much better informed about Scotland and who are committed to doing what they can in their own way to give something back.'

Moving away from Scotland has allowed him to see his native country with a new perspective. 'Too many of my preconceptions about the world beyond Scotland were wrong. For example, I went to America thinking it was an international cosmopolitan community. You only have to spend a little time in the US to realize that nothing could be further from the truth. Once you move away from the major population centres – and sometimes even within the larger metro areas – it is actually a very insular society.'

'I don't know if it is a particular Scottish attribute or not, but when I came to the US I had a tremendous fear of failure; I didn't want to let anyone down. If I was to be honest, it is a fear that is still with me to this day partly because there are so few safety nets in America. I knew I wanted to succeed of course but I think my initial ambitions were probably tempered by that Scottish character trait that tells you that you shouldn't "get above yourself". Fear of failure won the day though. That and the encouragement I was being given in America by friends and colleagues to raise my sights and ambitions. The fact is – and without actually realising it at the time – I was being coached to be more enterprising from the moment I set foot in the US. When I think about it now, that combination of work ethic, fear of failure and the sense of responsibility we have to other people probably goes a long way to explain the great contributions Scots have made overseas for generations.

'It is very easy to concentrate on the negatives but we are getting better and I firmly believe we are witnessing some remarkable and very positive changes in Scotland today.'

He believes devolution is the most important thing to have happened to Scotland in recent years, and although the media attention focuses on MSPs and the cost of the building, this has taken attention away from the fact that many real and dramatic changes are occurring. 'It is easier perhaps to see this when you are viewing the country from the outside. Devolution has prompted us to look at Scotland in a new way and brought about a period of self-analysis. Most of this has been positive. We are becoming much more active today in encouraging people to be enterprising; being all you can be regardless of your career path and making best use of whatever talents you have got. There is still a long way to go of course, but we are moving forward and we have a lot to be proud of. Devolution has helped us initiate something of a national audit and prompted us to look more closely at our strengths and weaknesses but it is an evolving process and, again, we have a long way to go.'

He is adamant that Scotland should not use the excuse that it is a small nation for not being able to tackle the issues and problems it faces. 'When I look at other small nations, whether Scandinavian or Irish or whatever, it is clear that we too we have many issues that are deeply embedded in our culture that are preventing us from realising our full potential. Devolution has helped highlight Scotland's many strengths; it has certainly raised the country's visibility overseas. But we also have to be willing to acknowledge that there are factors at play in our society that continue to hold us back. If we are to become the "great small country" that we aspire to be, we need to talk about these issues honestly. Traditionally our policy making tended to shy away from that approach and more often than not there was a tendency to turn a blind eye to some very real blights on our society.

Let's face it, sectarianism has been rife in some parts of Scotland for far too long and events of recent years have done away with the lie that we don't have any problem with race relations. The same might be said about other social issues in terms of health, law and order, and so on. The new Parliament has created a platform to discuss these types of problems and this openness is already influencing policy making. But there is still so much more to be done and some of the challenges involve issues that are complex and things that people aren't particularly comfortable talking about.'

It is apparent to him, from an overseas perspective, that there is a culture of dependency in Scottish society. 'We have always rightly taken great pride in the fact that we take care of those who cannot take care of themselves. But there is also the matter of personal responsibility. When you look at the socially deprived communities in America, more often than not it isn't money that effects change; change for the better typically only happens when the people in the local community are empowered and take responsibility. Change the mindset and the community will improve; it is a big challenge but it is the only real solution. We are a small country that fights above its weight and we are less inclined today to brush some of the less palatable features of life in Scotland under the carpet.'

However, he believes the future is bright for Scotland, especially if we seek advice from the diaspora. 'It goes against the grain for most Scots to ask for help in shaping our future but we are getting better at doing it. To my mind, that's where the Scottish diaspora has something to offer. The global Scot community wants to play its part.' On the whole, he is positive. 'Many of the things that prompted me to move overseas don't exist any more. I know many other Scots working internationally who feel the same way. From where I am sitting, there is a real vibrancy and energy about Scotland today. People are much more positive and it is those individuals who will be successful in Scotland, for Scotland.'

Interviewed by Henry McLeish
September 2005

Alan Esslemont
DIRECTOR OF TELEVISION
FOR TG4, GALWAY

The Confident Celt

THERE HAVE BEEN MANY STRANGE and unusual tales in this book so far and this one equally so. How does a Scotsman from an Anglophone community in the North East become fluent in Irish and Director of Television for the Irish language channel? It's a unique story, and given the debate about a Scottish Six, I am intrigued to hear from someone who is in charge of the strategic scheduling, presentation and acquired rights for a television station that runs almost continuously. When some in Scotland doubt that we can run a news programme I am proud to point out that I know a Scot who can run a whole television station.

A decade ago an Irish language channel, TG4, was launched and Alan Esslemont joined it. Now Director of Television, he travels all over the world sourcing programmes and acquiring rights. 'I am in charge of the presentation and the look of the channel. To a certain extent what you see is what we do. The way the schedule is put together and the way our brand comes across.'

Though provided with funding by the Irish government, the channel is required to earn additional revenue to survive. The channel is for the Irish language but deliberately screens programmes in English as well as Irish. 'If you don't have national resonance with your people then the native language becomes irrelevant. But for the communities that speak Irish daily – we also have to relate to them, we have to be special for them.'

When I switch on the channel in the hotel in the morning I find *EuroNews* being broadcast, in addition to an American police drama I had seen late the night before. It was in English but was new to me. Other English language programmes such as *The* OC are also on the schedule, as are live transmissions from the Dail, the Irish Parliament. Children's cartoons, a popular soap, documentaries and exclusive sports events, all in Irish, have become popular even with an Anglophone audience in Ireland. The channel aims for broad appeal not a narrow market. It seeks to promote the Irish language as a normal part of Irish life rather than making it exclusive.

Alan Esslemont and I go back a long way, first meeting at Edinburgh University in 1976. Two state school boys from 'small town' Scotland, we were somewhat overawed by the big city and the company of confident English public school boys. He was down from Brechin to study French and German, and I was through from Linlithgow to study Law. We became immediate kindred spirits and neither time nor distance has faded our friendship.

I fly out to Galway to meet him. Landing at the airport I take a taxi to my hotel. The driver has a south London accent and he tells me that his parents are from here and he has moved over to join them since they retired. It's symbolic of the return of the diaspora and the revival of this community, never mind Ireland as a whole.

I had first gone to Galway in 1986 for Alan's wedding. Emigration was the curse of Ireland and the west coast in particular. I vividly recall a billboard with an election poster for Fianna Fail that simply had an Irish passport and the words 'There has to be a better way'. It spoke volumes. The town was on its knees.

But all that has changed. Galway is booming: the median age is significantly lower than Scotland and a walk around before I go to bed sees a young town at play. Quay Street and High Street are jumping – and it's a Thursday night, not the weekend. I ask Alan later whether it's the students at the university but he tells me they have not returned as yet. These are just the locals. The contrast between this and a similar sized city in Scotland (such as Inverness) is palpable.

Alan now lives in the west of Connemara, in a village on the very edge of Europe, the Atlantic lapping at its shores. Irish is not just the medium of his work but the language of his home, with his wife Maire and their five children all native speakers.

His office is local, even if the work is global, with TG4 located nearer to Galway city but still in the Gaeltacht. I ask what his children think of Scotland, as they visit regularly.

'They feel they are Irish with a Scottish father. They speak Irish at home. They are interested in Scotland but feel a little bit superior. That's especially at football but also with the strong economy here. They always say that when they go back to Scotland the streets are full of old people. To a certain extent I think if you walk about Ireland it is full of young people. They all have self-confidence. It is something I see in our own kids as well. When they go to Scotland they don't feel it is as good a country as theirs. They feel they have more for them in Ireland.'

Alan Esslemont was born in Braemar. Both his parents are from the Deeside area and neither they nor any recent or remembered relative spoke Gaelic: it was an Anglophone family, never mind community.

Times were hard in Braemar and when he was six the family moved south and over the hills to Angus. His mother was a teacher at Aldbar and Careston Primary Schools and they lived in the schoolhouses attached. His father was a butcher and then a meat inspector at an abattoir in Brechin. Initially taught by his mother he recollects being belted by her but nothing further being said as they moved from the schoolroom to the adjacent schoolhouse. His last years in primary saw him move to a school in Brechin and from there to the high school in the town where he was Dux in Arts.

His childhood memories are of a rural community where farm life played a big part, even if his family were not themselves farmers. It was a rather innocent time in an area that had not changed much since the 1950s. He describes it as 'being in a bit of a time warp'.

His parents are now retired and have moved to Crieff – 'Dad has become expert at bridge playing but Mum has learned, and now teaches, elementary Gaelic.' He has a brother in the west of Scotland who is a town planner, and another in banking in northern England. Neither has learned Gaelic, let alone Irish.

He had decided to study French as it was his best subject and, despite his modesty, he is a gifted linguist. In his third year at university he went to France on an exchange year. He went to North Brittany where he met people who asked him about Scotland and the Gaelic language. Whilst there he met not just Breton speakers but Irish speakers. On his journey back from Brittany he passed through Ireland and travelled on his own road to Damascus. In Feeney's bar in the High Street he was surrounded by Irish speakers and was asked if, as a Scot, he spoke Gaelic. He decided there and then that he had to learn more about Scotland and its language.

Returning to complete his degree in French he also commenced a course in Gaelic. After graduating he went to Switzerland to work in a café and, as with others, simply improved his skiing. After nine months he returned home, intent on travelling around Europe. Tired from the journey home, he instead gave his brother his InterRail ticket and went to Skye to do a course in Gaelic. Thereafter, Alistair and Margaret MacKinnon, who ran the Post Office in Sleat, allowed him to park his father's caravan on their land and he got a job knitting jerseys on Sir Iain Noble's estate. The MacKinnons and his workmates all helped him learn the language and after two years he returned to Edinburgh University's Celtic department. A two year course was completed successfully in a year and whilst sitting in the exam room the Professor of Gaelic, Willie Gillies, asked him if he would like to go to Galway to teach Gaelic. He immediately accepted. He had loved his time in Skye and had become committed to the Gaelic language.

He anticipated a sojourn in Ireland and a return to Gaelic and the island. But in Galway he fell in love with an Irish lass, so Irish and Ireland it was to be.

His initial contract at Galway was renewed but, as with many children of teachers, he did not wish to teach. He was doing some part time work when he saw an advert for an audio visual course in Tralee. He applied successfully for it, surprising folk, then as now, by being a Scot fluent in Irish. After that he obtained some work for the Irish national broadcaster Radio Telefis Éireann (RTE) before moving to Telegael in Connemara where he continues to live.

RTE was the first successful Irish language media company in the west of Ireland and he stayed there for seven years. I had seen him at his work there many years ago but he took me back with him to visit them last year. The firm was celebrating having been nominated for two Emmys and having won one. The trophy was passed around and indeed had been, I was told, in the local pub the night before. I delight in asking broadcasters here in Scotland how many Emmys they have won and why lads from a village in Connemarra can do it while they cannot even run a news bulletin. From there it was onto TG4, where he has been for a decade.

It's a glorious day in Ireland when he comes to meet me at my hotel and we adjourn to the pub. Walking up the High Street we enter the same Feency's Bar that proved so pivotal in his life's journey. Irish theme bars are universal now – in our global world they rival Starbucks and McDonalds in ubiquity – but this is a distinctively Irish bar, not a plastic paddy imitation. It has a local feel and an individual air. Though Irish is commonly spoken in the pub I, by necessity, order in English and there is no animosity or hostility to the use of it or indeed to my being Scottish. It's a place that appears confident in its own identity: neither flaunting its Irishness nor resenting the use of English.

I ask him about the differences between Scots and Irish Gaelic. He briefly tells me that there are about one hundred common words that are different but almost all of the other words are the same, although the grammar can change quite a lot, and he confesses to some temporary difficulty when switching from one to the other. As with others in this book he is too modest: I know from speaking to many in the Gaelic community in Scotland that he is highly respected for his knowledge of the language. Though neither a native speaker nor even resident in the land he is extremely learned in it and masterful of it.

Despite the distance travelled in his life's journey he sees his roots in Scotland. 'At the end of the day there is a certain Scottishness that formed your community. There is the work ethic and to a certain extent attention to detail. Even though I didn't do science at school, the way I was taught languages showed me how logical systems can help make sense of a very complex world.'

Ireland is his home now but he remains committed to and concerned about Scotland. He has seen improvements in recent years but does fret over the loss of culture and the lack of confidence. Telling me what he thinks is the major difference between Scotland and Ireland he says, 'The Irish are multilateral. My own job brings me into contact with people all over the world. We see ourselves as a centre. We conduct our own business. We talk to Scots, we talk to the French. It's all about contact. Whereas in Scotland if I had a job in television the contacts would be within Scotland and then London would do your international contacts. I do take that and apply it to the whole of society. Scotland is just at the end of the train track to London. It is important but it doesn't have a clear picture. Whereas in Ireland you are in the centre of a global network.' Telegael's Emmy and the fact that the rights to show Scottish Premier League football on television have been acquired by a very small Irish media company, Setanta, epitomise that.

Ireland has changed a great deal since he first arrived. 'From the eighties onwards the whole industry in Ireland has been at the centre of the network rather than being a spur off the London network, if you like.' He mentions Charles Haughey, the former Irish Taoiseach, and Alan Dukes, the Fine Gael leader of the time. 'You have to think multilateral, global and world class. You need to do that to compete. It took 10 to 15 years. Looking around not just Galway but all of Ireland, they have done it. But it wasn't always like that.' I remind him of his wedding and the election poster. 'The big thing I have learned from Ireland is that things can change. When I came across in 1984 I would say that I was the only person coming into the country. Everyone else was leaving. As soon as people turned 16, 17 or 18 they flew to America. I remember a whole congregation coming out of church in Boston speaking Irish as they had all gone across. Ireland between 1984 and 1990 was in a dreadful state. No job prospects. People believed the country was banjaxed. So things can change, but they can only change with vision.'

In media terms he sees a difficulty for Scots trying to emulate TG4, Telegael or Setanta. 'The only way you can compete globally in UK television is to be in London, whereas in Ireland you can compete globally from Galway and we do. The one disadvantage is that television here is less well resourced. To a certain extent that allows people in the regions in Britain to take a slightly snooty view of the media in Ireland. If you look at the work produced though there is no reason for that attitude of superiority.' That seems clear to me. Scottish television channels may be well-funded, but they are far from globally competing.

'The one big difference between Scotland and Ireland is that Irish people are very confident. It is the success of the cultural projects which were kicked off years ago. Projects such as the native games, the music and the language. That was the basis for Ireland. Now these three cultural aspects have been linked to a successful economy. For the first time since the English came to Ireland, the Irish have a successful economy and they manage to link this successful economy with their own culture.'

I ask him for his take on Scotland and it is incisive but contains a stark warning. 'I don't see why Scotland can't emulate Ireland. It has to be itself but it could be a lot healthier if it was more culturally active and had more desire to look at things globally and look outside Scotland. At the end of the day, if they don't, Scotland will become a retirement home.' The hopes of Alan Esslemont or the fears of his children are the choices facing Scotland. However, the maxim he quoted of multilateral, global and world class seems one worth adopting. Rather than being big players in a British league there is a chance to be a major competitor in our own right on the international stage.

Interviewed by Kenny MacAskill
September 2005

Professor Fiona Davidson

PROFESSOR OF GEOSCIENCES AT
THE UNIVERSITY OF ARKANSAS

Arran to Arkansas

FIONA DAVIDSON SPENT HER EARLY YEARS on Arran, also known as 'Scotland in miniature' because it encompasses so many of the qualities of the Scottish mainland, from mountains and glens to lowland pastures, golf courses and palm trees. Because of that island background she feels, more than most exiles, the pull of homeland and a special sense of kinship with the islanders she left behind. Now, as Professor of Geosciences at the University of Arkansas, she says: 'Being Scottish in the US is a big plus factor. In fact, to use an Americanism, it's cool to be Scottish!' After 20 years in the United States, she still recalls the pangs of parting. 'There is no real gulf between Scots who go abroad and those who stay at home. Scots who stay have the same qualities, the same ambitions and they want to be successful; and Scots who go abroad are not running away from anything. Often, they leave their home country because they want to do some particular thing they cannot do there.'

I meet Fiona in Fayetteville in Arkansas, on the campus of the university at which she is based. Arkansas is a state which offers a different side of America to the conventional stereotype. It is also home to Walmart, the world's biggest retailer. Today is a beautiful October day, and Fayetteville is full of colour with its trees and greenery. It is a pleasure to meet Fiona here. She is the archetypal 'Scots lass in a high-powered job', who I previously did some teaching with in America around five years ago. I still remain impressed by her dynamism and enthusiasm.

Born on the Scottish mainland in January 1964, Fiona says in her soft west-coast Scottish accent, 'It meant I had my first Calmac trip when I was about three days old. At that time, and indeed now, no children are born in Arran unless it is an absolute emergency. Nowadays, that ferry journey back to Arran is so special for me.' The family lived on Arran until she was nine, when work took her father to Newcastle and Fiona says that childhood in the close-knit community created connections which still matter to her. 'Arran was a great place for a wee kid. We lived very close to the primary school where the roll was so small that three classes were taught together. Most of the family I grew up with was on my mum's side, whose ancestors go back to the mid eighteenth century. My dad's family have been on Arran since 1679, so I grew up with cousins, second cousins, third cousins, even fourteenth cousins.

However, living away from the central cities, Fiona found that youngsters were restless on Arran. 'A lot of my friends had a hard time there as teenagers because there is not a lot to do. Most of them moved away for one reason or another, just like we ended up doing. What tended to happen in Arran was that the girls in particular moved away because it was harder for them to get work and have careers. A lot of the boys stayed behind, learned a trade and now get work amongst the increasingly retired population. The older former islanders move back and re-populate, many buying former estate houses, just as my mother and father have done.'

For Fiona, however, the Arran connection was never really broken. 'Even while studying for my geography degree at Newcastle, I worked in a hotel, my uncle's chemist shop and in a bar all during summer vacations.' After studying at Nebraska for a graduate degree and a PhD, Fiona decided to stay on in the US and settled in Arkansas in 1992. 'They offered me a job with lots of money before anyone else did! It was also by far the most attractive environment that I had seen. It is hotter in Arkansas in the summer than Scotland but the vegetation is very similar – we have a backyard full of brambles, there are the green hills and I live in a small town where I can walk to work. The scale is very human and feels European to a certain degree.'

She is now Associate Professor of Geography in the Geosciences Department and Director of European Studies, co-ordinating an inter-disciplinary programme of geography, political science and international relations. In 2004, she married Tom Paradise, a fellow-professor of geosciences. She confesses: 'Although I have been in the US for 20 years, it never quite fits. Coming back to Scotland is like putting on an old jacket, you slide in and you are invisible, even with my accent – although it does gets hard hearing "you are not from here are you?".'

She has no doubt of the identity which Scotland gave her. 'It has always been there and contributes to who I am and where I come from. I never have any self-doubt about my place in the world. I find this is well-received and there is a lot of warmth for Scots. Also, as an academic, I feel part of a great history which is not so much about battles won and lost but things like the Enlightenment, Adam Smith, Robert Burns and the great periods of achievement, social and technological advance and intellectual activity in Scotland. Most of all, I will always have the strength of community and family, a lot of which comes from my island upbringing on Arran. I have lived in England, Hong Kong and the US and never lost it. That strength makes you self-reliant when you are abroad because you always know there is somewhere you belong. My upbringing also gave me the Scottish work ethic that if you worked hard, you would get your just reward – however, there can be good and bad to that if it means over-emphasis on work. That strong work ethic, self-reliance and confidence in your identity – these are qualities on which Scotland can build. Perhaps the difference is that those who leave are prepared to take a few more risks. They have a different perspective and there is such a thing as being too comfortable.

She sees the lack of confidence and optimism as a complete contrast to the attitudes of Americans. 'There is a lot in the Scottish culture that does not breed confidence. The highest form of praise is: "It's no' bad." It could actually be "brilliant" but we must never be allowed to get above ourselves. That and the "kent yer faither" attitude can be depressing. We can come across as cold and emotionless, part of the Calvinistic background of repressed emotions and suppressed feelings. Why do Scots always have to be harder? There can also be too much appearance of pessimism. In Scotland, the tendency is to see the glass as half-empty and it can only be drained; in the US, it's half-full and that means it can still be filled to the brim. Of course, in the US there are huge problems but there is still a mentality that they can make things better.

'We have to beware that some exiles justify their absence by criticising Scotland. I love Scotland in a way that could not be bettered by anyone living in Scotland. I suppose I'm a small 'n' nationalist. The Parliament is a new focus for Scottish life; it is good in itself, but it should also be the catalyst for further change. It should eventually help Scots become a bit more ambitious, more confident and more prepared to renew themselves. Scotland is a very welcoming place and the idea of attracting immigrants is not only good for Scotland but also for the workplaces.'

Like others, Fiona is only too aware of the problems of dependency, sectarianism and violence in Scotland. 'Ways have to be found to tackle the problems of alcohol and drugs and I welcome the programme to tackle sectarianism. The sentimental view cannot ignore the harshness of life in many social areas, drink, drugs, knife crime and deprivation. The US has these problems, but Scotland has a different kind of violence – a lot of it just seems to be so gratuitous where people go out for a night's entertainment, carrying knives and other weapons and are prepared to use them.'

She believes that in the future we must find the right mix between positives and negatives. 'As a nation, we have to be less negative, to want success, celebrate achievements and in the process take more risks.'

Fiona Davidson is proud of her native country and has valued views on its future. This is not just in words, but also in deeds: she cooked as well as hosted the first Burns' Supper in Arkansas. Now that is dedication to Scotland's cause!

Interviewed by Henry McLeish
October 2005

Bill Elder

CHAIRMAN OF SILICON
SEMICONDUCTOR TECHNOLOGIES,
CALIFORNIA

The Possil Boy

POSSILPARK IS ONE OF THE POOREST AREAS not just in the city of
Glasgow, but all of Scotland. Synonymous with deprivation, stories
concerning it are more likely to relate to the violence that stalks it
and the drug problem that afflicts it, rather than the triumphs of one
of its sons. When I heard of a hugely successful Scot who hailed from
there and was immensely proud of the area that nurtured him, I was
keen to meet him.

Bill Elder's name had been given to me by many as an émigré
Scot to meet. With limited funds and constraints on time I had initially decided against contacting him, as West Coast America seemed
a trip too far. But when a journey to the Golden State was arranged
it was the perfect opportunity to meet him.

I had spoken to him briefly before I departed. I cold-called him
on his mobile phone after the number had been provided by a mutual acquaintance. It was answered by a distinctive west of Scotland
accent. He was friendly and considerate, despite never having met
me nor indeed knowing the first thing about me. He listened to what
I had to say and was happy to oblige despite having to ask my name
again at the end of the call. Information was e-mailed over to him
and arrangements made to contact him on arrival.

Again my ignorance of American geography and underestima-
tion of the size of California showed through. Landing in Los

243

Angeles, I imagined a short journey to meet him. Closer investigation showed otherwise. He lives and works in Silicon Valley near San Jose, a six hour drive or at least an hour flight each way. Having endured an 11 hour flight I was suffering from cabin fever. With a return flight to Scotland beckoning the thought of either was too much to bear. Accordingly, a conference call was arranged. It might be ironic to travel across an ocean and a continent to conduct a telephone interview with me in my hotel room in Los Angeles and him in his office in Sunnyvale, but it was worth it.

Though spawned from humble roots in Possilpark, Bill Elder is now a big fish in a big pond. In 1982 he founded Genus Inc., a semiconductor company in Silicon Valley. They pioneered new manufacturing technologies into semiconductor fabrication, increasing the speed and density of the chips. In 1988 it became a public company and by 1995 had a turnover of $100 million. The firm has recently merged with a German giant, Aixtron, and he holds the position of Chairman of Silicon Semiconductor Technologies, operating out of Sunnyvale, California as well as Aachen, Germany. He also sits on the executive board of Aixtron in Germany.

Corporate baron he may be, braggart he is not. Bill Elder not only retains the accent of his upbringing but is proud of his background, retaining fond memories of Possilpark and an immense pride in Glasgow. Born in Denmark Street in 1938 he returns to Scotland regularly and takes his sons to see the area he grew up in. The old houses may be gone and the area is subdued but he detects a vibrancy in the city that did not exist in the post-war era he was brought up in.

Despite his current substantial personal wealth, as with others brought up in that area there was no silver spoon. His father was a supervisor in a local factory and his mother was a housewife caring for him and his brother. He attended the local primary school, followed by Possil High School. His father was from a big family and it was a close-knit community with numerous cousins in close proximity. His grandmother lived in nearby Hamiltonhill, so there were large Sunday family gatherings albeit in the constrained space of a Glasgow tenement. Being a war child he experienced rationing, retaining a fond memory of queuing for sweets and being able to get whatever you wanted once it ended. Scots still retain that sweet tooth till this day.

With the family moving to the new town of Linwood he found work in the Rootes car factory that had opened there. The factory and town were interlinked and its closure was to have a serious effect upon the whole community. However, he prospered there. Attending night school at Paisley Technical College, the company subsequently allowed him additional day release. It was to be to their mutual benefit and he graduated with a degree in Industrial Engineering. He has retained a connection with the College receiving an Honorary Doctorate from what is now the University of Paisley in 1995, lecturing on occasion at the institution on entrepreneurship and establishing a scholarship to assist those with the entrepreneurial spirit if not the necessary funds.

The Scotland of the sixties he found to be a desolate place even if warm in spirit. The economic problems meant that many were leaving for pastures new and he was no different. He had a yearning for the USA and in 1968 he emigrated there. He landed in San Francisco with neither family to support him nor work to go to. Indeed whilst waiting for his visa he had taken a job at Upper Clyde Shipbuilders thinking it would assist in gaining employment in the shipyards on west coast America only to find on his arrival that the industry was in decline and the work heading for Korea. However, within four weeks he had found employment and it has been onwards and upwards since then. His first job was with Blue Shield, a Californian company who dealt with the Medicare scheme for the elderly and Medicaid scheme for the poor. He was employed as an industrial engineer to try to break the gridlock grinding the scheme to a halt. Successfully integrating the computer systems with the health care scheme, he was managing 250 people within six months and became a director within two years.

He hankered, though, to return to manufacturing. Silicon Valley was just beginning to develop and he sensed not only an opportunity but what he felt was the future. Starting out as a manufacturing engineer with Fairchild, he was with them for 10 years, culminating as manager of the plant in Hong Kong, employing 1,300 people. In 1979 his former boss had left and gone into the semiconductor equipment and asked him to join. He accordingly moved to Kasper Instrument, a division of Eaton Corporation, as Vice President of Operations, gaining promotion to Division President within a year. Wanting to strike out on his own he left and formed Genus Inc. in 1982.

Hugely successful in business he has neither forsaken his roots nor other social commitments. He was appointed Britain's first ever Honorary Consul for Silicon Valley. That latter role had a remit of seeking to broaden and increase business relationships with counterpart businesses in the UK. As well as being Chairman of the Silicon Valley British American Business Council, he is also a patron of the Scottish North American Business Counci, and a founding member of the Global Scot network. All that and he's married with four sons and living in the San Jose area in a house where the guest cottage is bigger than the tenement flat he grew up in. He is ideally placed to comment on many matters and particularly business and entrepreneurship in Scotland.

As with others throughout this book he credits Scotland with providing him with a 'tremendous education'. But he feels it was more than just that. 'A tenacity and the desire to be the best one can be sums up the Scots. It's a bent I have given to my own boys, that they have to work and dedicate themselves.' A big football fan and a Rangers supporter to this day he uses a sporting analogy to define what he sees as an equally Scottish trait that is a drawback. 'Scots individually do well. At teams sports Scotland has never done anything on the world stage. We are more focussed on individual talents than collective team work.'

That leads him to contrast the fortunes of Silicon Valley and Silicon Glen. The former has gone from strength to strength whilst that latter has stumbled and fallen along the way. He believes the difference lies in risk-taking and the availability of venture capital. He tells me a story that he views as apocryphal about the situation. Giving a lecture at Paisley University he told his audience how he had needed $7 million to start up his own company and actually got

$9.5 million, receiving it in two stages of $5 million then $4.5 million. A young man in the audience said he didn't believe him and explained how he had tried to start up his own company in Scotland but had needed two loans and his house mortgaged to the bank. Bill Elder explains to me, 'if I fail then I fail. It hurts my pride but I am still here and I don't lose my home. That is one of the main differences between Scotland and America. Venture capital here is much more risk-taking than the banking community in Scotland. That is why Silicon Valley has really taken off and Silicon Glen didn't. Scottish venture capitalists are less risk-taking. When National Semiconductor, Hyundai or any others were moving into Silicon Glen they were driven by American companies going into manufacturing with very little spin-off. There was no venture capital. There was no infrastructure to allow it to grow.'

That failure is made all the more tragic when he correctly points out that the banking and funding institutions did and do exist here. 'All the venture capital in Scotland was going outwith and being invested elsewhere. Some entrepreneurs have driven through it but if business needs large capital investment to get off the ground then just forget it – it just won't happen in Scotland. That needs to change.'

That said, he sees room for optimism in Scotland. Change is happening and he sees this embodied in his native city, where he feels there is now a bounce and vibrancy that contrasts with the gloom and despondency when he left it. As well as changes he sees opportunities and in particular mentions research at Edinburgh University and spin-offs as a result in photonics which he sees as an emerging industry with talented Scots. Tragically, when I come to write this chapter the business pages in the newspaper carry a story on the demise of Photonic Materials based in Strathclyde Business Park, Bellshill. The company had 'gone into provisional liquidation after apparently running out of cash. Photonic, which employed 25 people, including seven PhD holders, originally intended to develop optical crystals for use in fibre optic communication components.' The story went on to narrate that 'an unnamed US based oil and gas business bought the company's unique oil well logging materials technology.'

I know that the comments Bill Elder makes are sentiments shared not simply by Henry and me but much of the business sector in Scotland. But when will we ever learn? How many jobs must go and ideas be lost before we change? And change there must be if the opportunity in photonics and other technologies are not to be passed up by us as we have done before.

He sees the need for a cultural as structural change in Scotland. 'In terms of changing Scotland, it is the psyche. There is a problem in that if you meet a friend in Scotland they will say things are "not bad". If you meet a friend in San Francisco they will say things are "fantastic". Clearly they are neither bad nor fantastic all the time but it is all about mentality and mindset. Scotland has an inferiority complex about itself. It should feel a lot better about its people.' I totally agree. We do need to feel better about ourselves and our own.

He sees the Scottish diaspora as an opportunity for Scotland, and he is well-placed to know. The corporate boardrooms and technical laboratories he knows are festooned with Scots, whether in the USA or elsewhere. Giving them the chance to return and contribute is vital but they will need a financial inducement and not just a reliance on national sentiment to return. 'We have to look at what China and others have done. China did it when it wanted to get into various sectors. The Chinese sought out talented people who had left and encouraged them to come back. They looked at the Chinese community abroad, they gave them big incentives to go back home.'

As with others, he sees the need for Scotland to get focused and then take action. 'If you have an understanding and a belief that something can work, then you do what is necessary to achieve it. To get the technical and managerial skills back – getting them back, whatever it takes. Identify the industry. Identify the materials. Korea and Taiwan did it. They gave signing on fees. We do that for a footballer. Would you give £1 million to a CEO of a potential company? Probably not, but you would do it for a footballer. Its industry that drives the economy and we don't invest to the extent we should do.'

Those comments are both astute and an indictment of current Scottish society. We have failed to invest in our industry and in our key people. Fat cat salaries are under a great deal of scrutiny and criticism. Exactly as our football clubs have been prepared to spend top dollar to bring in star players so must Scotland PLC. There is something bizarre about Scotland that the wages paid to a star footballer are unquestioned but those to a high-flying CEO inevitably criticised.

Top dollar salaries and signing on fees will be needed to lure back the talented diaspora. When you compete in a global economy you need to pay the global rate. Some will complain, but if we want them to come home we will need to pay the market rate and perhaps a bit more, not rest on their nostalgia or altruism. There are understandable worries about the growing gap between the rich and poor in our society, but a healthy and vibrant economy is a prerequisite to eradicating poverty, and talented people are vital to that aim. The wealth gap is a matter for fair taxation, not a salary cap. As long as they pay their fair share of taxes when they are back, then what is the problem? If Communist China can do it, so can Calvinist Scotland.

Bill Elder has risen high but remains a Possil boy, and proud of it. Now resident in the States he will not be returning but, as he says, if we got our act together – 'boy, Scotland could really motor'. It's time for Scotland to play as a team.

Interviewed by Kenny MacAskill
October 2005

Irene Dunlop

PA TO BILL ELDER, CALIFORNIA

A Lanarkshire Child

WHILE DISCUSSING THIS BOOK and its participants with Bill Elder, I lament the gender imbalance. Whilst it's possible to rationalise and perhaps even excuse it, it remains regrettable. So I enquire if he knows any Scottish women resident in California that I could interview. He immediately suggests his personal assistant Irene Dunlop, telling me with obvious pride that she's a Glasgow girl.

Following my initial speculative approach to him on his mobile phone, I agreed to call him at his office. That sees me being put straight through to Irene Dunlop, his PA of several years. Her Scottish accent is clear and distinctive and her voice warm and reassuring, especially when the difficulties caused by my naivety come to light. She remains unfazed by my geographical ineptitude and assists in working out a solution. I begin to understand why many American Scots have described their accent as a Caledonian attribute and an asset in America. Irene herself acknowledges that. 'The accent helps me out here, it does me lots of favours.' Even in the UK it's still prized by many organisations and particularly call centres despite the drift of such jobs to the Indian sub-continent. The sound of a warm Scots accent is a pleasure and a comfort. I have never cast eyes on her, but her soothing voice painted a very favourable picture.

Having sorted the arrangements out for her employer she indicates willingness in principle to participate, though as with others she questions what she can contribute. As I am to find out it is a great deal. Her perspective of ordinary life is as valid and interesting as the view from the boardroom or corridors of power. As a young working mother, her reflections on her childhood in Lanarkshire provide a contrast with her toddler's situation in the Bay Area today. Life as an office worker in the west of Scotland in comparison to that in the USA is fascinating. Quality of life figures highly for many emigrants in their decision to leave, and it is factors such as the ones she comments on that we also need to address. There is more to life than work and more to aspire to as a country than simply a competitive economy, no matter how important they may be. However, it transpires that the weekend I am in Los Angeles sees her away for a short break with her husband and young child. I am in fact back in Scotland before I am able to catch up with her.

Conscious of the time difference, I wait until early evening to call her. Waiting in my office it provides an opportunity to rummage through papers I had picked up in the USA. Flicking through the *Los Angeles Times* from the Monday of my departure the sports pages carry a banner headline and substantial report on Dario Franchitti's victory in the Californian Indy Car Race. The article gave a full account of the race and acknowledged him as a Scotsman of Italian descent. Sadly, this was not mirrored by equal praise and reporting back in his native land. Dario Franchitti has grasped an opportunity given to him as a youngster in Scotland and flourished at home and abroad. He was perhaps fortunate to have the chance to participate in motor sports as a result of a family interest. But by skill, hard work and determination he has succeeded. As I write, the Scots media are now awash with stories about the young Scottish tennis sensation Andy Murray. He too has grasped opportunities not afforded to most in Scotland. Victories by both Andy Murray and Dario Franchitti are welcomed by the Scots but we need to know about them and more importantly ensure that others have the chance to participate and perhaps excel as they are.

With a 16 month old son, Darren Stewart Ferguson, opportunity for youngsters is important to Irene and plays a big part in her preference for remaining in the USA. 'There is so much more for

Darren out here. If somebody said "go back", I don't think I would do so and that's as a result of my child. I have two nieces in Scotland and I know that at this time of year, with the short days and cold and rainy nights, they are constantly in the house and that will be them through to spring. Darren is frequently in the park and indeed I had him out in the park last night. There are some 23 parks nearby. I have only been to half of them. I see kids out playing soccer, basketball, football, baseball and even practising karate in the open fields – there is just so many more activities and facilities on offer.'

It's not simply the opportunities for her child that she appreciates, but the attitude towards children in Californian society. 'Everything is much more child-centred here – they have swim meets and barbecues in the park where kids come and meet and play. Kids' clubs are available regularly. All the kids go along. Most of the swimming classes and other things here are free or for a nominal fee.' Some of what she says is based upon the climate and is beyond our control. As I write this chapter the clocks are about to be set back, and as the Scottish saying goes, 'the nights are fair drawing in'. There is something about this time of year encapsulated in that couthy phrase that sees Scots and Scotland prepare physically and psychologically for winter, with its dark nights and what seems like ceaseless rain. Often said in good humour but it frequently carries some sense of foreboding. The weather is part of Scotland and it forges Scottish identity, and we simply need to accept it. There are advantages as well as disadvantages, though the former may often seem few! But there are things that can be done, as happens in other countries sharing the drawbacks of a northern climate. Indoor facilities may not be needed in sunny California but are standard in cold Canada and chilly Scandinavia. Facilities can be made available that are both affordable and accessible. That's certainly not the situation in Scotland where facilities are few and often expensive.

The Californian outlook on children has tangible and visible outcomes. As I drive around, parks are full of kids in supervised play, and sports and kids are welcomed everywhere. 'It is very child-orientated. In the neighbourhood there are loads of kids. It is Halloween at the moment and my house is decorated with lights, skeletons, pumpkins etc., and I am just keeping up with others! At Christmas the whole neighbourhood decorates their houses and streets.' An ageing society in Scotland has become less tolerant of children. It has never been a particularly child-orientated society but in many ways things have got worse. Life is more complicated than when either Irene or I were children in Scotland. Mass car ownership makes playing on the street problematic, if not downright dangerous. Parks are built over, and parents are wary of allowing their kids to venture forth. There is certainly a problem with youth disorder in many parts but they are minority. I can't help think that rather than berating our children for inactivity or misbehaviour we need to provide the opportunity for them to participate. It comes at a price but is cheaper than the costs of delinquency and poor health.

Andy Murray and Dario Franchitti have succeeded in spite of rather than because of the land of their birth. If we are to ensure that others can benefit from the excitement generated by their success we need to ensure that the facilities are there for them. That applies not simply in tennis and motor sport but in a whole range of other activities whether sporting or artistic. It's not just for the elite but to allow each child to be all they can be.

It's not just the opportunities for her child that she prefers but the time she is afforded with him. She works from home two days per week, something which is becoming common practice in the USA. Part of that is doubtless down to traffic congestion but whatever the reason for it she sees advantages to it. 'I have a good way of working. I enjoy telecommuting. Part of it is down to traffic but it also gives you a better balance between home and work life. That is one of the reasons it is encouraged. America is not as generous with vacation, but accordingly they provide more flexibility. Telecommuting is very common here. I have a friend who telecommutes five days a week. E-mail, voicemail and technology today allows her to telecommute. She can join meetings through teleconferencing. Myself, I only work three days in the office, and if it didn't work Bill would not be slow in telling me. Some people would say it can't be done, but it can; if you can work for a man in Bill's position and make it successful, then I don't think there is any problem for others.' It is certainly the case that holiday entitlement is significantly less in the USA than in Europe. There are, though, solid arguments about having a better balance between work and play. Productivity is, after all, not just about the amount you work but what the outcome is. It's working smarter, not necessarily harder, that matters. Improving our productivity is essential but social changes can add to, rather than detract from that goal.

The demographic time bomb facing Scotland has been commented on by many from the First Minister down. There is no one, simple solution. Encouraging immigrants and dissuading emigrants is part. Equally though, having kids must not be seen as either financially unaffordable or a huge obstacle to maintaining a career and lifestyle. Teleworking has opportunities for many in much of remote Scotland but equally for young mothers like Irene in central Scotland. If new technology can keep her in the labour market while also allowing her to enjoy the formative years with her child, that can be no bad thing for either her or wider society.

Irene Dunlop is from Uddingston, a Lanarkshire town which, though on the fringes of Glasgow, has its own distinct identity. She was born in Melbourne, Australia, her parents having moved there in the early sixties but subsequently returned. Perhaps it was those formative years in the sunshine that resulted in her seeking sunnier pastures in later life. Her father worked at the steel works in Ravenscraig and her mother was a housewife. One brother has returned to Australia and her sister lives in Dublin, while her other brother remains in Lanarkshire.

She attended primary school in the town, then Uddingtson Grammar School. After leaving school she went straight into an office job. Starting work in a legal office in the east end of Glasgow she not only enjoyed it but had an aptitude for it. A naturally bright girl she completed a para legal course at Strathclyde University and moved into conveyancing and wills from the criminal defence matters she had been involved in. After a spell in Inverness working with The North of Scotland Water Board in their legal department, she moved back to her native Lanarkshire when her husband obtained a job at Sun Microsystems in Linlithgow. When an opportunity came for him to move to California they decided to try life abroad. Moving here she had neither a job nor the green card needed for employment. Writing to the British Consulate in San Francisco she worked in their accounts department and soon after became the PA to the Consul General, arranging events for vesting dignitaries from Prince Andrew through to business executives. It was there she met Bill Elder, the British Honorary Consul. She had been working there under a diplomatic visa but when her work permit came through she moved to being his PA.

She has very fond memories of Scotland, crediting it with providing the education that she has benefited from. The Scottish weather is not something that she misses or laments. 'The dreich days in Scotland are something we are glad to see the back of. The weather changes the whole lifestyle.' That said, it is part of her fond memories of her childhood. 'I remember nice summer days. I think they stick out as they are so few and far between and we would always do something special on the sunny days.'

The Californian sunshine is an attractive option not just for many Scots but Americans too. Scotland can neither change its geographical location nor its climatic conditions. But it can take steps to offset the problems that arise as a result and maximise whatever benefits may spring forth from them. Speaking to Irene makes me realise that Scotland must offer social as well as economic opportunity. It's not just a competitive economy that is needed but a happy and healthy nation. Social attitudes must change and sporting and other facilities be provided if we are to allow the children of Scots who remain here the same chances as those abroad. Given exceptional talent and hard work, Scots can win through, as Dario Franchitti and Andy Murray have shown. However, whatever their natural talent we need to provide the opportunities in their native land. They must be available to all, not just the gifted or fortunate few, for health and social reasons as much as sporting success, if Irene Dunlop's nieces are to have the same chances as her son.

Interviewed by Kenny MacAskill
October 2005

Craig Ferguson

TELEVISION PRESENTER,
LOS ANGELES

From Cumbernauld to Hollywood

THROUGHOUT MY SOJOURNS TO THE STATES and meetings with expatriate Scots I had been implored to speak to Craig Ferguson, a big star with a hugely popular television show that beams coast to coast in America. Five nights a week on CBS, his *Late, Late Show with Craig Ferguson* is a mixture of chat and comedy and attracts an audience significantly larger than the entire population of his native Scotland. Immensely funny as well as a sharp interviewer, his accent on his night-time chat show had given a certain cache to being Scots, I was told.

I have been asked on many occasions how I managed to gain access to so many celebrities and important people in business and public life. The answer is quite simple; I contacted them and asked to meet them. Though there has been some soul searching and understandable criticism of our Scottish ways or attitudes throughout this book, our politeness is not one. Even those who declined to participate did so in a thoughtful and considerate manner. There is something about a Scottish upbringing that instils good manners and respect. Craig Ferguson may be a Hollywood star, but he remains a Scottish lad. An e-mail outlining the nature of the book brought an immediate offer of an interview. Accordingly, though the journey around the diaspora was nearing its conclusion, a last trip to California beckoned.

As with many others I had spoken to, Craig is far better known abroad than at home. Recollections of him in Scotland were more likely to be of his incarnation as the comedy character Bing Hitler in the eighties than of the major media celebrity he now is in Hollywood, the media capital of the world. It's not just his current show that has made him a star but also regular appearances on *The Drew Carey Show* as well as scriptwriting the feature films *The Big Tease* and *Saving Grace*. He has now branched out into directing, with the critically acclaimed movie *I'll Be There* and was hailed as Best New Director at the Napa Valley Film Festival. He has also just finished his first novel, *Between the Bridge and the River*, to be published by Chronicle next Spring. It's hardly surprising that American Scots were clamouring for me to approach him.

Still somewhat jet-lagged, I made my way to CBS studios at Television City on Beverley Boulevard, Los Angeles for a 10:30am meeting with Craig. He had a prior meeting with show staff and further meetings thereafter. As I was to find out, not only is he exceptionally talented, but extremely hard-working. The show goes out five nights a week, and doesn't commence until half past midnight. It's a gruelling schedule to maintain but one that he works diligently at, and very successfully so, as audience figures and reviews confirm. Waiting for him in the main office of the show outside his private office, my eye is immediately caught by four clocks showing times in different cities. Not the usual London, Paris, New York and Tokyo clocks, but Glasgow, Aberdeen, Inverness and Auchenshoogle, all displaying the current time in Scotland. A surreal start to what was to be a fascinating interview.

As the show staffers departed his room I was invited in. It was unpretentious, being a functioning office rather than a star's suite. Bounding out of the chair he beckoned me to sit down. A big guy, well over six feet, and adorned by a wild head of hair. Resplendent in a Scotland top, he retains a distinctive Scottish accent. He tells me that he has been castigated by some for allegedly losing his Scottish accent. If he had, it's not obvious to me, but it's part of the cycle of criticism successful Scots suffer. As he says, 'Two things; even if I had, what difference does it make? And if I have, it's news to the

Americans that I have lost it. If I was doing a talk show in France would they say "he's talking French not Scottish"?' It's a legitimate point. My own accent changes if I am meeting or speaking to visiting foreigners and when you appear on an American television show you can hardly talk as if you are at the Barras. It's symptomatic of a Scottish malaise that seeks to find fault rather than give praise.

He is very impressive at being charismatic and naturally comic. If I hadn't been concentrating on making notes I would have been chortling throughout. It became clear why he is such a fantastic comedian: he has an ability to notice the humour in what people – and Scots in particular – say or do. He realises the absurdity of much of it and his recounting of it makes us laugh. It's a gift possessed by others such as Billy Connolly, but the strength of it is that it is natural. We can all visualise the situation or recall like moments, but they have the ability to recount it in a humorous manner, making us laugh at things that are sometimes an indictment of Scottish society and often tragic. Whilst Craig has a deep affection for Scotland, his memories are not of the shortbread tin variety but of a Scotland in the raw. What he has to say I find to be trenchant and in some instances searing.

He makes immediate mention of the influence of Scotland worldwide in a forceful but funny way. 'Scots at home are becoming more aware of that. I drive downtown through the streets of LA past Bonnie Brae and Gretna Green. They are not called these names because the indigenous Indian population thought that would be a nice name. Or the conquering Spanish said "let's call this street Bonnie Brae". The Scottish influence is huge worldwide and no more so than in America.' Throughout the interview he is generous in his praise of fellow Scots who have assisted him on his way, whether in Scotland or America, but space is too short to refer to them all. But it's clear that not only does he have a lot to say, he also has some things to get off his chest.

Before I depart for my trip, a Sunday tabloid does focus to some extent on his success, though more on his relationship with the Hollywood actress Sharon Stone. 'Scots boy with American star' rather than 'Scots lad is star in America' – it's Scotland, after all, and it couldn't possibly be so! He tells me that he has had a difficult relationship with the Scottish tabloid press. Reflecting our society in general, they choose to denigrate rather than praise, preferring titillation to truth to the extent that he was once reported as dating 'Laurel Canyon', an LA street, not a US lady. His interview with me was an exception, given on the basis of what it was trying to achieve and what he wanted to say. I felt honoured, and he tells me why he is happy to assist in the venture embarked on by Henry and me. 'I am very proud of being Scottish. I am also aware of certain things that a wee bit of time and distance give you. The temptation to look back at the country and see it through rose-tinted glasses – I try not to do that. I think I was tempered to disappointment early just by watching the Scottish football team. I think I became almost immune to having defeats and all that stuff. It made me quite tough, not fighty tough, just a little harder. That helps. I think a determination – it gave me that. It also gave me an inner anger which fuelled an inclusive mind and sent me on a voyage which started as self-destruction and ended up as a discovery. It's not as if my journey is over yet.'

Originally from Springburn, his family moved to Cumbernauld when he was very young and he grew up in the New Town with his brother and two sisters. His father spent a lifetime in the Post Office and his mother was a primary school teacher. He had a happy home life with a loving family but remembers the time and town for dampness and an insipient threat of violence. 'The minute you went out the front door it went from yellow to orange in terror alert. All that Catholic/Protestant nonsense. The only place that wasn't violent was in my house. If it wasn't the actual violence it was the threat of it. The anger, the tension, I found unbearable.' Some may not like what he says as it dispels a myth of bonnie banks and misty glens. However, as I come to write this chapter, Cumbernauld had just been awarded an unfortunate accolade as an 'ugly town' and having grown up at the same time in central Scotland I know exactly where he is coming from. It was a time where status was often defined by how good a footballer you were, how much you could drink and how hard you were. As Scotland ponders its current difficulties with 'booze and blades' there is a historical aspect and a cultural under-current predicated on an almost veneration of the hard-drinking and hard-man image. We loathe its manifestations but wallow in its glory. That needs to change.

His journey to Hollywood was not fast-tracked, but hard-earned with the odd bit of good fortune. Starting as a drummer in a punk rock band he was encouraged to do stand-up comedy by Michael Boyd, the Artistic Director of the Tron Theatre in Glasgow. To make ends meet he was working part-time in a well known restaurant in Glasgow's west end, the Ubiquitous Chip. Moving to this area of Glasgow was a liberating experience for him and he again makes an astute comment in an otherwise humorous aside. 'That was the beginning of a huge awakening for me. The people there had a real bohemian sense of living. I remember the morning after a party one night, someone offering me a croissant. I said no at first because I thought it was a drug. When I found out it was something to eat, it was like wow. It changed my life. The band I was in played drums and the singer was Peter Capaldi who is a lovely guy and a fabulous actor.' The Bing Hitler character followed with shows and television appearances. He was on the up.

A move to London beckoned, where he worked with Harry Enfield amongst others. He recalls the night he left for London with poignancy. There must be many other exiled Scots for whom there is a similar moment of realisation of the permanence of their depar-ture. 'I took the sleeper from Central Station. I had done a gig and had some money so I got a first class sleeping compartment. I was still drinking at the time and I had some beer with me. Sitting drink-ing beer, leaving Glasgow on a lovely night, coming over the bridge over the Clyde – I remember thinking, "is that it?". It felt like I was leaving, and I was. That was the night.'

The London years were unhappy years for him. He had been reluctant to go but felt drawn to it. Echoing comments made by oth-ers, he describes London as 'a magnet rather than a destination'. A place Scots require to go to, rather than interact directly in the wide world beyond these shores. He contrasts it unfavourably with his current home in America which he sees as a more natural destination for many Scots. 'The vast majority of what I do is here in America, but I thought that when I was in Scotland, when I used to play cowboys and Indians. You go to the Barrowland ballroom and you would see a lot of pretend Americans. The movies were American. The television shows were American. The pop groups were by and large American. I lived in London for eight years before moving here. A lot of people ask, "well, why go to LA where it is so false?" I thought, "why would it be better than London?" Because the world is better. It is more natural for a Scotsman of my type, whatever that is, to come to America than it is to go to England. It is less alien for me to be here than it would be to be in my next door neighbour's house.'

Personal unhappiness and addiction problems followed but these were overcome. Feeling frustrated with life, he was challenged by a friend as to what he wanted to do in an ideal world. He said 'go to Hollywood', and then realised that he had to risk it. With two suitcases in hand, he flew over and slept on the couch of a friend he had met in Scotland. A deal with Disney soon followed and other work was found. Reading film scripts he considered that he could do no worse and wrote his own. The screenplay for *Saving Grace* followed and he was on the route to success in Hollywood.

His wearing of a Scotland top leads me to comment on the Scotland international I had been at the Saturday before. At five minutes to three we were heading for the World Cup in Germany. At five past three it was disaster for Scotland as Belarus had scored and by four forty five we were told we should be hanging up our boots as the game had been lost. As it was, Scotland played badly against what was a very good team and – as ever – on the following Wednesday when it was to late to matter the team went to Slovenia and recorded an excellent three nil victory. It was ever thus. The hopes and fears of a nation carried in a football team lead him to comment: 'There is too much wrapped up in the Scottish football team. Eleven guys, most of whom you wouldn't trust to walk your dog. Brazil has the best team in the world but would you really like to be like Brazil. Be careful where you place your trust is my theory. I don't think football is the best way of looking at national pride.' I couldn't agree more. I am a loyal foot soldier in the Tartan Army, but too much of national pride and self-confidence has been tied up with the fortunes of the national team. Social and economic matters could be ignored if the team won on the park and especially if they could secure a victory over the Auld Enemy. The confidence of a nation that had newly discovered oil drained away following a defeat in a World Cup tournament in Argentina. A successful team is no substitute for a vibrant economy or a healthy society. Too much responsibility for our nation's dreams has been placed on the shoulders of too few, and for all the wrong reasons.

The discussion on Scottish football leads us on to another aspect of Scottish society which relates to talent and hard work. 'There was a lie that I learned in Scotland that I feel has to go. It had to go for me. The lie is this: somehow talent is only useful if it is given to you in such quantities that you needn't do anything about it. Now I will give you an example of that. Jim Baxter – an extraordinarily gifted football player – saying things like, "well we never used to train – we were in the pub all night." That is a shocking admission and a stupid comment. The mentality of the Scots should be "stay out of the damn pub and get out there and train". I am damn sure the Brazilian guys aren't in the pub all night. The same attitude exists when someone "passed exams but had to swot" – what, really!' I can't help but agree that in Scotland there is a view that denies talent that is worked at and denigrates success that is achieved. Yet both are vital and necessary.

It leads him on to comment on Scottish attitudes not simply to work but success. 'The feeling I get from the press – and I even felt like this when I lived there – is that it is a place where mediocrity is seen as excellence and excellence is seen as treason. To strive for some kind of bigger, wider, enormous impact outside of Scotland is not to be trusted. I don't get that. Take the football analogy – in my game I score goals, that's what I do. Do I want to score goals for Partick Thistle or Chelsea or Man United? I want to play in the big league so that's why I am here.' Strong stuff, but sometimes the truth hurts. There exists in Scotland a perverse paradox in that whilst we encourage education and instil a work ethic, rising too far is almost breaking a social taboo. The comment that excellence is treason is as fine a way I have heard of defining the curse of the 'kent yer faither syndrome' as any.

The risk aversion that exists in Scottish society is the next aspect that he comments on. Again he uses a sporting analogy, but this time from the American sport of baseball. 'There is no shame in failure. I fail nearly all the time but when the ball cracks on the bat it goes into the car park and that is the way I play. You swing and you miss but when it connects the feeling it gives you is amazing. The worst phrase I have ever heard is "I cannae be bothered". You better be bothered, someone else can be bothered. It's alright to be afraid but this "cannae be bothered" – I hate it.' It's something that has been commented on by others and especially from the business community. It is, though, something which Craig sees as reflected throughout Scottish society and being an area where learning from the Americans and their 'can do' attitude is vital.

The Scots failure to celebrate success is something that must be overcome. He tells a tale that is a classic indictment of the worst aspects of that unfortunate trait. It was at a time when he was first coming to prominence as Bing Hitler. 'I remember walking down near the Trongate and some guy shouting to me, "Haw Bing. Yer shite," and I said to him, "Why are you saying that?". He said to me he was "keeping my feet on the ground" and I said, "Why should my emotional well-being be any of your business? Why are you keeping my feet on the ground – is it your job to keep my feet on the ground?"' A similar tale could be told by any Scot, not just a successful one. A put down, rather than a pat on the back. The words said not out of spite or hate but almost as an endearment if not faint praise. But how does that assist your self-confidence, and why is it assumed that you must be getting full of yourself just because you are succeeding? Can we not be successful and retain magnanimity? Can we not laud and praise our own? In any event should the criticism not come if you do become arrogant, not on the assumption that you will. It is a pernicious aspect of Scottish psychology that must be jettisoned. Craig Ferguson has narrated it in a humorous way, but it's not funny and it's fundamentally damaging.

He continues, 'I find myself confused by my Scottishness more than anything. My family motto is *"dulcius ex asperis"*, which means "sweeter after difficulty". I used to think that was great – but now I think it is awful. Why do things have to be difficult to be sweet?' He sees the Scots as having determination yet also an inner anger that drives them and describes waking up that morning and being asked by his partner how he felt. 'I felt the dragon move around me this morning and I think that is a Scottish thing – deep down in a dark lair somewhere something moved and I thought "I better get out before she gets a hard time." There is something very funny and very dark about being Scottish.' Scotland has a great deal to be proud of but equally a lot of soul searching to do. Many of the ills we face are not the consequence of Thatcherism or London rule but the inner devil within all of us. The demon drink and other darker aspects of the Scottish character can only be addressed by ourselves. They need to be acknowledged and faced before they can be overcome.

I have on occasion described Scotland as having a sort of bipolar disorder. One day, 'Bonnie Scotland, wha's like us', the next day, 'we are all doomed'. It has given us determination, yet inner demons. Craig has used what his native land provided him with to overcome what it deprived him of and saddled him with. He has triumphed through adversity. It's time for Scotland to emulate one of its most successful sons. To use its natural talents and gifts to overcome the difficulties faced or self-inflicted. Scotland needs to use its innate determination to overcome its inner demons. There is no one holding us back but ourselves.

Craig Ferguson describes himself now as a Scottish American. But he is someone we can call our own and be proud to do so. He does not rule out a return to his native land but opportunity and change would be necessary. It's up to us to give him the encouragement and that chance. Maybe when someone hails him in a Scottish street and says, 'Hey Craig, we are really proud of you,' we'll know we are finally on our way.

Interviewed by Kenny MacAskill
October 2005

Some other books published by **LUATH** Press

Agenda for a New Scotland: Visions of Scotland 2020
Introduced and compiled by Kenny MacAskill
ISBN 1 905222 00 9
PB £9.99

I commend Agenda for a New Scotland *to all who believe that our country has a bright future, and who want to play their part in making sure that it happens.*
GEORGE REID MSP

After a wait of nearly 300 years, Scotland finally has its own Parliament again. A legislature, albeit a devolved one, has been elected, and just like the iconic stone, Scottish destiny seems to back in the hands of its people and their representatives.

Yet rather than being the end point of centuries of struggle it serves to mark a new beginning. With destiny returned it is now the responsibility of Scotland's executive, as holders of the people's mandate, to begin the process of shaping Scotland's future. But first a more fundamental question needs to be answered, what should that future be?

Through a series of articles by Scotland's leading figures, *Agenda for a New Scotland* proposes an answer to that question. Contributors include: Susan Deacon MSP, Owen Dudley Edwards, Roger Houchin, Elaine C Smith, RT HON Henry McLeish, and a foreword by George Reid MSP.

By outlining the opportunities Scotland has before it, socially, economically and politically, as well as the tribulations, *Agenda for a New Scotland* sets out an exciting and compelling vision of the future of our nation.

'MacAskill nails his political colours firmly to the mast but one of the smartest things he has done is to invite key players from across the political spectrum...'
ROBERT BROWN, SCOTTISH STANDARD

Scots in Canada
Jenni Calder
ISBN 1 84282 038 9
PB £7.99

The story of the Scots who went to Canada, from the seventeenth century onwards.

In Canada there are nearly as many descendants of Scots as there are people living in Scotland; almost five million Canadians ticked the 'Scottish origin' box in the most recent Canadian Census. Many Scottish families have friends or relatives in Canada.

Thousands of Scots were forced from their homeland, while others chose to leave, seeking a better life. As individuals, families and communities, they braved the wild Atlantic ocean, many crossing in cramped under-rationed ships, unprepared for the fierce Canadian winter. And yet Scots went on to lay railroads, found banks and exploit the fur trade, and helped form the political infrastructure of modern day Canada.

Meticulously researched and fluently written... it neatly charts the rise of a country without succumbing to sentimental myths.
SCOTLAND ON SUNDAY

Scots in the usa
Jenni Calder
ISBN 1 905222 06 8
PB £7.99

Increasingly, Americans of Scottish extraction are visiting Scotland in search of their family history. All over Scotland and the United States there are clues to the Scottish-American relationship – the legacy of centuries of trade and communication as well as of departure and settlement.

The experiences of Scottish settlers in the United States varied enormously, but from the Constitution to cattle raising, from education to exploration, many made a striking impact on their adopted country.

Scots in the USA examines why so many left Scotland, where they went and what they did in the United States, and their contribution to the emerging nation.

[Calder's] judgements are also usually careful and sensible...The book is clearly written and takes account of the meagre recent publications on the subject.
T M DEVINE, SCOTTISH REVIEW OF BOOKS

Luath Press Limited

committed to publishing well written books worth reading

LUATH PRESS takes its name from Robert Burns, whose little collie Luath (*Gael.*, swift or nimble) tripped up Jean Armour at a wedding and gave him the chance to speak to the woman who was to be his wife and the abiding love of his life. Burns called one of *The Twa Dogs* Luath after Cuchullin's hunting dog in Ossian's *Fingal*. Luath Press was established in 1981 in the heart of Burns country, and is now based a few steps up the road from Burns' first lodgings on Edinburgh's Royal Mile.
Luath offers you distinctive writing with a hint of unexpected pleasures.

Most bookshops in the UK, the US, Canada, Australia, New Zealand and parts of Europe, either carry our books in stock or can order them for you. To order direct from us, please send a £sterling cheque, postal order, international money order or your credit card details (number, address of cardholder and expiry date) to us at the address below. Please add post and packing as follows: UK – £1.00 per delivery address; overseas surface mail – £2.50 per delivery address; overseas airmail – £3.50 for the first book to each delivery address, plus £1.00 for each additional book by airmail to the same address. If your order is a gift, we will happily enclose your card or message at no extra charge.

Luath Press Limited
543/2 Castlehill
The Royal Mile
Edinburgh EH1 2ND
Scotland

Telephone: 0131 225 4326 (24 hours)
Fax: 0131 225 4324
email: sales@luath.co.uk
Website: www.luath.co.uk